Rick Steves' ROME 2000

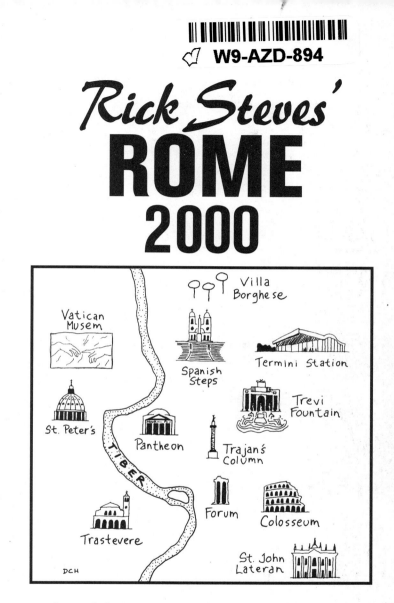

Villa Borghese

Vatican Musem

Termini Station

Spanish Steps

St. Peter's

Pantheon

Trevi Fountain

TIBER

Trajan's Column

Forum

Colosseum

Trastevere

St. John Lateran

DCH

by Rick Steves and Gene Openshaw

John Muir Publications
Santa Fe, New Mexico

Other JMP travel guidebooks by Rick Steves
Europe 101: History and Art for the Traveler (with Gene Openshaw)
Rick Steves' Europe Through the Back Door
Rick Steves' Mona Winks (with Gene Openshaw)
Rick Steves' Best of Europe
Rick Steves' France, Belgium & the Netherlands (with Steve Smith)
Rick Steves' Germany, Austria & Switzerland
Rick Steves' Great Britain & Ireland
Rick Steves' London (with Gene Openshaw)
Rick Steves' Italy
Rick Steves' Paris (with Steve Smith and Gene Openshaw)
Rick Steves' Postcards from Europe
Rick Steves' Scandinavia
Rick Steves' Spain & Portugal
Asia Through the Back Door (with Bob Effertz)
Rick Steves' Phrase Books: German, Italian, French,
    Spanish/Portuguese, and French/Italian/German

John Muir Publications, P.O. Box 613, Santa Fe, NM 87504
Copyright © 2000 by Europe Through the Back Door
Cover copyright © 2000 by John Muir Publications
All rights reserved.

Printed in the United States of America. First printing February 2000.

Portions of this book were originally published in *Rick Steves' Mona Winks*
© 1998, 1996, 1993, 1988 by Rick Steves and Gene Openshaw and in
Rick Steves' Italy © 2000, 1999, 1998, 1997, 1996, 1995 by Rick Steves.

ISBN 1-56261-525-4
ISSN 1527-4780

For the latest on Rick's lectures, guidebooks, tours, and public television series,
contact Europe Through the Back Door, Box 2009, Edmonds, WA 98020,
tel. 425/771-8303, fax 425/771-0833, www.ricksteves.com, or e-mail:
rick@ricksteves.com.

Europe Through the Back Door Editor: Risa Laib
John Muir Publications Editor: Dianna Delling
Production & Typesetting: Kathleen Sparkes, White Hart Design
Cover and Interior Design: Janine Lehmann
Maps: David C. Hoerlein
Photography: p. 57: Dominic Arizona Bonuccelli; all others: Rick Steves
    and Gene Openshaw
Printer: Publishers Press
Front cover photo: Colosseum, Rome, Italy; copyright © Blaine Harrington III

Distributed to the book trade by Publishers Group West, Berkeley, California

*Although the author and publisher have made every effort to provide accurate,
up-to-date information, they accept no responsibility for loss, injury, bad pasta,
or inconvenience sustained by any person using this book.*

CONTENTS
rome

ROME

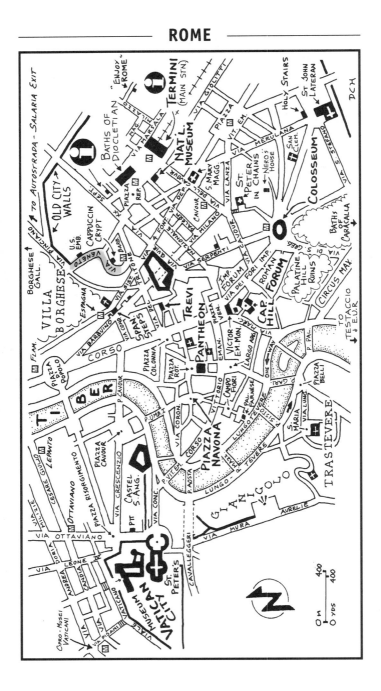

INTRODUCTION

1

r o m e

Rome is magnificent and brutal at the same time. Your ears will ring; if you're careless you'll be run down or pickpocketed; you'll be frustrated by the kind of chaos that only an Italian can understand. You may even come to believe Mussolini was a necessary evil. But Rome is required—and in the Jubilee Year 2000, it's more exciting than ever.

If your hotel provides a comfortable refuge (book in advance for 2000); if you pace yourself, accept and even partake in the siesta plan; if you're well organized for sightseeing; and if you protect yourself and your valuables with extra caution and discretion, you'll do fine. You'll see the sights and leave satisfied.

Rome at its peak meant civilization itself. Everything was either civilized (part of the Roman Empire, Latin- or Greek-speaking) or barbarian. Today Rome is Italy's political capital, the capital of Catholicism, and a splendid "junkpile" (okay, that's not quite the right word) of Western civilization. As you peel through its fascinating and jumbled layers, you'll find Rome's buildings, cats, laundry, traffic, and 2.6 million people endlessly entertaining. And then, of course, there are its magnificent sights.

Tour St. Peter's, the greatest church on earth, and scale Michelangelo's 100-yard-tall dome, the world's largest. Learn something about eternity by touring the huge Vatican Museum. You'll find the story of creation—bright as the day it was painted—in the newly restored Sistine Chapel. Do the "Caesar Shuffle" walk through ancient Rome's Forum and Colosseum. Savor Europe's most sumptuous building, the Borghese Gallery, and take an early evening "Dolce Vita Stroll" down the Via del Corso with Rome's beautiful people. Enjoy an after-dark walk from Campo de' Fiori to the Spanish Steps, lacing together Rome's Baroque and bubbly night spots.

This Information Is Accurate and Up-to-Date

This book is updated every year. Most publishers of guidebooks can afford an update only every two or three years (and even then, it's often by letter). Since this book is selective, I'm able to personally update it. Even with an annual update, things change. But if you're traveling with the current edition of this book, I guarantee you're using the most up-to-date information available. This book will help you have an inexpensive, hassle-free trip. Your trip costs about $10 per waking hour. Your time is valuable. This guidebook saves lots of time.

Welcome to My Rome City Guide

This book is organized this way:

Orientation includes tourist information and public transportation. The "Planning Your Time" section offers a suggested schedule with thoughts on how to best use your limited time.

Sights provides a succinct overview of Rome's most important sights, arranged by neighborhood, with ratings: ▲▲▲— Don't miss; ▲▲—Try hard to see; ▲—Worthwhile if you can make it; No rating—Worth knowing about.

The **Night Walk across Rome** connects Rome's great monuments and atmospheric squares.

The **Self-Guided Tours** lead you through Ancient Rome, with tours of the Colosseum, the Roman Forum, Palatine Hill, Trajan's Column, the Pantheon, and the Baths of Diocletian. You'll tour the pilgrimage churches, including the grandest of all: St. Peter's. And you'll see the great museums: the Vatican Museum, the National Museum of Rome, and the exciting Borghese Gallery.

Day Trips covers nearby sights: Tivoli, Ostia Antica, Naples, and Pompei.

Sleeping is a guide to my favorite budget hotels, mainly in several convenient (and for Rome, relatively quiet) neighborhoods near the sights.

Eating offers good-value restaurants ranging from inexpensive eateries to splurges, with an emphasis on good value.

Rome with Children contains tips on visting Rome with kids, **Shopping in Rome** has advice on shopping, and **Nightlife in Rome** is a brief guide to Rome's best evening activities.

Transportation Connections covers connections by train and by plane (with information on Rome's airport), laying the groundwork for your smooth arrival and departure.

The **Appendix** includes history, a climate chart, and a handy list of Italian survival phrases.

Throughout this book, when you see a ✪ in a listing, it means that the sight is covered in much more detail in one of my tours—a page number will tell you just where to look to find more information.

Browse through this book and choose your favorite sights. Then have a great trip! You'll become your own guide with my tours. Traveling like a temporary local, you'll get the absolute most out of every mile, minute, and dollar. You won't waste time on mediocre sights because, unlike other guidebooks, this one covers only the best. Since your major financial pitfall is lousy, expensive hotels, I've worked hard to assemble the best accommodations values.

Trip Costs

Six components make up your trip costs: airfare, surface transportation, room and board, sightseeing/entertainment, shopping/miscellany, and gelato.

Airfare: Don't try to sort through the mess. Find and use a good travel agent. A basic, round-trip United States-to-Milan (or Rome) flight should cost $700 to $1,000, depending on where you fly from and when. Always consider saving time and money in Europe by flying "open jaws" (flying into one city and out of another).

Surface Transportation: For a typical one-week visit, allow $60 to $100 for taxis (which can be shared by up to four people); if you opt for buses and the Metro, figure about $20 per person. The cost of round-trip transportation to day trip destinations ranges from minimal ($6–10 for Tivoli, about $6 for Ostia Antica) to affordable ($50 for Naples and Pompeii). For a one-way trip between Rome's airport and the city center, allow $9 per person by train or up to $45 by taxi (can be shared).

Room and Board: You can thrive in Rome on $80 a day per person for room and board. This allows $10 for lunch, $20 for dinner, and $50 for lodging (based on two people splitting the cost of a $100 double room that includes breakfast). If you've got more money, I've listed great ways to spend it. Students and tightwads can enjoy Rome for as little as $40 a day ($20 for a bed, $20 for meals and snacks). But budget sleeping and eating require the skills covered later in this chapter (and in greater detail in my book *Rick Steves' Europe Through the Back Door*).

Sightseeing and Entertainment: Figure about $7 per major sight (Colosseum, museums), $2 for minor ones (climbing church towers), and $25 for splurge experiences (e.g., tours). An overall average of $15 a day works for most. Don't skimp here. After all, this category directly powers most of the experiences all the other expenses are designed to make possible.

Shopping and Miscellany: Figure $1 per postcard, coffee, and soft drink and $2 per gelato. Shopping can vary in cost from nearly nothing to a small fortune. Good budget travelers find that this category has little to do with assembling a trip full of lifelong and wonderful memories.

Exchange Rate

I've priced things in lire (L) throughout the book.

> L1,900 = about $1

Many tourists are mind-boggled by the huge prices: 30,000 lire for dinner! L120,000 for the room! L136,000 for the taxi ride! To figure lire quickly and easily, cover the last three digits and cut what's left by a half (e.g., a L24,000 dinner costs $12). That L30,000 dinner costs $15 in U.S. money; the L120,000 room, $60; and the taxi ride...uh-oh!

Beware of the "slow count." After you buy something you may get your change back in batches. The salesperson (or bank teller) hopes you're so confused by all the zeros that you'll gather up your money and say *"grazie"* before he or she finishes the count. Always do your own rough figuring beforehand and understand the transaction. Never part with a 100,000-lire note (say "CHEN-toh MEE-lah") without making clear you know it's not a 10,000. Wait for the last bits of money to straggle over to you, then deliberately count your change.

There are legitimate extras (café prices as much as double when you sit down instead of stand at the bar, taxis get L5,000 extra after 22:00, and so on), to which paranoid tourists wrongly take offense. But the waiter who charges you L70,000 for a pizza and beer assumes you're too polite to involve the police. If you have any problem with a restaurant, hotel, or taxi, get a cop to arbitrate. Rome is trying to civilize itself.

Prices, Times, and Discounts

The prices in this book, as well as the hours and telephone numbers, are accurate as of mid-1999—but once you pin Rome down, it wiggles. I know you'll understand that this, like any other guidebook, starts to yellow even before it's printed.

In Rome—and in this book—you'll use the 24-hour clock. It's the same through 12:00 noon, then keep going—13:00, 14:00... For anything over 12, subtract 12 and add p.m. (14:00 is 2:00 p.m.)

This book lists peak-season hours for sightseeing attractions (June–October). Off-season, roughly November through May, expect shorter hours, more lunchtime breaks, and fewer activities. Confirm your sightseeing plans locally, especially when traveling between November and May.

While discounts for sights and transportation are not listed in this book, seniors (60 and over), students (with International Student Identity Cards), and youths (under 18) may snare a deal—although these days many discounts are limited to European residents.

When to Go

Rome's best travel months are May, June, September, and October. Between November and April you can usually expect pleasant weather, and generally none of the sweat and stress of the tourist season. Peak season (July–October) offers the longest hours and the most exciting slate of activities—but terrible crowds and, at times, suffocating heat. In August, many hotels drop their prices.

In Rome, temperatures hit the high 80s and 90s in summer and drop to the 40s and 50s in winter. Spring and fall can be chilly, and many hotels do not turn on their heat. Air conditioning, when available, usually doesn't kick in until June 1. Most mid-range hotels come with air conditioning—a worthwhile splurge in the summer. (See climate chart in the Appendix.)

Red Tape and Business Hours

You need a passport, but no visa or shots, to travel in Italy.

Business Hours: Traditionally, Rome uses the siesta plan. People work from 8:00 or 9:00 to 13:00 and from 15:30 to 19:00, six days a week. Many businesses have adopted the government's new recommended 8:00-to-14:00 workday. In tourist areas, shops are open longer. If you're buying more than $200 worth of souvenirs, ask in the shops about getting the 10 to 19 percent tax back at the airport upon departure.

Banking

You'll want to spend local hard cash. The fastest way to get it is by using plastic: your ATM, credit, or debit card. Banks are slow and cash machines are fast. Bring some traveler's checks as a back-up.

Regular banks have the best rates for cashing traveler's checks. For a large exchange it pays to compare rates and fees. Bank of Sicily consistently has good rates. Banking hours are generally Monday through Friday 8:30 to 13:30 and 15:30 to 16:30, but they can vary wildly. Post offices and the train station usually change money if you can't get to a bank.

To get a cash advance from a bank machine, you'll need a four-digit PIN (numbers only, no letters, seven-digit PINs won't work) with your bank card. Before you go, verify with your bank that your card will work.

Visa and MasterCard are more commonly accepted than American Express. Just like at home, credit or debit cards work easily at larger hotels, restaurants, and shops, but smaller businesses prefer payment in hard lire.

Use a money belt. Thieves target tourists. A money belt (call 425/771-8303 for our free newsletter/catalog) provides peace of mind and allows you to carry lots of cash safely.

Don't be petty about changing money. The greatest avoidable money-changing expense is having to waste time every few days returning to a bank. Change a week's worth of money, get big bills, stuff them in your money belt, and travel!

Travel Smart

Many people travel through Rome thinking it's a chaotic mess. They feel any attempt at efficient travel is futile. This is dead wrong—and expensive. Rome, which seems as orderly as spilled spaghetti, actually functions quite well. Only those who understand this and travel smart can enjoy Rome on a budget.

Buy a phone card and use it for reservations and double-checking hours of sights. Enjoy the friendliness of the local people. Ask questions. Most locals are eager to point you in their idea of the right direction. Learn the currency and develop a simple formula to quickly estimate prices in dollars. Pack along a pocket-size notebook to organize your thoughts. Those who expect to travel smart, do.

Museums and sights, especially large ones, usually stop admitting people 30 to 60 minutes before closing time. Sundays have the same pros and cons as they do for travelers in the United States: Sightseeing attractions are generally open but with shorter hours; shops and banks are closed. City traffic is light. Rowdy evenings are rare on Sundays. Saturdays are virtually weekdays with earlier closing hours. Hotels are often booked up on Easter, April 25, May 1, in August, and on Fridays and Saturdays. Religious holidays and train strikes can catch you by surprise anywhere in Italy.

Really, this book can save you lots of time and money. But to have an "A" trip, you need to be an "A" student. Read the entire thing before your trip and take notes. As you read this book, note the days when museums are closed and if reservations are mandatory. For instance, if you want to see the Borghese Gallery or Nero's Golden House, you must reserve ahead. If you go to the Vatican Museum on a Sunday, you'll run smack into closed doors, or—if it's the last Sunday of the month—huge crowds. Day-tripping to Ostia Antica on Monday is bad news. A smart trip is a puzzle—a fun, doable, and worthwhile challenge.

Italian Tourist Offices in the United States

Before your trip, contact the nearest Italian TI and briefly describe your trip and request information. You'll get the general packet and, if you ask for specifics (city map, calendar of festivals, etc.), an impressive amount of help. If you have a specific problem, they're a good source of sympathy.

Write, call, or fax the office nearest you...

In New York: 630 5th Ave. #1565, New York, NY 10111, brochure hotline tel. 212/245-4822, tel. 212/245-5618, fax 212/586-9249.

In Illinois: 500 N. Michigan Ave. #2240, Chicago, IL 60611, brochure hotline tel. 312/666-0990, tel. 312/644-0996, fax 312/644-3019.

In California: 12400 Wilshire Blvd. #550, Los Angeles, CA 90025, brochure hotline tel. 310/820-0098, tel. 310/820-1898, fax 310/820-6357.

Web sites on Italy: www.italiantourism.com (Italian Tourist Board in U.S.), www.museionline.it (museums in Italy), and www.fs-on-line.com (train info and schedules).

Web sites on Rome: www.roma2000.it (site listings and itineraries), www.comune.roma.it/comunicazione/evento/ (music, exhibitions, and events), www.wantedinrome.com (job openings and real estate, but also festivals and exhibitions), www.informaroma.it (general Rome info), and www.vatican.va (the pope's Web site).

Recommended Guidebooks

For most travelers, this book is all you need. The tall green Michelin guide to Rome has solid, encyclopedic coverage of sights, customs, and culture, though nothing on room and board (sold in English in Italy).

The well-researched Access and the colorful Eyewitness guides to Rome are very popular with travelers. Eyewitness is fun for its great, easy-to-grasp graphics and photos, and it's just right for people who want only factoids. But the Eyewitness books are relatively skimpy on content and they weigh a ton. I buy them in Rome (no more expensive than in the U.S.) or simply borrow them for a minute from other travelers at certain sights to make sure I'm aware of that place's highlights. *Let's Go Rome* is youth-oriented with good coverage of nightlife, hosteling, and cheap transportation deals. If you'll be traveling elsewhere in Italy, consider *Rick Steves' Italy 2000*.

In Rome, the American Bookstore sells all the major guidebooks (Via Torino 136, Metro: Repubblica, tel. 06-474-6877).

Rick Steves' Books and Videos

Rick Steves' Europe Through the Back Door 2000 (John Muir Publications) gives you budget travel skills on minimizing jet lag, packing light, planning your itinerary, traveling by car or train, finding budget beds without reservations, changing money, avoiding rip-offs, outsmarting thieves, hurdling the language barrier, staying healthy, taking great photographs, using your bidet, and much more. The book also includes chapters on 34 of my favorite "Back Doors," five of which are in Italy.

Rick Steves' Country Guides are a series of seven guidebooks that cover the best of Europe, Italy, Britain/Ireland, France/Belgium/Netherlands, Spain/Portugal, Germany/Austria/Switzerland (with Prague), and Scandinavia. All are updated annually and come out each January.

Rick Steves' City Guides include this book (new for 2000), Paris, and London. For thorough coverage of Europe's three greatest cities, complete with extensive self-guided tours through the greatest museums, consider these handy, easy-to-pack guidebooks.

Europe 101: History and Art for the Traveler (co-written with Gene Openshaw, John Muir Publications), which gives you the story of Europe's people, history, and art, is heavy on Italy's ancient, Renaissance, and modern history. Written for smart people who were sleeping in their history and art classes before they knew they were going to Europe, *101* helps resurrect the rubble.

Rick Steves' Mona Winks: Self-Guided Tours of Europe's Top Museums (co-written with Gene Openshaw, John Muir Publications, 1998) gives you one- to three-hour self-guided tours through Europe's 20 most exhausting and important museums. Nearly half of the book is devoted to Italy, with tours of Venice (St. Mark's, Doge's Palace, and Accademia Gallery) and Florence (Uffizi Gallery, Bargello, Michelangelo's *David*, and a Renaissance walk through the town center). If you want to enjoy these great sights and museums, *Mona* will be a valued friend.

In Italy a phrase book is as fun as it is necessary. My *Rick Steves' Italian Phrase Book* (John Muir Publications, 1999) will help you meet the people and stretch your budget. It's written by a monoglot who, for 25 years, has fumbled through Italy struggling with all the other phrase books. Use this fun and practical communication aid to make accurate hotel reservations over the telephone, ask for a free taste of cantaloupe-flavored gelato at the *gelatería*, have the man in the deli make you a sandwich, and tell your cabbie that if he doesn't slow down you'll throw up.

My public television series, *Travels in Europe with Rick Steves*, includes six half-hour shows on Italy. A new series of 13 shows, including two on Rome, airs in 2000. All 52 of the earlier shows air throughout the United States on public television stations and the Travel Channel. Each episode is also available on an information-packed home video, as is my two-hour slideshow lecture on Italy (call us at 425/771-8303 for our free newsletter/catalog or check www.ricksteves.com).

Rick Steves' Postcards from Europe (John Muir Publications, 1999), my autobiographical book, packs 25 years of travel anecdotes and insights into the ultimate 3,000-mile European adventure. Through my guidebooks, I share my favorite European discoveries with you. In *Postcards* I introduce you to my favorite European friends. Half of the book is set in Italy: Rome, Venice, Florence, and the Cinque Terre.

Maps

The maps in this book, designed and drawn by Dave Hoerlein, are concise and simple. Dave is well traveled in Rome and Italy and has designed the maps to help you orient quickly and get to where you want to go painlessly. In Rome, pick up a map at the tourist information office or your hotel and you're ready to travel.

Transportation

Transportation concerns within Rome are limited to the Metro, buses, and taxis, all covered in the Orientation chapter. If you have a car, stow it. You don't want to drive in Rome. Transportation to day trip destinations is covered in the Day Trips chapter. For all the specifics on transportation throughout Italy by train or car, see *Rick Steves' Italy 2000*.

In Rome, get train tickets and railpass-related reservations and supplements at travel agencies rather than dealing with the congested train station. The cost is the same. Your hotel can direct you to the nearest travel agency.

Telephones and Mail

Smart travelers use the telephone every day—especially in Rome—to confirm hotel reservations, call sights to check opening hours, and phone home. Dialing long distance is easy with an Italian phone card.

Italy's phone cards aren't credit cards, just handy cards you insert in the phone instead of coins. The L5,000, L10,000, or L15,000 phone cards are much easier to use than coins for long-distance calls. Buy phone cards at post offices, tobacco shops, and machines near phone booths (many phone booths indicate where the nearest phone-card sales outlet is located). Tear off the perforated corner to "activate" the card. Insert it into the phone. Dial slowly and deliberately, as if the phone doesn't understand numbers very well. Repeat as needed. Italian phone numbers vary in length; a hotel can have, say, a 10-digit phone number and 11-digit fax number. When spelling out a proper noun on the phone, "i" (pronounced "ee" in Italian) and "e" (pronounced "ay") are confusing. Say "i, Italia" and "e, Enrico" to clear up that problem.

Dialing Direct: Italy recently dispensed with area codes. To call anywhere within Italy, just dial the number. For example, the number of one of my recommended Rome hotels is 06-482-4696. To call it from the Rome train station, dial 06-482-4696. If you call it from Venice, it's the same: 06-482-4696. (All normal Rome telephone numbers—not including toll-free or cell phone numbers—start with 06. In 2001 Rome's initial "06" is expected to change to "46.")

When dialing internationally, dial the international access code (of the country you're calling from), the country code (of the country you're calling to), and the local number. To call the Rome hotel from the United States, dial 011 (the U.S. international access code), 39 (Italy's country code), then 06-482-4696. To call my office from Italy, I dial 00 (Italy's international access code), 1 (the U.S. country code), 425 (Edmonds' area code), and 771-8303. For international access codes and country codes, see the Appendix. If you plan to access your voice mail from Italy, be advised that you can't dial extensions or secret codes once you connect (here you're on vacation—relax).

Orange SIP public telephones are everywhere and take coins or cards. Hotel-room phones are reasonable for calls within Italy (the faint beeps signal L200 phone units) but a terrible rip-off for calls to the United States (unless you use a PIN card—see below—or your hotel allows toll-free access to your USA Direct service—see below). If you have phone-card phobia, you'll find easy-to-use "talk now, pay later" metered phones in some bars or in the central post office or train station in Rome. European time is six/nine hours ahead of the east/west coast of the United States.

Calling the United States from Italy is now cheapest with new PIN cards (sold in hole-in-the-wall long-distance phone shops). Buy these, scratch off and reveal your personal identification number, dial the toll-free number, punch in your PIN, and talk. You'll get about three minutes per dollar. Because you don't insert these cards into a phone, you can use them at any phone, even in your hotel room.

USA Direct Services such as AT&T, MCI, and Sprint, while still convenient, are no longer a good value. It's much cheaper to call the United States using an Italian phone card or PIN card, but some people prefer to use their easier, pricier calling cards. Each card company has a toll-free number in each European country (for Italy: AT&T—tel. 172-1011, MCI—tel. 172-1022, Sprint—tel. 172-1877) that puts you in touch with an English-speaking operator who takes your card number and the number you want to call, puts you through, and bills your home phone number for the call (at the rate of about $2.50 for the first minute and $1.50 per additional minute, plus a $4 service charge). Oddly, you need to use a 200-lire coin or Italian phone card to dial the toll-free number. Hanging up when you hear an answering machine is expensive ($6.50). First use a coin or an Italian phone card to call home for five seconds—long enough to say "call me," or to make sure an answering machine is off so you can call back, using your USA Direct number to connect with a person. It's a rip-off to use USA Direct for calls between European countries; it's much cheaper to call direct using an Italian phone card.

Mail: Mail service is miserable throughout Italy. Postcards get last priority. If you must have mail stops, consider a few pre-reserved hotels along your route or use American Express offices. Most American Express offices in Italy will hold mail for one month. This service is free to anyone using an AmEx card or traveler's checks (and available for a small fee to others). Allow 14 days for U.S.-to-Italy mail delivery, but don't count on it. Federal Express makes pricey two-day deliveries. Phoning is so easy that I've completely dispensed with mail stops. If possible, mail nothing precious from Italy. But if you must, use the Vatican's mail service.

Sleeping

For hassle-free efficiency, I favor hotels and restaurants handy to your sightseeing activities. Rather than listing hotels scattered throughout Rome, I describe my favorite neighborhoods and recommend the best accommodations values in each, from $15 bunks to plush, with-all-the-comforts $200 doubles.

Sleeping in Rome is expensive. Cheap big-city hotels can be depressing. Tourist information services cannot give opinions on quality. A major feature of this book is its extensive listing of good-value rooms. I like places that are clean, small, central, quiet at night, traditional, inexpensive, and friendly, with firm beds— and those not listed in other guidebooks. (In Rome, for me, six out of nine is a keeper.)

Hotels

Double rooms listed in this book will range from about $50 (very simple, toilet and shower down the hall) to $200 (maximum plumbing and more), with most clustering around $120 (with private bathrooms). Three or four people economize by sharing larger rooms. Solo travelers find that the cost of a *camera singola* is often only 25 percent less than a *camera doppia*. Most listed hotels have rooms for anywhere from one to five people. If there's room for an extra cot, they'll cram it in for you. Prices are often soft— especially if you are arriving direct. If there's no middleman you're in a stronger position to bargain. Offer cash as a bargaining chip.

Hotels often give a 10 percent discount for cash (they'll avoid the credit card fee, but—more importantly—they can pocket the cash without paying the high local taxes). Consider the supply-and-demand situation. Breakfasts are legally supposed to be optional, but initial prices quoted often include breakfast and a private bathroom. Offer to skip breakfast for a better price.

Prices are fairly standard, and you normally get close to what you pay for. Shopping around earns you a better location and more character but rarely a cheaper price.

You'll save $10 to $20 if you ask for a room without a shower and just use the shower down the hall. Generally rooms with a bath or shower also have a toilet and a bidet (which Italians use for quick sponge-baths). Tubs usually come with a frustrating "telephone shower" (hand-held nozzle). If a shower has no curtain, the entire bathroom showers with you. The cord that dangles over the tub or shower is not a clothesline. You pull it when you've fallen and can't get up.

Double beds are called *matrimoniale*, even though hotels aren't interested in your marital status. Twins are *due letti singoli*. A few places have kept the old titles, *locanda* or *pension*, indicating that they offer budget beds. The Italian word for "hotel" is *albergo*.

When you check in, the receptionist will normally ask for your passport and keep it for a couple of hours. Hotels are legally required to register each guest with the local police. Relax. Americans are notorious for making this chore more difficult than it needs to be.

The hotel breakfast, while convenient, is often a bad value—$8 for a roll, jelly, and usually unlimited *caffè latte*. You can always request cheese or salami (L5,000 extra). I enjoy taking breakfast at the corner café. It's OK to supplement what you order with a few picnic goodies.

Rooms are safe. Still, zip cameras and keep money out of sight. More pillows and blankets are usually in the closet or available on request. In Italy towels and linen aren't always replaced every day. Hang your towel up to dry.

Making Reservations

Reserve your Rome room with a phone call, fax, or e-mail as soon as you can commit to a date. It's possible to visit Rome without reservations, but given the high stakes, the quality of the gems I've found for this book, and the fact that this is a Jubilee Year, I'd highly recommend making reservations.

To reserve from home, telephone first to confirm availability, then fax or e-mail your formal request. It's easy to reserve by phone. I've taken great pains to list telephone numbers with

Sleep Code

To give maximum information in a minimum of space, I use
this code to describe accommodations listed in this book.
Prices listed are per room, not per person.

- **S** = Single room (or price for one person in a double)
- **D** = Double or Twin room. "Double beds" are often two
  twins sheeted together and are usually big enough for
  nonromantic couples.
- **T** = Triple (generally a double bed with a single)
- **Q** = Quad (usually two double beds)
- **b** = Private bathroom with toilet and shower or tub
- **t** = Private toilet only (the shower is down the hall)
- **s** = Private shower or tub only (the toilet is down the hall)
- **CC** = Accepts credit cards (**V** = Visa, **M** = MasterCard,
  A= American Express). If CC isn't mentioned, assume
  you'll have to pay cash.
- **SE** = Speaks English. This code is used only when it seems
  predictable that you'll encounter English-speaking
  staff.
- **NSE** = Does not speak English. Used only when it's unlikely
  you'll encounter English-speaking staff.

According to this code, a couple staying at a "Db-
L140,000, CC:V, SE" hotel would pay a total of L140,000
(about $73) for a double room with a private bathroom. The
hotel accepts Visa or Italian cash. The staff speaks English.

long-distance instructions (see "Telephones," above; also see the
Appendix). Most hotels listed are accustomed to English-only
speakers. Fax costs are reasonable, e-mail's a steal, and simple
English is usually fine. To fax, use the handy form in the Appendix; for e-mailers, it's online at www.ricksteves.com/reservation.
If you don't get an answer to your fax request, consider that a
"no." (Many little places get 20 faxes a day after they're full and
can't afford to respond.) If you're writing, add the zip code and
confirm the need and method for a deposit. A two-night stay in
August would be "2 nights, 16/8/00 to 18/8/00" (Europeans write
the date day/month/year and hotel jargon uses your day of departure). You'll often receive a letter back requesting one night's
deposit. A credit card will usually be accepted, though you may
need to send a personal check, signed traveler's check, or a bank
draft in the local currency. If your credit card is the deposit, you
can pay with your card or cash when you arrive; if you don't show

up, you'll be billed for one night. Always reconfirm your reservations a day in advance by phone.

Honor (or cancel by phone) your reservations. Long distance is cheap and easy from public phone booths. Don't let these people down—I promised you'd call and cancel if for some reason you can't show up. Don't needlessly confirm rooms through the tourist office; they'll take a commission.

Eating

The Italians are masters of the art of fine living. That means eating…long and well. Lengthy, multi-course lunches and dinners and endless hours sitting in outdoor cafés are the norm. Americans eat on their way to an evening event and complain if the check is slow in coming. For Italians, the meal is an end in itself, and only rude waiters rush you. When you want the bill, mime-scribble on your raised palm or ask for it: *"Il conto?"*

Even those of us who liked dorm food will find that the local cafés, cuisine, and wines become a highlight of our Italian adventure. Trust me, this is sightseeing for your palate, and even if the rest of you is sleeping in cheap hotels, your taste buds will relish an occasional first-class splurge. You can eat well without going broke. But be careful; you're just as likely to blow a small fortune on a disappointing meal as you are to dine wonderfully for $20.

Roman Cuisine

In Rome you'll enjoy risotto from the north and pasta from the south. And while you'll eat wonderfully "Italian" while in Rome, you'll also find a few typically Roman dishes. Uniquely "Roman cuisine" originated as food for poor people—hearty servings of fresh local produce, simply prepared. Basic ingredients are tomatoes, garlic, cheese, and peppers. The meat is often the "fifth quarter"— organ meats. Try to venture away from the tourist-friendly pastas and grilled meats with potatoes. Here are some ideas:

Antipasto (appetizer): *Antipasto misto* (a mixed appetizer plate of cold sliced meats and cold cooked vegetables) is the popular standard here. Many restaurants display a grand buffet, and eaters are often welcome to assemble "salad bar–style" their own plate of whatever looks good. Try *caprese* (tomato and fresh mozzarella topped with basil and drizzled with olive oil) and *bruschetta* (crunchy toasted garlic bread with olive oil—impossible to duplicate outside of Italy).

Primo Piatto (first course): Among many pasta options, local specialties include *fettucini* (ribbon noodles), *spaghetti alla carbonara* (with chopped bacon, cheese, and egg), *penne all' arrabbiata* (pasta tubes with a spicy tomato/garlic/parsley sauce, literally "angry pasta"), *pasta alla amatriciana* (with spicy tomato sauce and bacon bits), and *spaghetti alla puttanesca* (with peppers, black olives, tomato, and garlic—early fast-food, literally "prostitute's spaghetti"...they could slurp it down between jobs). *Gnocchi alla Romana* is another good Roman standby (little oven-cooked potato dumplings with tomatoes or butter).

Secondi Piatto (main course): Typical main courses include *abbacchio* (milk-fed baby lamb, cooked various ways), *saltimbocca alla Romana* (veal with sage and ham cooked in butter and wine), and *fritto misto* (a mix of deep-fried meats and vegetables).

Contorno (vegetables): Along with *patate arrosto* (the standard roasted potatoes), be sure to try grilled vegetables (especially zucchini) and artichokes—*carciofi* (pressed flat and fried, served with oil and garlic) or *carciofi alla guidia* (served "Jewish style" with an anchovy garlic sauce).

Wines: The only distinctive local wine is Frascati (a light white) which is not good enough to merit ignoring other better Italian wines.

Dessert: I'll see you at the *gelatería*.

Restaurants

When restaurant hunting, choose places filled with locals, not the place with the big neon signs boasting, "We speak English and accept credit cards." Restaurants parked on famous squares generally serve bad food at high prices to tourists. Locals eat better at lower-rent locales. Family-run places operate without hired help and can offer cheaper meals. The word *osteria* (normally a simple local-style restaurant) makes me salivate. For unexciting but basic values, look for a *menù turistico*, a three- or four-course set-price menu. Galloping gourmets order à la carte with the help of a menu translator. (The *Marling Italian Menu Master* is excellent. *Rick Steves' Italian Phrase Book* has enough phrases for intermediate eaters.)

A full meal consists of an appetizer (*antipasto*, L5,000–L10,000), a first course (*primo piatto*, pasta or soup, L8,000–14,000), and a second course (*secondo piatto*, expensive meat and fish dishes, L10,000–20,000). Vegetables (*contorni, verdure*) may come with the *secondo* or cost extra (L6,000) as a side dish. Restaurants normally pad the bill with a cover charge (*pane e coperto*, around L2,000) and a service charge (*servizio*, 15 percent); these charges are listed on the menu. Italian waiters are paid well and tipping is not expected.

As you will see, the lire add up in a hurry. Light and budget eaters get by with a *primo piatto* each and sharing an *antipasto*. Italians admit that the *secondo* is the least interesting aspect of the local cuisine.

Alternatives to Restaurants

Try deli food from *rosticcerîe*, simple sandwiches in bars (below), easy meals from self-service cafeterias, and stand-up or take-out pizza from Pizza Rustica shops.

A *rosticcería* is like a deli with great cooked food to go. American-style fast food is like you know it—but with better salad bars and beer. Self-service eateries feed you without the add-ons.

Pizza is cheap and everywhere. Key pizza vocabulary: *capricciosa* (generally ham, mushrooms, and artichokes), *funghi* (mushrooms), *margherita* (tomato sauce and mozzarella), *marinara* (tomato sauce, oregano, garlic, no cheese), *quattro formaggi* (four different cheeses), and *quattro stagioni* (different toppings on each of the four quarters: ham, mushrooms, olives, and artichokes). Kids like *margherita* (cheese only) and *diavola* (closest thing in Italy to American "pepperoni"). If you ask for *peperoni* on your pizza, you'll get green or red peppers, not sausage. At Pizza Rustica take-out shops, slices are sold by weight (100 grams, or *un etto*, is a hot cheap snack; 200 grams, or *due etti*, make a light meal).

For a fast, cheap, and healthy lunch, find a *tavola calda* bar with a buffet spread of meat and vegetables and ask for a mixed plate of vegetables with a hunk of mozzarella (*piatto misto di verdure con mozzarella*). Don't be limited by what you can see. If you'd like a salad with a slice of cantaloupe and a hunk of cheese, they'll whip that up for you in a snap. Belly up to the bar and, with these key words and a pointing finger, you can get a fine *piatto misto di verdure* (mixed plate of vegetables). "*Scaldare, per favore*" means "Heated, please." Ask for *carciofo* (artichoke), *asparagi* (asparagus), *fagioli* (beans), *fagiolini* (string beans), *broccoli, carote, funghi* (mushrooms), *patate* (potato), *spinaci, zucchine, pomodoro* (tomato), *verdure miste* (mixed vegetables), mozzarella, or *grissini* (breadsticks). If something's a mystery, ask for *un assaggio* (a little taste).

Cafés and Bars

Italian "bars" are not taverns but cafés. These local hangouts serve coffee, mini-pizzas, sandwiches, and cartons of milk from the cooler, and many dish up plates of fried cheese and vegetables from under the glass counter, ready to reheat. This is my budget choice, the Italian equivalent of English pub grub. For quick meals, bars usually have trays of cheap ready-made sandwiches (*panini* or *tramezzini*)—some kinds are delightful grilled. To save time for sightseeing and room for dinner, my favorite lunch is a ham and cheese *panini* at a bar (called *tost*, grilled twice to get really hot). To get food "to go," say, "*Da portar via*" ("for the road").

Bars serve great drinks—hot, cold, sweet, or alcoholic. Half-liters of bottled water (*natural* or *frizzante*) are cheap.

If you ask for *"un caffè"* your *barista* will assume you want espresso. Cappuccino—espresso topped with foamed milk—is served to locals before noon and to tourists any time of day. (To an Italian, cappuccino is a breakfast drink and a travesty after anything with tomatoes.) Italians like it only warm. To get it hot, request *"molto caldo"* (very hot) or *"più caldo, per favore"* (hotter, please). Experiment with a few of the options...

- *caffè Americano*: espresso diluted with water
- *caffè lungo*: same as caffè Americano
- *caffè corretto*: espresso with a shot of liqueur
- *caffè freddo*: sweet and iced espresso
- *cappuccino freddo*: iced cappuccino
- *caffè hag*: espresso decaf (decaf is easily available for any coffee drink)
- *macchiato*: with only a little milk
- *caffè latte*: coffee with lots of hot milk, no foam
- *latte*: milk only

Beer on tap is *"alla spina."* Get it *piccola* (33 cl), *media* (50 cl) or *grande* (a liter). To order a glass of red (*rosso*) or white (*bianco*) wine say, *"Un bicchiere di vino rosso/bianco."* House wine comes in quarter-liter carafes (*un quarto litro*).

All bars have a WC (*bagno, toilette*) in the back and the public is entitled to use it.

Prices: You'll notice a two-tiered price system. Drinking a cup of coffee while standing at the bar is cheaper than drinking it at a table. If you're on a budget, don't sit without first checking out the financial consequences.

If the bar isn't busy, you'll often just order and pay when you leave. Otherwise (1) decide what you want; (2) find out the price by checking the price list on the wall, the prices posted near the food, or asking the barman; (3) pay the cashier; and (4) give the receipt to the barman (whose clean fingers handle no dirty lire) and tell him what you want.

Picnics

In Rome picnicking saves lots of lire and is a great way to sample local specialties. In the process of assembling your meal you get to deal with the Italians in the market scene. On days you choose to picnic, gather supplies early. You'll probably visit several small stores or market stalls to put together a complete meal, and many close around noon.

While it's fun to visit the small specialty shops, a local *alimentari* is your one-stop corner grocery store (most will slice and stuff your sandwich for you if you buy the ingredients there). A *supermercato* gives you more efficiency with less color for less cost.

Juice lovers can get a liter of O.J. for the price of a Coke or coffee. Look for "100% *succo*" (juice) on the label. Hang onto the half-liter mineral water bottles (sold everywhere for about L1,000). Buy juice in cheap liter boxes, drink some and store the extra in your water bottle. (I drink tap water—*acqua del rubinetto.)*

Picnics can be an adventure in high cuisine. Be daring. Try the fresh mozzarella, presto pesto, shriveled olives, and any UFOs the locals are excited about. Shopkeepers are happy to sell small quantities of produce, but in a busy market, a merchant may not want to weigh and sell small, three-carrot-type quantities. In this case, estimate generously what you think it should cost, and hold out the lire in one hand and the produce in the other. Wear a smile that says, "If you take the money, I'll go." He'll grab the money. A typical picnic for two might be fresh rolls, 100 grams of cheese, 100 grams of meat (100 grams = about a quarter-pound, called *un etto* in Italy), two tomatoes, three carrots, two apples, yogurt, and a liter box of juice. Total cost: $10.

Culture Shock—Accepting Italy as a Package Deal

We travel all the way to Italy to enjoy differences—to become temporary locals. You'll experience frustrations. Certain truths that we find "God-given" or "self-evident," like cold beer, ice in drinks, bottomless cups of coffee, hot showers, body odor smelling bad, and bigger being better, are suddenly not so true. One of the benefits of travel is the eye-opening realization that there are logical, civil, and even better alternatives. A willingness to go local ensures that you'll enjoy a full dose of Italian hospitality.

If there is a negative aspect to the image Italians have of Americans, it is that we are big, loud, aggressive, impolite, rich, and a bit naive. While Italians, flabbergasted by our Yankee excesses, say in disbelief, "*Mi sono cadute le braccia!*" ("I throw my arms down!"), they nearly always afford us individual travelers all the warmth we deserve.

Tours of Italy

Travel agents will tell you about normal tours of Italy, but they won't tell you about ours. At Europe Through the Back Door, we offer one-week winter getaways to Rome (maximum 20 people) and 20-day tours of Italy (departures April through October, 26 people on a big bus with lots of empty seats). For more information, see www.ricksteves.com or call 425/771-8303.

Send Me a Postcard, Drop Me a Line

If you enjoy a successful trip with the help of this book and would like to share your discoveries, please fill out and send the survey at the end of this book to me at Europe Through the Back Door, Box 2009, Edmonds, WA 98020. I personally read and value all feedback. Thanks in advance—it helps a lot.

For our latest travel information on Italy, tap into our Web site at www.ricksteves.com. To check on any updates for this book, go to www.ricksteves.com/update. My e-mail address is rick @ricksteves.com. Request a free issue of our Back Door quarterly newsletter.

Judging from all the happy postcards I receive from travelers who have used this book, it's safe to assume that you're on your way to a great, affordable vacation—with the finesse of an independent, experienced traveler. Thanks, and *buon viaggio!*

BACK DOOR TRAVEL PHILOSOPHY
As Taught in *Rick Steves' Europe Through the Back Door*

Travel is intensified living—maximum thrills per minute and one of the last great sources of legal adventure. Travel is freedom. It's recess, and we need it.

Experiencing the real Europe requires catching it by surprise, going casual... "Through the Back Door."

Affording travel is a matter of priorities. (Make do with the old car.) You can travel—simply, safely, and comfortably—anywhere in Europe for $70 a day ($80 for Rome) plus transportation costs. In many ways, spending more money only builds a thicker wall between you and what you came to see. Europe is a cultural carnival and, time after time, you'll find that its best acts are free and the best seats are the cheap ones.

A tight budget forces you to travel close to the ground, meeting and communicating with the people, not relying on service with a purchased smile. Never sacrifice sleep, nutrition, safety, or cleanliness in the name of budget. Simply enjoy the local-style alternatives to expensive hotels and restaurants.

Extroverts have more fun. If your trip is low on magic moments, kick yourself and make things happen. If you don't enjoy a place, maybe you don't know enough about it. Seek the truth. Recognize tourist traps. Give a culture the benefit of your open mind. See things as different but not better or worse. Any culture has much to share.

Of course, travel, like the world, is a series of hills and valleys. Be fanatically positive and militantly optimistic. If something's not to your liking, change your liking. Travel is addicting. It can make you a happier American, as well as a citizen of the world. Our Earth is home to 6 billion equally important people. It's humbling to travel and find that people don't envy Americans. They like us, but with all due respect, they wouldn't trade passports.

Globetrotting destroys ethnocentricity. It helps you understand and appreciate different cultures. Travel changes people. It broadens perspectives and teaches new ways to measure quality of life. Many travelers toss aside their hometown blinders. Their prized souvenirs are the strands of different cultures they decide to knit into their own character. The world is a cultural yarn shop. And Back Door Travelers are weaving the ultimate tapestry. Come on, join in!

ORIENTATION

Sprawling Rome actually feels small once you get to know it. It's the old core—within the triangle formed by the train station, the Colosseum, and the Vatican. Consider it in these layers:

The ancient city had a million people. Tear it down to size by walking through just the core. The best of the classical sights stand in a line from the Colosseum to the Pantheon.

Medieval Rome was little more than a hobo-camp of 50,000—thieves, mean dogs, and the pope, whose legitimacy required a Roman address. The medieval city, a colorful tangle of lanes, lies between the Pantheon and the river.

Window shoppers' Rome twinkles with nightlife and ritzy shopping near Rome's main drag, Via del Corso—in the triangle formed by Piazza del Popolo, Piazza Venezia, and the Spanish Steps.

Vatican City is a compact world of its own with two great, huge sights: St. Peter's Basilica and the Vatican Museum.

Trastevere, the seedy, colorful, wrong-side-of-the-river neighborhood/village, is Rome at its crustiest—and perhaps most "Roman."

Baroque Rome is an overleaf that embellishes great squares throughout the town with fountains and church facades.

Since no one is allowed to build taller than St. Peter's dome, the city has no modern skyline. And the Tiber River is ignored. After the last floods (1870), the banks were built up very high and Rome turned its back on its naughty, unnavigable river.

Planning Your Time
After considering Rome's major tourist sights, I've covered just my favorites. You won't be able to see all of these, so don't try. You'll keep coming back to Rome. After several dozen visits, I still have a healthy list of excuses to return.

GREATER ROME

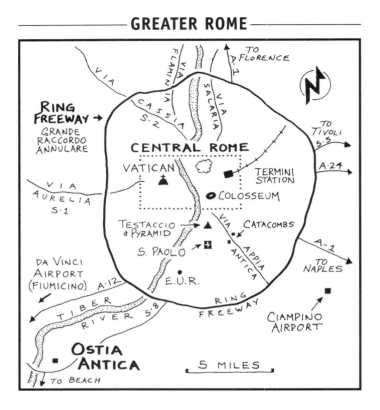

Rome in a Day

Some actually try to "do" Rome in a day. Crazy as that sounds, if all you have is a day, it's a great one. See the Vatican City (2 hours in the Vatican Museum and Sistine Chapel, 1 hour in St. Peter's), taxi over the river to the Pantheon (picnic on its steps), then hike over Capitol Hill, through the Forum, and to the Colosseum. Have dinner on Campo de' Fiori and dessert on Piazza Navona.

Rome in Two to Three Days

Do the "Caesar Shuffle" from the Colosseum to the Forum, then over Capitol Hill to the Pantheon. After a siesta, join the locals strolling from Piazza del Popolo to the Spanish Steps (see my recommended Dolce Vita Stroll, page 198). Have dinner near your hotel. On the second day, see the Vatican City (St. Peter's, climb the dome, tour the Vatican Museum). Have dinner on the atmospheric Campo de' Fiori, then walk to the Trevi Fountain

Daily Reminder

Sunday: These sights are closed today: Vatican Museum (except for the last Sunday of the month, when it's free) and the Catacombs of San Sebastian. The Pantheon and E.U.R.'s Museum of Roman Civilization close early in the afternoon. The Porta Portese flea market hops in the morning.

Monday: These sights are closed today: Borghese Gallery, Capitol Hill Museums, Octagonal Hall (of Diocletian Baths), Etruscan Museum, Castel Sant' Angelo, Protestant Cemetery, E.U.R.'s Museum of Roman Civilization, Ostia Antica, and Villa d'Este. All the ancient sites, National Museum of Rome, Vatican Museum, among others, *are* open.

Tuesday: All sights are open in Rome. Not a good day to sidetrip to Naples (its archaeological museum is closed).

Wednesday: Catacombs of San Callisto closed.

Thursday: Cappuccin Crypt closed.

Friday/Saturday: All sights are open in Rome.

and Spanish Steps (see my recommended Night Walk across Rome, page 50). With a third day, add the Borghese Gallery (reservations required) and the National Museum of Rome.

Rome in Seven Days

Rome's a great one-week getaway. Its sights can keep even the most fidgety traveler well entertained for a week.

Day 1–City orientation tour (walking tour or bus tour), then the Baths of Diocletian (Octagonal Hall) and the National Museum of Rome. Afternoon: Dolce Vita stroll and shopping.

Day 2–Do the "Caesar Shuffle" from Nero's Golden House (reservation required), to the Colosseum, Forum, Mammertine Prison, Trajan's Forum, Capitol Hill, and Pantheon.

Day 3–Vatican City: St. Peter's Basilica, climb the dome, Vatican Museum. (Note: The museum is less crowded in the afternoon but last admission is often at 14:00.)

Day 4–Sidetrip to Ostia Antica. Evening floodlit hike from Trastevere to the Spanish Steps.

Day 5–Borghese Gallery (reservation required) and Pilgrims' Rome (the churches Santa Maria Maggiore, San Clemente, and San Giovanni in Laterano).

Day 6–Sidetrip to Naples and Pompeii.

Day 7–Personal choice—Hadrian's Villa, Appian Way with Catacombs, E.U.R., Testaccio sights, more shopping, or more time at the Vatican.

Arrival in Rome

For a rundown on Rome's train station and airport, see Transportation Connections, page 200.

Tourist Information

While Rome has three main tourist information offices (abbreviated in this book as TI), the dozen or so handy TI kiosks scattered around the town at major tourist centers are handier and just as helpful. If all you need is a map, forget the TI and pick one up at your hotel.

You'll find the main TIs at the airport (tel. 06-6595-6074) and the train station (daily 8:15–19:15, near track #1, very crowded, only one open on Sun, marked with a large "i" in middle of station, tel. 06-487-1270 or 06-482-4078). The helpful central office covers the city and the region (Mon–Fri 8:15–19:15, Sat 8:15–13:45, next to Saab dealership, Via Parigi 5, tel. 06-4889-9253, www.comune.roma.it, e-mail: mail@informaroma.it).

The central TI office, near Piazza della Repubblica's huge fountain, is a five-minute walk out the front of the train station. It's air-conditioned, less crowded, and more helpful than the station TI, and it has a table to plan on—or sit under to overcome your frustration. Ask for the better "long stay" city map and *L'Evento*, the bimonthly periodical entertainment guide for evening events and fun. All hotels list an inflated rate to cover the hefty commission any TI room-finding service charges. Save money by booking direct.

The smaller TIs (daily 9:00–16:00) include kiosks near the entrance to the Forum (on Piazza del Tempio della Pace), at Via del Corso (on Largo Goldoni), in Trastevere (on Piazza Sonnino), on Via Nazionale (at Palazzo delle Esposizione), at Castel Sant' Angelo, and at St. John in Lateran.

Romanc'e is a cheap little weekly entertainment guide with a helpful English section on musical events and the pope's schedule for the week. It's sold at newsstands. Fancy hotels carry a free English monthly, *Un Ospite a Roma* (A Guest in Rome).

Enjoy Rome is a free and friendly—if entrepreneurial—information service providing maps, a free useful city guide, a room-finding service, and lots of tours—see "Tours of Rome," below (Mon–Fri 8:30–14:00, 15:30–18:30, Sat 8:30-14:00, closed Sun, 3 blocks northeast of train station at Via Varese 39, tel. 06-445-1843, fax 06-445-0734, www.enjoyrome.com).

Helpful Hints

Plan Ahead: The marvelous Borghese Gallery and newly opened Nero's Golden House both require reservations. For the Borghese

The Jubilee Year—2000

Whether you're a pilgrim or a tourist or a little of both, Rome's the place to be in 2000. It's a Jubilee Year.

While Rome sees thousands of pilgrims every year, Jubilee Years are festival years, offering Catholics around the world the Roman pilgrimage of a lifetime. The Jubilee Year comes from an Old Testament belief that God said that every 50 years we should free slaves, forgive debts, and return land to the original owners. In 1470 the Church shortened the time between Jubilee Years from 50 to 25 years.

The year 2000 happens to be the granddaddy of all Jubilee Years. Rome and the Vatican expect millions of extra visitors. As this is the first Holy Year since the fall of the USSR, this Jubilee will be huge among Eastern European Catholics, finally free to travel.

Secular travelers will be coming to Rome on a cultural pilgrimage—to see the grand city of Western Civilization all dolled up with newly restored monuments.

While some predict pandemonium, most are now expecting manageable crowds, and some hoteliers even fear a Jubilee Year bust with the expected crowds avoiding the expected crowds. I predict huge crowds of pilgrims, who will stay in institutions outside the city (at massive places recommended by the Church), but otherwise a city with more than ever to show off, better equipped than ever to do it. You'll find fleets of new buses, tourist info kiosks scattered all over town, well-organized sights with extended opening hours, a pedestrian-friendly old town, and lots of healthy competition keeping service up and prices reasonable. For the latest, check www.jubil2000.org.

If you're thinking this Jubilee commotion is outdated, consider its origin. The purpose of this redistribution of wealth is based on the notion that it takes about fifty years for aggressive people, when left unbridled, to create such an imbalance that society as a whole becomes threatened. Ignoring that imbalance can lead to a regrettably violent redistribution of wealth. (Central America's history substantiates this point. Roughly twice a century, rather than celebrate a Jubilee Year, landowners violently put down uprisings by their "unruly poor.") The pope's wish for this Jubilee Year is for the rich world to forgive the Third World debt (see page 211). While Jubilee 2000 has become a tourist event, it's still a global celebration...and a necessity.

Gallery, it's safest to make reservations well in advance before your trip (for specifics, see page 109). You can wait until you're in Rome to call for a reservation time at Nero's Golden House, though it's wise to book farther ahead (see page 32).

Museum Hours: Outdoor sights like the Colosseum, the Forum, and Ostia Antica are open roughly 9:00 to 18:00. For 2000, museum hours will probably be extended into the evening. Hours listed anywhere can vary. Confirm sightseeing plans each morning with a quick L200 telephone call asking, "Are you open today?" (*"Aperto oggi?"*; ah-PER-toh OH-jee) and "What time do you close?" (*"A che ora chiuso?"*; ah kay OH-rah kee-OO-zoh). I've included telephone numbers for this purpose. The last pages of the daily *Messaggero* newspaper list current events, exhibits, and hours.

Churches: Churches generally open early (around 7:00), close for lunch (roughly 12:00–15:00), and close late (around 19:00). Kamikaze tourists maximize their sightseeing hours by visiting churches before 9:00 and seeing the major sights that stay open during the siesta (St. Peter's, Colosseum, Forum, Capitol Hill Museums, National Museum of Rome) while all good Romans are taking it cool and easy. Many churches have "modest dress" requirements, which means no bare shoulders, miniskirts, or shorts—for men or women (although you'll find many tourists in shorts touring many churches). Many dark interiors can be lit with a coin. Whenever possible, let there be light.

Dealing with (and Avoiding) Problems

Theft Alert: With sweet-talking con artists meeting you at the station, well-dressed pickpockets on buses, and thieving gangs of children at the ancient sites, Rome is a gauntlet of rip-offs. There's no great physical risk, but green tourists will be ripped off. Thieves strike when you're distracted. Don't trust kind strangers. Keep nothing important in your pockets. Assume you're being stalked. (Then relax and have fun.) Be most on guard while boarding and leaving buses and subways. Thieves crowd the door, then stop and turn while others crowd and push from behind. The sneakiest thieves are well-dressed business men (generally with something in their hands); lately many are posing as tourists with Tevas, fannypacks, and cameras. Scams abound: Don't give your wallet to self-proclaimed "police" who stop you on the street, warn you about counterfeit (or drug) money, and ask to see your wallet.

If you know what to look out for, the gangs of children picking the pockets and handbags of naive tourists are no threat but an interesting, albeit sad, spectacle. Gangs of city-stained children (sometimes as young as 8 to 10 years old), too young to prosecute but old enough to rip you off, troll through the tourist crowds around the Colosseum, Forum, Piazza Repubblica, and train and Metro stations. Watch them target tourists distracted with a video camera or overloaded with bags. The kids look like beggars and use newspapers or cardboard signs to confuse their victims. They scram like stray cats if you're onto them. A fast-fingered mother with a baby is often nearby. The terrace above the bus stop near the Colosseum Metro stop is a fine place to watch the action and maybe even pick up a few moves of your own.

Reporting Losses: To report lost or stolen passports and documents or to file an insurance claim, you must file a police report (Carabinieri or Polizia offices at train station near platform 1, also at Piazza Venezia). To replace a passport, file the police report, then go to your embassy (see below). To report lost traveler's checks, call your bank (Visa tel. 800-874-155, Thomas Cook/Mastercard tel. 800-872-050, American Express tel. 800-872-000), then file a police report. To report stolen or lost credit cards, call the company (Visa tel. 800-877-232, Mastercard tel. 800-870-866, American Express tel. 06-7228-0371), then file a police report.

Embassies: United States (Mon–Fri 8:30–13:00, 14:00–17:30, Via Veneto 119, tel. 06-46741), Canada (Via Zara 30, tel. 06-445-981), Australia (Corso Trieste 25, tel. 06-852-721), Great Britain (Via XX Septembre 80, tel. 06-482-5441).

Emergency Numbers: Police tel. 113. Ambulance tel. 112 and 118.

Hit and Run: Walk with extreme caution. Scooters don't need to stop at red lights, and even cars exercise what drivers call the "logical option" of not stopping if they see no oncoming traffic. As Vespa scooters become electric, they'll get quieter (hooray) but more dangerous for pedestrians. Follow locals like a shadow when you cross a street (or spend a good part of your visit stranded on curbs).

Staying Healthy: The siesta is a key to survival in summertime Rome. Lie down and contemplate the extraordinary power of gravity in the eternal city. I drink lots of cold, refreshing water from Rome's many drinking fountains (the Forum has three). There's a pharmacy (marked by a green cross) in every neighborhood, including a handy one in the train station (open 7:30–22:00). A 24-hour pharmacy is on Piazza dei Cinquecento 51 (next to the train station on Via Cavour, tel. 06-488-0019). Embassies can recommend English-speaking doctors. Anyone is entitled to free emergency treatment at public hospitals. The hospital closest to the train station is Policlinico Umberto 1 (entrance for emergency treatment on Via Lancisi, translators available, Metro: Policlinico).

Getting around Rome

Sightsee on foot, by city bus, or by taxi. I've grouped your sight-seeing into walkable neighborhoods.

Public transportation is efficient, cheap, and part of your Roman experience. It starts running around 5:30 and stops around 23:30 (sometimes earlier). After midnight there are a few very crowded night buses, and taxis become more expensive and hard to get. Don't try to hail one—go to a taxi stand.

Buses and subways use the same ticket. You can buy tickets at newsstands, tobacco shops, or at major Metro stations or bus stops, but not on board (L1,500, good for 75 minutes—one Metro ride and unlimited buses). All-day bus/Metro passes cost L6,000.

Buses (especially the touristic #64) and the subway are havens for thieves and pickpockets. Assume any commotion is a thief-created distraction.

By Subway: The Roman subway system (Metropolitana) is simple, with two clean, cheap, fast lines. While much of Rome is not served by its skimpy subway, these stops are helpful: Termini (train station, National Museum of Rome at Palazzo Massimo, recommended hotels), Repubblica (Baths of Diocletian/Octagonal Hall, main tourist office, recommended hotels), Barberini (Cappuc-cin Crypt, Trevi Fountain), Spagna (Spanish Steps, Villa Borghese, classy shopping area), Flaminio (Piazza del Popolo, start of recommended Via del Corso Dolce Vita stroll), Ottaviano (St. Peter's and Vatican City), Cipro-Musei Vaticani (Vatican Museum, recommended hotels), Colosseo (Colosseum, Roman Forum, recommended hotels), and E.U.R. (Mussolini's futuristic suburb).

By Bus: Bus routes are clearly listed at the stops. Punch your ticket in the orange stamping machine as you board—or you are cheating. Riding without a stamped ticket on the bus, while rela-tively safe, is stressful. Inspectors fine even innocent-looking tourists L100,000. If you hop a bus without a ticket, locals who use tickets rather than a monthly pass can sell you a ticket from their wallet bundle. Ideally buy a bunch of tickets so you can hop a bus without first having to search for an open tobacco shop.

Learn which buses serve your neighborhood. Here are a few worth knowing about:

#64: Termini (train station), Piazza della Repubblica, Via Nazionale (recommended hotels), Piazza Venezia (near Forum), Largo Argentina (near Pantheon), St. Peter's Basilica. Ride it for a city overview and to watch pickpockets in action (can get horribly crowded).

#8: This tram connects Largo Argentina with Trastevere (get off at Piazza Mastai).

#492: Stazione Tiburtina, Termini, Piazza Barberini, Piazza

ROME'S METRO

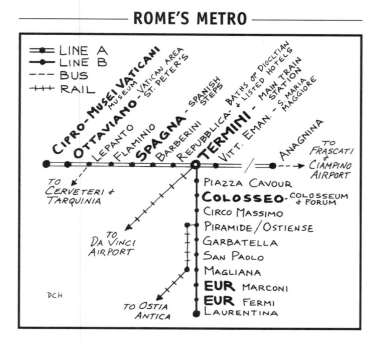

Venezia, Corso Rinascimento, Piazza Cavour (Castel Sant' Angelo), Piazza Risorgimento (near Vatican Museum).

#714: Termini, Santa Maria Maggiore, San Giovanni in Laterano, Terme di Caracalla.

Rome has cute "*electrico*" minibuses which wind through the narrow streets of old and interesting neighborhoods. These are handy for sightseeing and fun for simply joyriding:

Electrico #116: Through the medieval core of Rome from Campo de' Fiori to Piazza Barberini via the Pantheon.

Electrico #117: San Giovanni in Laterano, Colosseo, Via dei Serpenti, Trevi Fountain, Piazza di Spagna, Piazza del Popolo.

By Taxi: Taxis start at about L5,000 (surcharges of L2,000 on Sun, L5,000 for night hours of 22:00–7:00, L2,000 surcharge for luggage, L14,000 for airport, tip about 10 percent by rounding up to the neareast thousand lire). Sample fares: Train station to Vatican–L16,000; train station to Colosseum–L10,000; Colosseum to Trastevere–L12,000. Three or four companions with more money than time should taxi almost everywhere. It's tough to wave down a taxi in Rome. Find the nearest taxi stand. (Ask a local or in a shop "*Dov'è* [DOH-vay] *una fermata dei tassi?*" They're listed on my maps.) Unmarked, unmetered taxis at train stations and the airport are usually a rip-off. Taxis listing their telephone number on the door have fair meters—use them. To save time and energy, have your hotel call a taxi (the meter starts when the call is received). (Some Rome cab telephone numbers: 06-6645, 06-8822, 06-3570.)

Tours of Rome

You can choose from an assortment of walking tours or a bus tour.

Enjoy Rome—This company offers several English-only city walking tours daily, such as greatest ancient and Baroque hits, Vatican, Rome at night, Trastevere, and Jewish Ghetto (3 hrs, L30,000 per tour, L25,000 if under 26, kids under 15 free). Ask about their bike tours of Rome (3 hrs, L35,000 includes bike rental, helmet, and guide) or air-conditioned bus to Pompeii (L70,000, 3-hr drive each way, offered every other day, tour and admission not included, tel. 06-445-1843, also see listing on page 24).

Walks of Rome—Lately students working for "Walks of Rome" have been giving free 45-minute tours of the Colosseum in order to promote their other guided walks. The tours bring the Colosseum to life and they hope you'll join—and pay for—their other walks: Forum (2 hrs), Vatican City (full-day church, museum, Sistine), night tour (great Renaissance and Baroque squares, nightly at 19:00), and catacombs (3 hrs by bus with some of city included). Their pub crawl tour meets at 20:00 on the Spanish Steps and finishes at a disco six pubs later around midnight. I've never seen 50 young, drunk people having so much fun (tel. 06-484-853 or 0347-795-5175, e-mail: walkingtours@yahoo.com).

Scala Reale—Tom Rankin (an American architect in love with Rome and his Roman wife) runs Scala Reale, a small company committed to sorting out the rich layers of Rome for small groups with a longer-than-average attention span. Their excellent walking tours vary in length from two to four hours and start at L30,000 per person. Try to book in advance since their small groups are limited to six and fill up fast. Their fascinating "Rome Orientation" walks lace together lesser-known sights from antiquity to the present, helping you get a sense of how Rome works (U.S. tel. 888/467-1986, Italy tel. 06-445-1477, fax 06-4470-0898, www.scalareale.org, e-mail: scalareale@mail.nexus.it).

Bus Tour—The ATAC city bus tour offers your best budget orientation tour of Rome. In 2.5 hours you'll have 80 sights pointed out to you (by a live guide in English and maybe one other language) and get out for 15-minute stops at St. Peter's Square, Colosseum, and Piazza Venezia (L15,000, bus #110 departs daily at 10:30, 14:00, 15:00, 17:00, and 18:00 from in front of train station from platform C, buy tickets at information kiosk there, tel. 06-4695-2252).

ROME
SIGHTS

I've clustered Rome's sights into walkable neighborhoods, some quite close together. The Colosseum and the Forum are a few minutes' walk from Capitol Hill. Beyond that is the Pantheon, a 10-minute walk. I like to group these sights in one great day, starting at the Colosseum and ending at the Pantheon. (Note that the Pantheon closes at 13:00 on Sunday.)

Note that in this chapter, Rome's most important sights have the shortest listings and are marked with a ✪ (and page number). These sights are covered in much more detail in one of the tours included in this book.

In Italian museums, art is dated with A.C. (for Avanti Cristo, or B.C.) and D.C. (for Dopo Cristo, or A.D.). O.K.?

To connect sights by night, try my Night Walk Across Rome (page 50), which includes the Trevi Fountain and Spanish Steps. To join the parade of people strolling down Via del Corso every evening, take my recommended Dolce Vita Stroll (page 198).

Ancient Rome: The Colosseum and Forum Area

The core of the ancient city, where the grandest monuments were built, is between the Colosseum and Capitol Hill. Rome hopes to eventually close down its main drag, Via dei Fori Imperiali (a plan controversial for the traffic problems this would create) and turn this entire area into a vast archaeological park.

Beware of gangs of young theives, particularly between the Colosseum and the Forum; they're harmless if you know what to look for (see "Theft Alert" on page 26).

The following sights are listed in roughly geographical order from the Colosseum area to Capitol Hill. Except for St. Peter-in-Chains Church, the sights date from ancient Rome. St. Peter-in-Chains is included here because it's close to the Colosseum.

▲**St. Peter-in-Chains Church (San Pietro in Vincoli)**—Built in the fifth century to house the chains that held St. Peter, this church is most famous for its Michelangelo statue. Check out the much-venerated chains under the high altar, then focus on Moses (free, but pop in L500 to light the statue, Mon–Sat 7:00–12:30, 15:30–19:00, Sun 7:30–12:30, a short walk uphill from the Colosseum, modest dress required).

Pope Julius II commissioned Michelangelo to build a massive tomb that had 48 huge statues and was crowned by a grand statue of this egomaniac pope. When Julius died, the work had barely been started, and no one had the money or concern for Julius to finish the project. Michelangelo finished one statue, the one of Moses, and left a few unfinished statues: Leah and Rachel flanking Moses in this church, the "prisoners" now in Florence's Accademia, and the "slaves" now in Paris' Louvre.

Study the powerful statue; it's mature Michelangelo. He worked on it in fits and starts for 30 years. Moses has received the Ten Commandments. As he holds the stone tablets, his eyes show a man determined to stop his tribe from worshiping the golden calf and idols... a man determined to win salvation for the people of Israel. Why the horns? Centuries ago, the Hebrew word for "rays" was mistranslated as "horns."

▲**Nero's Golden House (Domus Aurea)**—The remains of Emperor Nero's "Golden House" are newly opened to the public. The original entrance to the house was all the way over at the Arch of Titus in the Forum. The massive house once sprawled across the valley (where the Colosseum now stands) and up the hill—the part you tour today. Larger even than Bill Gates' place, it was a pain to vacuum. A colossal, 100-foot bronze statue of Nero towered over eveything. The house incorporated an artificial lake (where the Colosseum was later built) and a forest stocked with game. Every building used the best multicolored marble and walls held the finest frescoes. No expense was too great for Nero—his mistress bathed daily in the milk of 500 wild asses kept for the purpose.

Nero (ruled A.D. 54–68) was Rome's most notorious emperor. He killed his own mother, kicked his pregnant wife to death, crucified St. Peter, and—most galling to his subjects—was a bad actor. When Rome burned in A.D. 64, Nero was accused of torching it to clear land for an even bigger house. The Romans rebelled, and Nero stabbed himself in the neck, crying, "What an artist dies in me!"

While only hints of the splendid, colorful frescoes survive, the towering vaults and the basic immensity of the place are impressive. As you wander through rooms that are now underground, look up at the holes in the ceiling. Imagine how much of old Rome still hides underground ... and why the subway is limited to two lines. Visits are allowed only with an escort (25 people every 15 minutes) and a reservation (L12,000, daily 9:00–20:00, last entry at 19:00, tour lasts 40 min, escort speaks Italian, audio guides-L3,000, 200 yards northeast of Colosseum, through a park gate, up a hill and on the left). To reserve a place, call 06-3974-9907 or 199-199-100 (Mon–Sat 8:00–20:00, information tel. 06-481-5576).

▲▲▲**Colosseum**—This 2,000-year-old building is *the* great example of Roman engineering (L10,000, daily 9:00–19:00, off-season 9:00–15:00, tel. 06-481-5576 or 06-700-4261). ✪ See Colosseum Tour on page 55.

▲**Arch of Constantine**—The well-preserved arch, which stands between the Colosseum and the Forum, commemorates a military coup and, more importantly, the acceptance of Christianity in the Roman Empire. In A.D. 312 an ambitious general named Constantine (who had a vision he could win under the sign of the cross) defeated the Emperor Maxentius. Constantine became Emperor and promptly legalized Christianity. ✪ See Colosseum Tour on page 55.

▲▲▲**Roman Forum (Foro Romano)**—This is ancient Rome's birthplace and civic center, and the common ground between Rome's famous seven hills (free, daily 9:00–19:30 or an hour before darkness, off-season 9:00–15:00, tel. 06-699-0110). ✪ See Forum Tour on page 60.

▲**Palatine Hill**—The hill overlooking the Forum was the home of the emperors and contains scant remains of imperial palaces. The newly opened Palatine museum has sculptures and fresco fragments but is nothing special. From a pleasant garden, you'll get an overview of the Forum; on the far side, look down into an emperor's private stadium and then beyond at the dusty Circus Maximus (L12,000, daily 9:00–19:30 or an hour before darkness, off-season 9:00–15:00, entrance is near Arch of Titus at south end of the Forum). ✪ See Palatine Hill Tour on page 71.

▲**Mammertine Prison**—The 2,500-year-old, cistern-like prison that once held Saints Peter and Paul is worth a look (donation requested, daily 9:00–12:00, 14:30–18:00, at the foot of Capitol Hill, near Forum's Arch of Septimius Severus). When you step into the room you'll hit a modern floor. Ignore that and look up at the hole in the ceiling, from which prisoners were lowered. Then take the stairs down to the actual prison floor-level. As you descend, you'll walk past a supposedly miraculous image of Peter's face, created when a guard pushed him into the wall. Downstairs you'll see the column that Peter was chained to. It's said that in this room a miraculous fountain sprang up so Peter could baptize other prisoners. The upside-down cross commemorates Peter's upside-down crucifixion.

Imagine humans, amid rotting corpses, awaiting slow deaths. On the walls near the entry are lists of notable prisoners (Christian and non-Christian) and the ways they were executed: *strangolati*, *decapitato*, *morto di fame* . . .

▲**Trajan's Column and Forum**—This is the grandest column and best example of "continuous narration" we have from antiquity. More than 2,500 figures on the 40-meter-high column tell of Trajan's victorious Dacian campaign (circa A.D. 103, in present-day Romania), from the assembling of the army at the bottom to the victory sacrifice at the top. (Free, always open and viewable, on Piazza Venezia across street from Victor Emmanuel Monument).
✪ See Trajan's Column and Forum Tour on page 79.

Capitol Hill Area

There are several ways to get to the top of Capitol Hill. From the north (Piazza Venezia), take the grand stairs located to right of the big white Victor Emmanuel Monument (described below). From the south (the Forum), take either the steep staircase of winding road, which converge at a great Forum overlook and a refreshing water fountain. Block the spout with your fingers; water spurts up for drinking. Romans call this *il nasone* (the nose). A cheap Roman boy takes his date out for a drink at *il nasone*.

▲▲**Capitol Hill (Campidoglio)**—This hill was the religious and political center of ancient Rome. It's still the home of the city's government. Michelangelo's Renaissance square is bounded by two fine museums and the mayoral palace. Its centerpiece is a copy of the famous equestrian statue of Marcus Aurelius (the original is behind glass in the adjacent museum). To approach the great square the way Michelangelo wanted you to, enter from the grand stairway off Piazza Venezia. Coming up the stairs, you'll see the new Renaissance face of Rome with its back to the Forum, facing the new city. Notice how Michelangelo gave the buildings the "giant order"—huge pilasters make the existing two-story buildings feel one-storied and more harmonious with the new square. Notice also how the statues atop these buildings welcome you and then draw you in. The terraces just downhill (past either side of the mayor's palace) offer fine views of the Forum.

Capitol Hill Museums—These two museums, Palazzo dei Conservatori and Palazzo Nuovo, are in two buildings that face each other atop Capitol Hill (one L10,000 ticket is good for both museums, free entrance on last Sun of month, while closed in 1999 they plan to open for 2000, Tue–Sun 9:00–19:00 or later, closed Mon, tel. 06-6710-2071).

The 500-year-old **Palazzo dei Conservatori** is one of the world's oldest museums (it's the building nearest the river, to the right of Marcus Aurelius as you face him). Outside the entrance, notice the marriage announcements and, very likely, wedding parties taking advantage of the photo opportunity. Inside the free courtyard, have a look at giant chunks of a statue of Emperor Constantine. (A rare public toilet hides near the museum ticket-taker.) The museum is worthwhile, with lavish rooms housing several great statues. Tops is the original (500 B.C.) Etruscan *Capitoline Wolf* (the little statues of Romulus and Remus were added in the Baroque age). Don't miss the *Boy Extracting a Thorn* or the enchanting *Commodus as Hercules.* The second-floor painting gallery—except for one Caravaggio—is forgettable.

Palazzo Nuovo, across the square, houses mostly portrait busts of forgotten emperors. But it has two must-sees: the *Dying Gaul* (first floor up) and the restored, gilded bronze equestrian statue of Marcus Aurelius (behind glass in the museum courtyard). This greatest surviving equestrian statue of antiquity was the original centerpiece of the square. While most such pagan statues were destroyed by Dark-Age Christians, Marcus (the great pagan philosopher-emperor) was mistaken as Constantine (the first Christian emperor) and therefore spared.

Descend the stairs leading to Piazza Venezia. At the bottom of the stairs, look up the long stairway on your right (which pilgrims climb on their knees) for a good example of the earliest style of Christian church. While pilgrims find it worth the climb, sightseers can skip it.

Also from the bottom of the stairs, look left down the street several blocks to see a condominium actually built around surviving ancient pillars and arches of Teatro Marcello—perhaps the oldest inhabited building in Europe. Facing Piazza Venezia, look down into the ditch on your right to see how everywhere modern Rome is built on the forgotten frescoes and mangled mosaics of ancient Rome.

Piazza Venezia—This vast square is the focal point of modern Rome. The Via del Corso, which starts here, is the city's axis, surrounded by Rome's classiest shopping district. From the Palazzo Venezia's balcony above the square (to your right with back to Victor Emmanuel Monument), Mussolini whipped up the nationalistic fervor of Italy. Fascist masses filled the square screaming, "Four more years!" or something like that. (Fifteen years later, they hung him from a meat hook in Milan.)

Victor Emmanuel Monument—This oversized monument to an Italian king was part of Italy's rush to overcome the new country's strong regionalism and to create a national identity after

unification in 1870. Romans think of it not as an altar of the
fatherland but as "the wedding cake," "the typewriter," or "the
dentures." It wouldn't be so bad if it weren't sitting on a priceless
acre of ancient Rome and if they had chosen better marble (this is
too in-your-face white and picks up the pollution horribly),
though one of this book's authors happens to like the monument.
Soldiers guard Italy's Tomb of the Unknown Soldier as the eternal
flame flickers. Stand with your back to it and see how Via del
Corso bisects Rome.

Pantheon Area

▲▲▲**Pantheon**—For the greatest look at the splendor of Rome,
antiquity's best-preserved interior is a must. Built two millennia
ago, this influential domed temple served as the model for Michelangelo's dome of St. Peter's, the dome of Florence's Duomo, and
many domes that grace U.S. state capitol buildings (free, Mon–Sat
9:00–18:30, Sun 9:00–13:00, tel. 06-6830-0230). ✪ See Pantheon
Tour on page 83.

▲▲**Churches near the Pantheon**—✪ For more information on
the following churches, see page 85. The **Church of San Luigi
dei Francesi** has a magnificent chapel painted by Caravaggio
(free, Fri–Wed 7:30–12:30, 15:30–19:00, Thu 7:30–12:30, sightseers should avoid Mass at 7:30 and 19:00, modest dress recommended). The only Gothic church in Rome is **Santa Maria sopra
Minerva**, with a little-known Michelangelo statue, *Christ Bearing
the Cross* (the church is on a little square behind the Pantheon to
the east). The **Church of St. Ignazio**, a church several blocks east
of the Pantheon, is a riot of Baroque illusions with a false dome.
(Both churches open early, take a siesta: Sopra Minerva closes
at 12:00, St. Ignazio at 12:30, and both reopen from around 15:30
to 19:00; modest dress recommended.)

A few blocks away, back across Corso Vittorio Emmanuele,
is the rich and Baroque **Gesu Church**, headquarters of the Jesuits
in Rome. The Jesuits powered the Church's Counter-Reformation.
With Protestants teaching that all roads to heaven didn't pass
through Rome, the Baroque churches of the late 1500s were
painted with spiritual road maps that said they did.

Walk out the Gesu Church and two blocks down Corso V.
Emmanuele to the **Sacred Area** (Largo Argentina), an excavated
square facing the boulevard, about four blocks south of the Pantheon. Walk around this square and look into the excavated pit at
some of the oldest ruins in Rome. Near here, Caesar was assassinated. Today this is a refuge for cats—some 250 of them are cared
for by volunteers. You'll see them (and their refuge) at the far (west)
side of the square.

HEART OF ROME

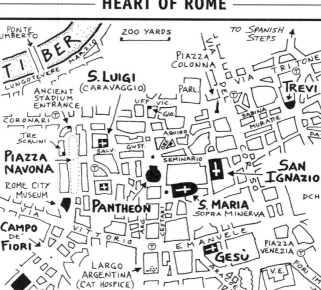

▲**Trevi Fountain**—This bubbly Baroque fountain of Neptune with his entourage is a minor sight to art scholars but a major nighttime gathering spot for teens on the make and tourists tossing coins. ✪ See Night Walk across Rome on page 50.

East Rome: Near the Train Station

These sights are within a 10-minute walk of the train station. By Metro, use the Termini stop for the National Museum and the Piazza Repubblica stop for the rest.

▲▲▲**National Museum of Rome in Palazzo Massimo**—This museum houses the greatest collection of ancient Roman art anywhere, including busts of emperors and a Roman copy of the Greek Discus Thrower (L12,000, daily 9:00-19:45, tel. 06-481-5576, the second floor can be visited only with escort, get time for 45-minute tour upon arrival, not possible to reserve in advance). ✪ See National Museum of Rome Tour on page 96.

— EAST ROME —

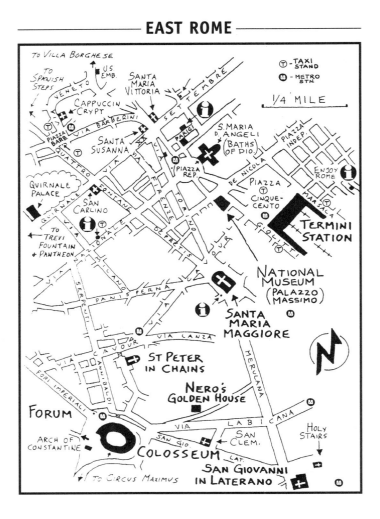

Baths of Diocletian—Around A.D. 300 Emperor Diocletian built the largest baths in Rome. This sprawling meeting place, with baths and schmoozing spaces to accommodate 3,000 bathers at a time, was a big deal in ancient times. While most of it is still closed, two sections—both facing Piazza della Repubblica—are open and worth a visit: (1) the Church of Santa Maria degli Angeli, once the great central hall of the baths, now a church; and (2) the Octagonal Hall, once a gymnasium, now a free gallery showing off fine bronze and marble statues—the kind that would have decorated the baths of imperial Rome (free, Tue–Sat 9:00–14:00, Sun 9:00–13:00, closed Mon). ✪ See Baths of Diocletian Tour on page 91.

▲**Santa Maria della Vittoria**—This church houses Bernini's statue of a swooning *St. Teresa in Ecstasy* (free, daily 7:00–12:00, 16:00–19:00, on Largo Susanna, about 5 blocks northwest of train station, Metro: Repubblica). Once inside the church, you'll find Teresa to the left of the altar.

Teresa has just been stabbed with God's arrow of fire. Now the angel pulls it out and watches her reaction. Teresa swoons, her eyes roll up, her hand goes limp, she parts her lips…and moans. The smiling, Cupid-like angel understands just how she feels. Teresa, a 16th-century Spanish nun, later talked of the "sweetness" of "this intense pain," describing her one-ness with God in ecstatic, even erotic, terms.

Bernini, the master of multimedia, pulls out all the stops to make this mystical vision real. Actual sunlight pours through the alabaster windows; bronze sunbeams shine on a marble angel holding a golden arrow. Teresa leans back on a cloud and her robe ripples from within, charged with her spiritual arousal. Bernini has created a little stage-setting of heaven. And watching from the "theater boxes" on either side are members of the family that commissioned the work.

North Rome: Villa Borghese and nearby Via Veneto

▲**Villa Borghese**—Rome's unkempt "Central Park" is great for people watching (plenty of modern-day Romeos and Juliets). Take a row on the lake or visit its fine museums.

▲▲▲**Borghese Gallery**—This private museum, filling a cardinal's mansion in the park, is newly restored and offers one of Europe's most sumptuous art experiences. Observe its slick mandatory reservation system and you'll enjoy a collection of world-class Baroque sculpture, including Bernini's *David* and his excited statue of Apollo chasing Daphne, as well as paintings by Caravaggio, Raphael, Titian, and Rubens—without any crowds.

Cost, Hours, and Reservations: L12,000, Tue–Fri 9:00–21:00, Sat 9:00–23:30, Sun 9:00–20:00, closed Mon. Reservations are easy to get in English over the Internet (www.ticketeria.it) or by phone (dial 06-32810; if you get a recording, English follows the Italian, Mon–Fri 9:00–19:00, Sat 9:00–13:00). Entry times: 9:00, 11:00, 13:00, 15:00, 17:00, 19:00 (Jun–Sept the museum may stay open until 23:30, info tel. 06-854-8577). ✪ For more on reservations, as well as a self-guided tour, see Borghese Gallery Tour on page 109.

Etruscan Museum (Villa Giulia Museo Nazionale Etrusco)—
The Etruscan civilization thrived in this part of Italy around
600 B.C., when Rome was an Etruscan town. The Etruscan civilization is fascinating but the Villa Giulia Museum is hard to get
to, extremely low-tech, and in a state of disarray. I don't like it,
and Etruscan fans will prefer the Vatican Museum's Etruscan
section. Still, the Villa Giulia does have the famous "husband and
wife sarcophagus" (a dead couple seeming to enjoy an everlasting
banquet from atop their tomb; 6th century B.C from Cerveteri),
the Apollo from Veio statue (of textbook fame), and an impressive
room filled with gold sheets of Etruscan printing and temple statu-
ary from the Sanctuary of Pyrgi (L8,000, Tue–Sun 9:00–19:00,
closed Mon, open late on summer weekends and closes early off-
season, Piazzale di Villa Giulia 9, tel. 06-321-7224).
▲**Cappuccin Crypt**—If you want bones, this is it. The crypt is
below the church of Santa Maria della Immaculata Concezione on
Via Veneto, just up from Piazza Barberini. The bones of more than
4,000 monks who died between 1528 and 1870 are in the basement,
all artistically arranged for the delight—or disgust—of the always-
wide-eyed visitor. The soil in the crypt was brought from Jerusalem
400 years ago, and the monastic message on the wall explains that
this is more than just a macabre exercise. Pick up a few of Rome's
most interesting postcards (donation, Fri–Wed 9:00–12:00, 15:00–
18:00, closed Thu, Metro: Barberini). A painting of St. Francis by
Caravaggio is upstairs. Just up the street you'll find the American
embassy, Federal Express, and fancy Via Veneto cafés filled with
the poor and envious looking for the rich and famous.
Ara Pacis (Altar of Peace)—In 9 B.C, after victories in Gaul and
Spain, Emperor Augustus celebrated the beginning of the Pax
Romana by building this altar of peace. Peace is almost worshiped
here. The north and south walls show a procession with realistic
portraits of the imperial family in Greek Hellenistic style. It's a
fine combination of Roman grandeur and Greek elegance. While
the altar is likely to be closed for restoration, you can see much of
it through the windows at any hour (a long block west of Via del
Corso on Via di Ara Pacis, on east bank of river near Ponte
Cavour, nearest Metro: Spagna).

West Rome: Vatican City Neighborhood

Vatican City is actually a tiny independent country (just over 100
acres) that contains the huge Vatican Museum (with Michelangelo's
Sistine Chapel) and St. Peter's Basilica (with Michelangelo's exquisite *Pietà*). A helpful tourist office is just to the left of St. Peter's
Basilica (Mon–Sat 8:30–19:00, closed Sun, tel. 06-6988-4466, Vatican switchboard tel. 06-6982, www.vatican.va). The entrances to

VATICAN AREA

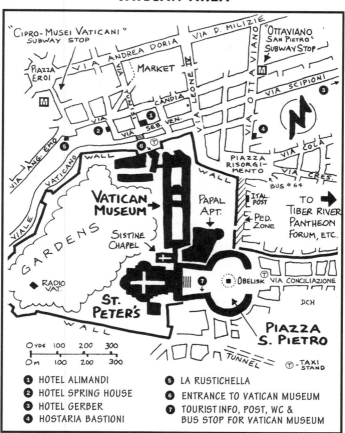

1 HOTEL ALIMANDI
2 HOTEL SPRING HOUSE
3 HOTEL GERBER
4 HOSTARIA BASTIONI

5 LA RUSTICHELLA
6 ENTRANCE TO VATICAN MUSEUM
7 TOURIST INFO, POST, WC &
    BUS STOP FOR VATICAN MUSEUM

St. Peter's and to the Vatican Museum are a 15-minute walk apart (follow the outside of the Vatican wall). The neighborhood's new Metro stop, Cipro-Musei Vaticani, is closer to the Vatican Museum, while the Ottaviano stop is closer to St. Peter's.

▲▲▲St. Peter's Basilica—There is no doubt: This is the richest and most impressive church on earth. To call it vast is like calling God smart. Don't miss Michelangelo's *Pietà* (behind bulletproof glass) to the right of the entrance. Bernini's altar work and seven-story-tall bronze canopy (*baldacchino*) are brilliant. The church strictly enforces its dress code. Dress modestly—a dress or long pants, shoulders covered (men and women).

Hours: Daily May–Sept 7:00–19:00, until 18:00 Oct–Apr (ticket booth to treasury closes one hour earlier). All are welcome to join in the hour-long Mass at the front altar (Mon–Sat at 17:00, Sun at 17:45). The view from the dome is worth the climb (L8,000 elevator plus 300-step climb, allow an hour to go up and down, daily May–Sept 8:30–19:00, Oct–Apr daily 8:30–18:00, ticket booth closes half hour earlier). ⚫ See St. Peter's Basilica Tour on page 141.

▲▲▲**Vatican Museum**—The four miles of displays in this immense museum—from ancient statues to Christian frescoes to modern paintings—are topped by the Raphael Rooms and Michelangelo's glorious Sistine Chapel.

Cost and Hours: L18,000, Apr–mid-Jun and Sept–Oct: Mon–Fri 8:45–16:30, Sat 8:45–13:45, closed Sun, except last Sun of month when museum is free; the rest of the year it's open Mon–Sat 8:45–13:45. Last entry 45 minutes before closing. The Sistine Chapel closes 30 minutes before the rest of the museum. Closed May 1, Jun 29, Aug 15, Nov 1, Dec 8, and on church holidays. Tel. 06-6988-3333. ⚫ See Vatican Museum Tour on page 117.

▲**Castel Sant' Angelo**—Built as a tomb for the emperor; used through the Middle Ages as a castle, prison, and place of last refuge for popes under attack; and today a museum, this giant pile of ancient bricks is packed with history.

Ancient Rome allowed no tombs—not even the emperor's—within its walls. So Hadrian grabbed the most commanding position just outside the walls and across the river and built a tomb (c. A.D. 139) well within view of the city. His mausoleum was a huge cylinder (64 meters wide, 21 meters high) topped by a cyprus grove and crowned by a huge statue of Hadrian himself riding a chariot. For nearly a hundred years (from Hadrian to Caracalla in A.D. 217), Roman emperors were buried here.

In 590 the Archangel Michael appeared above the mausoleum to Pope Gregory the Great. Sheathing his sword, the angel signaled the end of a plague. The fortress that was Hadrian's mausoleum eventually became a fortified palace, renamed for the "holy angel."

After Dark Age centuries as a fortress and prison, the pope built the elevated corridor connecting Castel Sant' Angelo with the Vatican (1277). Since Rome was repeatedly plundered by invaders, Castel Sant' Angelo was a handy place of last refuge for threatened popes. In anticipation of long sieges, rooms were decorated with papal splendor (you'll see paintings by Crivelli, Signorelli, and Mantegna). In the 16th century, during a sack of Rome by troops of Charles V of Spain, the pope with his entourage of hundreds lived for months inside the castle (an unimaginable ordeal considering the food service at the top-floor bar).

After you walk around the entire base of the castle, take the small staircase down to the original Roman floor. In the atrium, study the model of the castle in Roman times and imagine the niche in the wall filled with a towering "welcome to my tomb" statue of Hadrian. From here a ramp leads to the right spiraling 125 meters. Fine brickwork and bits of mosaic survive (but the holes in the wall held a long-gone marble veneer). At the end of the ramp, stairs climb to the room where the ashes of the emperors were kept. These stairs continue to the top, where you'll find the papal apartments. Don't miss the Sala del Tesoro (treasury), where the wealth of the Vatican was locked up in a huge chest. Miss the 58 rooms of the military museum. The views from the top are great—pick out landmarks as you stroll around—and a restful coffee with a view of St. Peter's is worth the price (admission–L10,000, Tue–Fri 9:00–21:00, Sat 9:00–24:00, Sun 9:00–20:00, closed Mon, tel. 06-681-9111, Metro: Lepanto, bus #64, #80, #87, #280 or #492).

Ponte Sant' Angelo, the bridge leading to Castel Sant' Angelo, was built by Hadrian for quick and regal access from downtown to his tomb. The three middle arches are actually Roman originals and a fine example of the empire's engineering expertise. The angels were designed by Bernini and finished by his students.

Southwest Rome: Trastevere

Trastevere is the colorful neighborhood across (*tras*) the Tiber (*tevere*) river. Trastevere offers the best look at medieval-village Rome. The action all marches to the chime of the church bells. Go there and wander. Wonder. Be a poet. This is Rome's Left Bank.

This proud neighborhood was long a working-class area. Now becoming trendy, high rents are driving out the source of so much color. Still, it's a great people scene, especially at night.

Start your exploratory stroll at **Piazza di Santa Maria in Trastevere**. While today's fountain is from the 17th century, there's been a fountain here since Roman times.

Santa Maria in Trastevere, one of Rome's oldest churches, was made a basilica in the fourth century when Christianity was legalized (free, daily 7:30–13:00, 15:00–19:00). It was the first church dedicated to the Virgin Mary. The portico (covered area just outside the door) is decorated with fascinating ancient fragments filled with early Christian symbolism. Most of what you see today dates from around the 12th century, but the granite columns come from an ancient Roman temple, and the ancient basilica floor plan (and ambience) survives. The 12th-century mosaics behind the altar are striking and notable for their portrayal of Mary—the first to show her at the throne with Jesus in Heaven. Look below the scenes from the life of Mary to see ahead-of-their-time paintings (by Cavallini, from 1300), predating the Renaissance by 100 years.

To get to Trastevere, taxi or ride the bus (from Vatican area—#23; from Via Nazionale hotels—take #64, #70, #115, or #640 to Largo Argentina, then transfer to #8 and get off at Piazza Mastai for Trastevere).

Before leaving Trastevere, wander the back streets (if hungry, see Eating chapter). If you want to walk from Trastevere to Campo de' Fiori to link up with the Night Walk across Rome (page 50): From Trastevere's church square (Piazza di Santa Maria), take Via del Moro to the river and cross on Ponte Sisto, a pedestrian bridge with a good view of St. Peter's dome. Continue straight ahead for one block. Take the first left, which leads down Via di Capo di Ferro through the scary and narrow darkness to Piazza Farnese, with the imposing Palazzo Farnese. Michelangelo contributed to the facade of this palace, now the French embassy. The fountains on the square feature huge, one-piece granite hot tubs from the ancient Roman Baths of Caracalla. One block from there (opposite the palace) is the atmospheric square Campo de' Fiori.

South Rome: Testaccio and the Pyramid

Three fascinating lesser sights cluster at the Piramide Metro stop between the Colosseum and E.U.R. in the gritty Testaccio neighborhood. (This is a quick and handy stop as you return from E.U.R. or when changing trains en route to Ostia Antica.)

Working-class since ancient times, Testaccio has recently gone trendy bohemian and visitors will wander through an awkward mix of yuppie and proletarian worlds not noticing—but perhaps feeling—the "keep Testaccio for the Testaccians" graffiti.

Pyramid of Gaius Cestius—The Marc Antony/Cleopatra scandal (around the time of Christ) brought exotic Egyptian styles into vogue. A rich Roman magistrate, Gaius Cestius, had a pyramid built as his tomb. Made of brick covered in marble, it was completed in just 330 days (as stated in its Latin inscription) and fell far short of Egyptian pyramid standards. It was later incorporated into the Aurelian Wall (located next to Piramide Metro stop).

Porta Ostiense—This formidable gate (also next to Piramide Metro stop) is from the Aurelius Wall, begun in the third century under Emperor Aurelius, marking the beginning of the end of the Roman Empire. The wall encircled the city and was 12 miles long and 25 feet high, with 14 main gates and 380 hundred-foot-tall towers. Most of what you'll see today is circa A.D. 400. This gate was reconstructed by the barbarians in the sixth century. (A Museum of the Roman Wall at Porta San Sebastian is due to reopen soon; see "Ancient Appian Way," below).

——— TESTACCIO ———

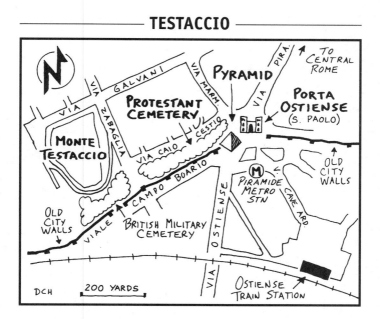

Protestant Cemetery—The Cimitero Acattolico per gli Stranieri al Testaccio (cemetery for the burial of non-Catholic foreigners) is a Romantic tomb-filled park running along the wall just beyond the pyramid. From the Piramide Metro stop, walk between the pyramid and the Roman gate on Via Persichetti, then go left on Caio Cestio to the gate of the cemetery. Ring the bell (donation box, Tue–Sun 9:00–18:00, Oct–Mar 9:00-17:00, closed Mon).

Originally, none of the Protestant epitaphs were allowed any mention of heaven. Signs direct visitors to the graves of notable non-Catholics who died in Rome since 1738. Many of the buried were diplomats. And many, such as Shelley and Keats, were from the Romantic Age; they came on the Grand Tour and—"captivated by the fatal charms of Rome," as Shelley wrote—never left. Head left toward the pyramid. Keats lies in the far corner. At the pyramid, look down on Matilde Talli's cat hospice (flier at the gate). Volunteers use donations to care for these "Guardians of the Departed" who "provide loyal companionship to these dead."

Monte Testaccio—Just behind the Protestant Cemetery (as you leave, turn left and continue two blocks down Caio Cestio) is a 110-foot-tall ancient trash mountain. It's made of broken *testae*— broken earthenware jars used to haul mostly wine 2,000 years ago when this was a gritty port warehouse district. After 500 years of sloppy dock work, Rome's lowly eighth hill was built. Because the caves dug into the hill stay cool, trendy bars, clubs, and restaurants compete with gritty car repair places for a spot. The neighborhood was once known for a huge slaughterhouse and a Gypsy camp squatting inside an old military base. Now it's home to the Villagio Globale, a site for concerts and techno-raves. For a youthful and lively night scene, adventurers might consider a trip out to Monte Testaccio.

Ancient Appian Way (Via Appia Antica)

Since the fourth century B.C this has been Rome's gateway to the East. The first section was perfectly straight. It was the largest, widest, fastest road ever, the wonder of its day, called the "Queen of Roads." Eventually this most important of Roman roads stretched 700 kilometers to the port of Brindisi—where boats sailed for Greece and Egypt. Twenty-nine such roads fanned out from Rome. Just as Hitler built the autobahn system in anticipation of an empire, the emperors realized the military and political value of a good road system. A central strip accommodated animal-powered vehicles and elevated sidewalks served pedestrians. As it left Rome, the road was lined with tombs and funerary monuments. Imagine a funeral procession passing under the pines and cypress and past a long line of pyramids, private mini-temples, altars, and tombs.

Hollywood created the famous image of the Appian Way lined with Spartacus and his gang of defeated and crucified slave rebels. This image is only partially accurate. Regardless of Kirk Douglas, Spartacus was killed in battle.

Tourist's Appian Way: The road starts about two miles south of the Colosseum at the massive San Sebastian Gate. There's a Museum of the Roman Wall here (closed but hoping to open soon, interesting look at Roman defense and chance to scramble along a stretch of the ramparts). Half a mile down the road are the two most historic and popular catacombs, those of San Callisto and San Sebastian (described below). Beyond that the road gets pristine and traffic-free, popular for biking and evocative hiking.

To reach the Appian Way, take the Metro to the Colli Albani stop, then catch bus #660 to Via Appia Antica—its last stop and the start of an interesting stretch of Via Appia Antica (conveniently, the stop is next to a café that rents bikes). The stretch between the third and 11th milestones is most interesting.

▲▲**Catacombs**—The catacombs are burial places for (mostly) Christians who died in ancient Roman times. By law, no one was allowed to be buried within the walls of Rome. While pagan Romans were into cremation, Christians preferred to be buried.

But land was expensive and most Christians were poor. A few wealthy landowning Christians allowed their land to be used as burial places.

The 40 or so known catacombs circle Rome about three miles from its center. From the first through the fifth centuries, Christians dug an estimated 360 miles of tomb-lined tunnels with networks of galleries as many as five layers deep. The Christians burrowed many layers deep for two reasons: to get more mileage out of the donated land and to be near martyrs and saints already buried there. The tufa—soft and easy to cut but becoming very hard when exposed to air—is perfect for the job. Bodies were wrapped in linen (like Christ). Since they figured the Second Coming was imminent, there was no interest in embalming the body.

When Emperor Constantine became a Christian in 312, Christians had a new, interesting problem. There would be no more persecuted martyrs to bind them and inspire them. Thus the early martyrs and popes assumed more importance, and Christians began making pilgrimages to their burial places in the Catacombs.

In the 800s, when barbarian invaders started ransacking the tombs, Christians moved the relics of saints and martyrs to the safety of churches in the city center. For a thousand years the catacombs were forgotten. Around 1850 they were excavated and became part of the romantic Grand Tour of Europe.

Finding abandoned plates and utensils from ritual meals in the candlelit galleries led Romantics to guess that persecuted Christians hid out and lived in these catacombs. This Romantic legend grew. But Catacombs were not used for hiding out. They are simply early Christian burial grounds. With a million people in Rome, the easiest way for the 10,000 or so early Christians to hide out was not to camp in the Catacombs (which everyone, including the government, knew about), but to melt into the city.

The underground tunnels, while empty of bones, are rich in early Christian symbolism which functioned as a secret language. The dove symbolized the soul. You'll see it quenching its thirst (worshiping), with an olive branch (at rest), or happily perched (in paradise). Peacocks, known for their "incorruptible flesh," symbolized immortality. The shepherd with a lamb on his shoulders was the "good shepherd," the first portrayal of Christ as a kindly leader of his flock. The fish was used because in Greek the first letters of these words—"Jesus Christ, Son of God, Savior"—spelled "fish." You'll see pictures of people praying with their hands raised up—the custom at the time. And the anchor is a cross in disguise. A second-century bishop had written on his tomb: "All who understand these things, pray for me." Catacomb tours are essentially the same. Which one you visit is not important.

E.U.R.

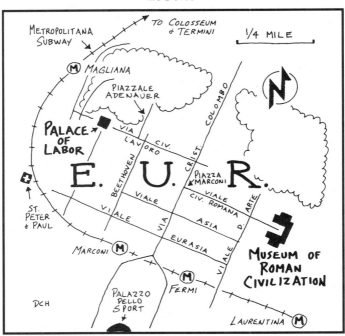

The Catacombs of San Callisto, the official cemetery for the Christians of Rome and burial place of third-century popes, is the most historic. Sixteen bishops (early popes) were buried here. Buy your L8,000 ticket and wait for your language to be called. They move lots of people quickly. If one group seems ridiculously large (over 50 people), wait for the next English tour (Thu–Tue 8:30–12:00, 14:30–17:30, closed Wed, Via Appia Antica 110).

The Catacombs of San Sebastian are 300 meters farther down the road (L8,000, Mon–Sat 8:30–12:00, 14:30–17:30, closed Sun, Via Appia Antica 136). Dig this: The catacombs have a Web site—www.catacombe.roma.it.

E.U.R.

In the late 1930s Italy's dictator Mussolini planned an international exhibition to show off the wonders of his fascist society. But these wonders brought us World War II, and Il Duce's celebration never happened. The unfinished mega-project was completed in the 1950s and now houses government offices and big obscure museums.

If Hitler and Mussolini won the war, our world might look like E.U.R. (pronounced "ay-oor"). Hike down E.U.R.'s wide, pedestrian-mean boulevards. Patriotic murals, aren't-you-proud-to-be-an-extreme-right-winger pillars, and stern squares decorate the soulless planned grid and stark office blocks. Boulevards named for Astronomy, Electronics, Social Security, and Beethoven are more exhausting than inspirational. Today E.U.R. is worth a trip for its Museum of Roman Civilization.

The Metro skirts E.U.R. with three stops (10 minutes from the Colosseum): Use E.U.R. Magliana for the "Square Colosseum" and E.U.R. Fermi for the Museum of Roman Civilization (both described below). Consider walking 30 minutes from the palace to the museum through center of E.U.R.

From the Magliana subway stop, stairs lead uphill to the **Palace of the Civilization of Labor (Palazzo del Civilta del Lavoro)**—the essence of Fascist architecture. With its giant, no-questions-asked, patriotic statues and its black and white simplicity, this is E.U.R.'s tallest building and landmark. It's understandably nicknamed the "Square Colosseum." Around the corner, Café Palombini is still decorated in the 1930s style and is now quite trendy with young Romans (7:00–24:00, good gelato, pastries and snacks, Piazzale Adenauer 12, tel. 06-591-1700).

▲**Museum of Roman Civilization (Museo della Civilta Romana)**—With 59 rooms filled with with plaster casts and models illustrating the greatness of classical Rome, this vast and heavy museum gives a strange, lifeless, close-up look at Rome. Each room has a theme, from military tricks to musical instruments. One long hall is filled with casts of the reliefs of Trajan's Column. The highlight is the 1:250 scale model of Constantine's Rome—c. A.D. 300 (L5,000, Tue–Sat 9:00–19:00, Sun 9:00–13:30, closed Mon, Piazza G. Agnelli, from Metro: E.U.R. Fermi, walk 10 minutes up Via dell Arte, you'll see its colonnade on the right, tel. 06-592-6041).

Rome can be grueling. But a fine way to enjoy this historian's rite of passage is an evening walk lacing together Rome's floodlit night spots. Fine urban spaces, real-life theater vignettes, sitting so close to a Bernini fountain that traffic noises evaporate, water flickering its mirror on the marble, jostling with local teenagers to see all the gelato flavors, enjoying lovers straddling more than the bench, jaywalking past flak-proof-vested *polizia*, marveling at the ramshackle elegance that softens this brutal city for those who were born here and can imagine living nowhere else—these are the flavors of Rome best tasted after dark.

Campo de' Fiori

Start at the Campo de' Fiori (Field of Flowers), my favorite outdoor dining room after dark (see the Eating chapter). The statue of Giordano Bruno, a heretic who was burned in 1600 for believing the world was round and not the center of the universe, marks the center of this great and colorful square. Bruno overlooks a busy produce market in the morning and strollers after sundown. This neighborhood is still known for its free spirit and occasional demonstrations. When the statue of Bruno was erected in 1889, local riots overcame Vatican protests against honoring a heretic. Bruno faces his executioner, the Vatican Chancellory (the big white building in the corner a bit to his right), while his pedestal reads: "And the flames rose up."

At the east end of the square (behind Bruno), the ramshackle apartments are built right into the old outer wall of ancient Rome's mammoth Theater of Pompey. This entertainment complex covered several city blocks, stretching from here to Largo Argentina. Julius Caesar was assassinated here while the Senate was renting meeting space.

NIGHT WALK ACROSS ROME

The square is lined with and surrounded by fun eateries. Bruno also faces La Carbonara, which gave birth to pasta carbonara. The Forno, nest door, is a popular place for hot and tasty take-out *pizza bianco* (plain but spicy pizza bread).

•*If Bruno did a hop, step, and jump forward, then turned right on Via dei Baullari and marched 200 yards, he'd cross the busy Corso Vittorio Emanuele and find...*

Piazza Navona

Rome's most interesting night scene features street music, artists, fire-eaters, local Casanovas, ice cream, fountains by Bernini, and outdoor cafés (splurge worthy if you've got time to sit and enjoy the human river of Italy).

This oblong square retains the shape of the original racetrack that was built by the emperor Domitian. (You can still see the ruins of the original entrance. Exit the square at the north end, take an immediate left and look down to the left 20 feet below the current street level.) Since ancient times, the square has been a center of Roman life. In the 1800s, the city would flood the square to cool off the neighborhood.

The **Four Rivers fountain** in the center is the most famous fountain by the man who remade Rome in Baroque style, Gian Lorenzo Bernini. Four burly river gods (representing the four continents that existed in 1650) support an obelisk, while the water of the world gushes everywhere. The Nile has his head covered (since the head-waters were unknown then). The Ganges holds an oar. The Danube turns to admire the obelisk, which originally stood here in Domitian's stadium. And the Rio de la Plata from Uruguay tumbles backward in shock, wondering how he ever made the top four. Bernini enlivens the fountain with exotic flora and fauna from these newly discovered lands. Homesick Texans may want to find the armadillo.

The Plata river god is gazing upward at the church of Saint Agnes, worked on by Bernini's former student turned rival, Borromini. Borromini's concave facade helps reveal the dome and epitomizes the curved symmetry of Baroque. Tour guides say that Bernini designed his river god to look horrified at Borromini's work. Or he may be shielding his eyes from St. Agnes' nakedness, as she was stripped before being martyred. But the fountain was completed two years before Borromini even started work on the church.

At the **Tre Scalini café** (near the fountain), sample some *tartufo* "death-by-chocolate" ice cream, world-famous among connoisseurs of ice cream and chocolate alike (L5,500 to go, L12,000 at a table). Seriously admire a painting by a struggling artist. Request "Country Roads" from an Italian guitar-player, and don't be surprised when he knows it. Listen to the white noise of gushing water and exuberant humans.

• *Leave Piazza Navona directly across from Tre Scalini café, go (east) past rose peddlers and palm readers, jog left around the guarded building, and follow the brown sign to . . .*

The Pantheon

The Pantheon is straight down Via del Salvatore (cheap pizza place on left just before the Pantheon, easy WC at McDonald's). Sit for a while under the floodlit and moonlit Pantheon's portico.

The 40-foot single-piece granite columns of the Pantheon's entrance show the scale the ancient Romans built on. The columns support a triangular, Greek-style roof with an inscription that says that "M. Agrippa" built it. In fact, it was built *("fecit")* by Emperor Hadrian (A.D. 120) who gave credit to the builder of an earlier structure. This impressive entranceway gives no clue that the greatest

wonder of the building is inside—a domed room that inspired later domes, from Michelangelo's St. Peter's to our U.S. state capitols. Notice how the pavement slants down from McDonald's to the Pantheon, showing how high modern Rome has built on ancient rubble. ✪ For more information, see Pantheon Tour on page 83.
• *With your back to the Pantheon, veer two o'clock to the right down Via Olfeni.*

From the Pantheon to Piazza Colonna

After passing Bar Pantheon, you'll see **Tazza d'Oro Casa del Caffè**, one of Rome's top coffee shops, dating back to the days when this area was licensed to roast coffee beans. Look back at the fine view of the Pantheon from here. Via Olfeni leads to Piazza Capranica.

Piazza Capranica is home to the big, plain Florentine Renaissance–style Palazzo Capranica. Big shots, like the Capranica family, built stubby towers on their palaces—not for any military use, but just to show off. Leave the piazza to the right of the palace, between the palace and the church. Via in Aquiro leads to a sixth-century B.C. **Egyptian obelisk** (taken as a trophy by Augustus after his victory in Egypt over Mark Antony and Cleopatra). Walk into the guarded square past the obelisk and face the huge parliament building. A short detour to the left (past Albergo National) brings you to some of Rome's best gelato. **Gelatería Caffè Pasticceria Giolitti** is cheap to-go or elegant and splurge-worthy for a sit among classy locals (open daily until very late, your choice: cone or *bicchierini* cup, Via Uffici del Vicario 40). Or head directly from the parliament into the next, even grander square.

Piazza Colonna features a huge second-century column honoring Marcus Aurelius. The big, important-looking palace is the prime minister's residence.
• *Cross Via del Corso, Rome's noisy main drag, jog right (around the Y-shaped shopping gallery from 1928), and head down Via dei Sabini to the roar of the water, light, and people of the Trevi fountain.*

The Trevi Fountain

The Trevi fountain is an example of how Rome took full advantage of the abundance of water brought into the city by its great aqueducts. This watery Baroque avalanche was built in 1762 by Nicola Salvi, hired by a pope celebrating his reopening of the ancient aqueduct that powers it. Salvi used the palace behind the fountain as a theatrical backdrop for Neptune's "entrance" into the square. Neptune surfs through his watery kingdom while Triton blows his conch shell.

The square is always lively, with lucky Romeos clutching

dates while unlucky ones clutch beers. Romantics toss a coin over their shoulder, thinking it will give them a wish and assure their return to Rome. That may sound silly, but every year I go through this touristic ritual...and it actually seems to work.

Take some time to people watch (whisper a few breathy *bellos* or *bellas*) before leaving.

• *Face the fountain, then go past it on the right down Via delle Stamperia to Via del Triton. Cross the busy street and continue to the Spanish Steps (ask, "Dov'è Piazza di Spagna?"—Spagna rhymes with "lasagna"), a few blocks and thousands of dollars of shopping opportunities away.*

Spanish Steps (Piazza di Spagna)

The Piazza di Spagna, with the very popular Spanish Steps, got its name 300 years ago when this was the site of the Spanish Embassy. It's been the hangout of many Romantics over the years (Keats, Wagner, Openshaw, Goethe, and others). The British poet John Keats pondered his mortality then died in the building on the right side of the steps.

The Boat Fountain at the foot of the steps, which was done by Bernini's father, Pietro Bernini, is powered by an aqueduct. All of Rome's fountains are aqueduct-powered; their spurts are determined by the water pressure provided by the various aqueducts. This one, for instance, is much weaker than Trevi's gush.

The piazza is a thriving night scene. Window-shop along Via Condotti which stretches away from the Steps. This is where Gucci and other big names cater to the trend-setting jet set. Facing the Spanish Steps, you can walk right about a block to tour one of the world's biggest and most lavish McDonald's (clean WC). There's a taxi stand in the courtyard outside McDonald's. Or the Spagna Metro stop is just to the left of the Steps (usually open until 23:30) to zip you home.

COLOSSEUM
TOUR

Rome has many layers—modern, Baroque, Renaissance, Christian—but let's face it, "Rome" is Caesars, gladiators, chariots, centurions, _"Et tu, Brute,"_ trumpet fanfares, and thumbs up or thumbs down. That's the Rome we'll look at. Our "Caesar Shuffle" begins with the downtown core of ancient Rome, the Colosseum. A logical next stop is the Forum, just next door, past the Arch of Constantine.

Orientation

Cost: L10,000
Hours: Daily 9:00–19:00, off-season 9:00–15:00.
Getting there: The Metro stop, Colosseo, lets you out just across the street from the monument. Look out for young street thieves (see page 26).
Information: Outside the entrance of the Colosseum, vendors sell handy little _Rome, Past and Present_ books with plastic overlays to un-ruin the ruins (marked L20,000, pay no more than L15,000). For a fee, the modern-day gladiators pose for photos. A WC is behind the Colosseum (facing ticket entrance, go right; WC is under stairway). Tel. 06-481-5576 or 06-700-4261.
Tours: As you stand in the ticket line, students may offer you a free tour. The tours are good (and free because they'll try to get you to pay for their other tours—see "Tours of Rome" at the end of the Orientation chapter).
Tour length: Allow 45 minutes.

Exterior of Colosseum

• _View the Colosseum from the Forum fence near the grassy patch across the street from the "Colosseo" subway station._

Built when the Roman Empire was at its peak (A.D. 80), the Colosseum represents Rome at its grandest. The Flavian Amphitheater

ANCIENT ROME

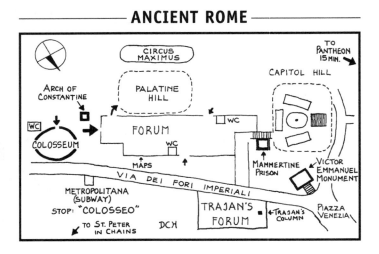

(its real name) was an arena for gladiator contests and public spectacles. When killing became a spectator sport, the Romans wanted to share the fun with as many people as possible. They did this by sticking two Greek theaters together. The outside (the grassy patch) was decorated with a 100-foot bronze statue that gleamed in the sunlight. The final structure was colossal—a "coloss-eum," the wonder of its age. It could accommodate 50,000 roaring fans (100,000 thumbs).

The Romans pioneered the use of the rounded arch and concrete, enabling them to build on this colossal scale. They made a shell of brick, then filled it in with concrete. Inside, you'll see this clearly among the ruins. Iron pegs held the larger stones together—notice the small holes that pockmark the sides. When it was done, the whole thing was faced with shining travertine marble (still visible on the top level).

The exterior says a lot about the Romans. They were great engineers, not artists. While the essential structure is Roman, the facade is Greek, decorated with the three types of Greek columns—Doric (bottom), Ionic (middle), and Corinthian (top). Originally, copies of Greek statues stood in the arches of the upper two stories. The Colosseum

was designed to be functional more than beautiful. If ancient Romans visited the United States today as tourists, they'd send home postcards of our greatest works of "art"—freeways.

Only a third of the original Colosseum remains. Earthquakes destroyed some of it, but most was carted off as easy pre-cut stones for other buildings during the Middle Ages and Renaissance.

• *Enter by the south entrance—to your right, past the Arch of Constantine. Buy your ticket and go inside. Move up to a railing overlooking the arena.*

Interior of Colosseum

You're on arena level. What we see now are the underground passages beneath the playing surface. The oval-shaped arena (86 by 50 yards) was originally covered with boards, then sprinkled with sand (*arena* in Latin). Like modern stadiums, the spectators ringed the playing area. The brick masses around you supported the first small tier of seats, and you can see two larger, slanted supports higher up. A few marble seats survive on the opposite side. Wooden beams stuck out from the top to support an enormous canvas awning that could be hoisted across by armies of sailors to provide shade for the spectators—the first domed stadium.

"Hail, Caesar! We who are about to die salute you!" The gladiators would enter the arena from the west end (to your left), parade around to the sound of trumpets, stop at the emperor's box at the "50-yard line" (where you're standing), raise their weapons, shout this salute—and the fights would begin. The fights pitted men against men, men against beasts, and beasts against beasts.

The gladiators were usually slaves, criminals, or poor people who got their chance for freedom, wealth, and fame in the ring. They learned to fight in training schools, then battled their way up the ranks. The best were rewarded like our modern sports stars with fan clubs, great wealth, and product endorsements.

The animals came from all over the world: lions, tigers, bears, oh my, crocodiles, elephants, and hippos (not to mention exotic human "animals" from the "barbarian" lands). They were kept in cages beneath the arena floor, then lifted up in elevators; released

at floor-level, the animals would pop out from behind blinds into the arena—the gladiator didn't know where, when, or by what he'd be attacked. Nets ringed the arena to protect the crowd. The stadium was inaugurated with a 100-day festival in which 2,000 men and

9,000 animals were killed. Colosseum employees squirted perfumes around the stadium to mask the stench of blood. For a lighthearted change of pace between events, the fans watched dogs bloody themselves fighting porcupines.

If a gladiator fell helpless to the ground, his opponent would approach the emperor's box and ask: Should he live or die? Sometimes the emperor left the decision to the crowd, who would judge based on how valiantly the man had fought. They would make their decision—thumbs up (Latin word: *siskel*) or thumbs down (*ebert*).

And Christians? Did they throw Christians to the lions like in the movies? Christians were definitely thrown to the lions, made to fight gladiators, crucified, and burned alive...but probably not here in this particular stadium. Maybe, but probably not.

Rome was a nation of warriors that built an empire by conquest. The battles fought against Germans, Egyptians, barbarians, and strange animals were played out daily here in the Colosseum for the benefit of city-slicker bureaucrats who got vicarious thrills watching brutes battle to the death. The contests were always free, sponsored by politicians to buy votes or to keep Rome's growing mass of unemployed rabble off the streets.

• *With these scenes in mind, wander around. Climb to the upper deck for a more colossal view (stairs near the exit, at north end).*

As you exit, the Roman Forum is directly in front of you, the subway stop is on your right, and the Arch of Constantine is on your left.

Arch of Constantine

If you are a Christian, were raised a Christian, or simply belong to a so-called "Christian nation," ponder this arch. It marks one of the great turning points in history—the military coup that made Christianity mainstream. In A.D. 312 an upstart general named Constantine defeated the Emperor Maxentius in one crucial battle. The night before, he'd seen a vision of a cross in the sky. Constantine became emperor and promptly legalized Christianity. With this one battle, a once-obscure Jewish sect with a handful of followers was now the state religion of the entire Western world.

In A.D. 300 you could be killed for being a Christian; by 400 you could be killed for not being one. Church enrollment boomed.

By the way, don't look too closely at the reliefs decorating this arch. By the fourth century Rome was on its way down. Rather

than struggle with original carvings, the makers of this arch plugged in bits and pieces scavenged from existing monuments. The arch is newly restored and looking great. But any meaning read into the stone will be very jumbled.

• *The Roman Forum (Foro Romano) is to the right of the Arch, 100 yards west. If you're ready for a visit, see the next chapter.*

ROMAN FORUM TOUR

6

rome

Heart of the Empire

The Forum was the political, religious, and commercial center of the city. Rome's most important temples and halls of justice were here. This was the place for religious processions, elections, important speeches, and parades by conquering generals. As Rome's empire expanded, these few acres of land became the center of the civilized world.

Orientation

Cost: Free. (There's a L12,000 charge to visit the Palatine Hill; see next chapter.)

Hours: Daily 9:00–19:30 or an hour before darkness, off-season 9:00–15:00.

Getting there: The closest Metro stop is Colosseo. The Forum has two entrances: one on Via dei Fori Imperiali, and the other—where this tour begins—near the Colosseum (about 100 yards west of the Arch of Constantine). WCs are at either entrance. Tel. 06-699-0110.

Tour length: Allow one hour.

Overview

● *Start at the entrance nearest the Colosseum. Hike up the ramp marked "Via Sacra." Stand next to the triumphal Arch of Titus and look out over the rubble-littered valley called the Forum.*

The hill in the distance with the bell tower is Capitol Hill. Immediately to your left, with all the trees, is Palatine Hill. The valley in between is rectangular, running roughly east (the Colosseum end) to west (Capitol Hill). The rocky path at your feet is the Via Sacra, which runs through the the valley—through the trees, past the large brick Senate building, under the Arch of Septimius Severus—#13 on map—and (originally) up Capitol Hill.

THE FORUM

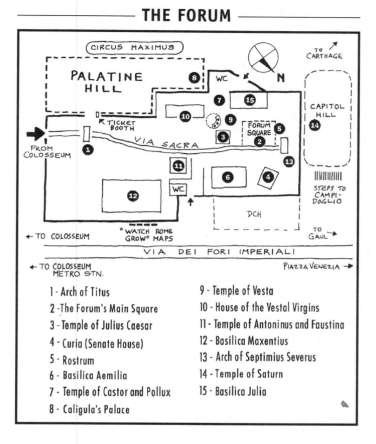

1 - Arch of Titus
2 - The Forum's Main Square
3 - Temple of Julius Caesar
4 - Curia (Senate House)
5 - Rostrum
6 - Basilica Aemilia
7 - Temple of Castor and Pollux
8 - Caligula's Palace

9 - Temple of Vesta
10 - House of the Vestal Virgins
11 - Temple of Antoninus and Faustina
12 - Basilica Maxentius
13 - Arch of Septimius Severus
14 - Temple of Saturn
15 - Basilica Julia

Picture being here when a conquering general returned to Rome with crates of booty. The valley was full of gleaming white buildings topped with bronze roofs. The Via Sacra—Main Street of the Forum—would be lined with citizens waving branches and carrying torches. The trumpets would sound as the parade began. First came porters, carrying chests full of gold and jewels. Then came a parade of exotic animals from the conquered lands—elephants, giraffes, hippopotamuses—for the crowd to "ooh" and "ahh"

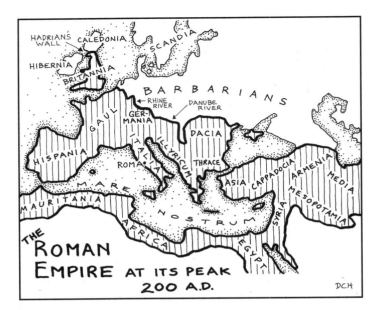

at. Next were the prisoners in chains, with the captive king on a wheeled platform so the people could jeer and spit at him. Finally, the conquering hero himself would drive down in his four-horse chariot, with rose petals strewn in his path. The whole procession would go the length of the Forum and up the face of Capitol Hill to the Temple of Saturn (the eight big columns midway up the hill— #14 on map), where they'd place the booty in Rome's coffers. They'd continue up to the summit to the Temple of Jupiter (not visible today) to dedicate the victory to the King of the Gods.

1. Arch of Titus (Arco di Tito)

The Arch of Titus commemorated the Roman victory over the province of Judea (Israel) in A.D. 70. The Romans had a reputation as benevolent conquerors who tolerated the local customs and rulers. All they required was allegiance to the Empire, which could be shown by worshiping the current emperor as a god. No problem for most conquered people, who already had half a dozen gods on their prayer lists. But the Israelites' god was jealous and refused to let his people worship the emperor. Israel revolted. After a short but bitter war, the Romans defeated the rebels, took Jerusalem, and sacked their temple.

The propaganda value of Roman art is demonstrated on the inside of this arch, where a relief shows the emperor Titus in a

Rome — Republic and Empire (500 B.C.–A.D. 500)

Ancient Rome spanned about a thousand years, from 500 B.C. to A.D. 500. In that time Rome expanded from a small tribe of barbarians to a vast empire, then dwindled slowly to city size again. For the first 500 years, when Rome's armies made her ruler of the Italian peninsula and beyond, Rome was a republic governed by elected senators. During the next 500 years, a time of world conquest and eventual decline, Rome was an empire ruled by a military-backed dictator.

Julius Caesar bridged the gap between republic and empire. This ambitious general and politician, popular with the people because of his military victories and charisma, suspended the Roman constitution and assumed dictatorial powers around 50 B.C., until he was assassinated by a conspiracy of senators. His adopted son, Augustus, succeeded him, and soon "Caesar" was not just a name but a title.

Emperor Augustus ushered in the Pax Romana, or Roman peace (A.D. 100–200), a time when Rome reached her peak and controlled an empire that stretched even beyond Eurail—from Scotland to Egypt, from Turkey to Morocco.

chariot being crowned by the Goddess Victory. (Thanks to the tolls of modern pollution, they both both look like they've been through the wars.) The other side shows the sacking of the temple—soldiers carrying a Jewish candelabrum and other plunder. The two (unfinished) plaques on poles were to have listed the conquered cities.

The brutal crushing of this rebellion (and another one 60 years later) devastated the nation of Israel. With no temple as a center for their faith, the Jews scattered throughout the world (the Diaspora). There would be no Jewish political entity again for two thousand years, until modern Israel was created after World War II.

• *Stroll into the Forum, down the Via Sacra. Pass through the trees and between ruined buildings until it opens up to a flat, grassy area.*

2. The Forum's Main Square

The original Forum, or main square, was this flat patch about the size of a football field, stretching to the foot of Capitol Hill. Surrounding it were once temples, law courts, government buildings, and triumphal arches.

Rome was born right here. According to legend, twin brothers Romulus (Rome) and Remus were orphaned in infancy and raised by a she-wolf on top of the Palatine. Growing up, they found it hard to get dates. So they and their cohorts attacked the nearby Sabine tribe, fought them here in this valley, and kidnapped their women. After they made peace, the marshy valley became the meeting place and then the trading center for the scattered tribes on the surrounding hillsides.

The square was the busiest and most crowded—and often the seediest—section of town. Besides the senators, politicians, and currency exchangers, there were even sleazier types—souvenir hawkers, fortune-tellers, gamblers, slave marketers, drunks, hookers, lawyers, and tour guides.

The Forum is now rubble, no denying it, but imagine the Forum in its prime: blinding white marble buildings with 40-foot columns and shining bronze roofs; rows of statues painted in realistic colors; chariots rattling down the Via Sacra. Mentally replace tourists in T-shirts with tribunes in togas. Imagine the buildings towering and the people buzzing around you while an orator gives a rabble-rousing speech from the Rostrum. If things still look like just a pile of rocks, at least tell yourself, "But Julius Caesar once leaned against these rocks."

• *At the east end of the main square sit the foundations of a temple now capped with a peaked wood-and-metal roof . . .*

3. The Temple of Julius Caesar (Templo del Divo Giulio, or "Ara di Cesare")

On this spot—right under the metal roof—Julius Caesar's body was burned after his assassination.

Caesar (100–44 B.C.) changed Rome—and the Forum—dramatically. He cleared out many of the wooden market stalls and began to ring the square with even grander buildings. (Caesar's house was located right behind the temple, near that clump of trees.)

However, not everyone liked his urban design or his politics. When he assumed dictatorial powers, he was ambushed and stabbed to death by a conspiracy of senators, including his adopted son Brutus (*Et tu, Brute?*).

The funeral was held here, facing the main square. The citizens gathered and speeches were made. Mark Antony stood up to say (in Shakespeare's words), "Friends, Romans, countrymen, lend me your ears. I come to bury Caesar, not to praise him." When Caesar's body was burned, the citizens who still loved him threw anything at hand on the fire, requiring the fire department to come put it out. Then the very people who had killed him dedicated this temple in his name, making him the first Roman to be a god.

• *Head down the Via Sacra towards the arch of Septimius Severus. Stop at the big, well-preserved brick building with the triangular roof. If the door's open, look in.*

4. The Curia

The Senate House (Curia) was the most important political building in the Forum. Three hundred senators, elected by the citizens of Rome, met here to debate and create the laws of the land. Their wooden seats once circled the building in three tiers; the Senate president's podium sat at the far end. The marble floor is from ancient times. Listen to the echoes in this vast room—the acoustics are great.

Rome prided itself on being a republic. Early in its history,

the people threw out the king and established rule by elected representatives. Each Roman citizen was free to speak his mind and have a say in public policy. Even when emperors became the supreme authority, the Senate was a power to be reckoned with.

(Note: Although Julius Caesar was assassinated in "the Senate," it wasn't here—the Senate was temporarily meeting across town.)

A statue and two reliefs inside the Curia help build our mental image of the Forum. The statue, made of porphyry marble in about A.D. 100, with its plugged-in head, arms, and feet missing, was a tribute to an emperor, probably Hadrian or Trajan. The two relief panels may have decorated the Rostrum. One shows a government amnesty on debt, with people burning their debt records, while the other shows intact architecture and the latest fashion in togas.

• *Go back down the Senate steps to the metal guardrail and look right to a 10-foot-high wall marked . . .*

5. Rostrum (Rostri)

Nowhere was Roman freedom more apparent than at this "Speaker's Corner." The Rostrum was a raised platform, 10 feet high and 75 feet long, decorated with statues, columns, and the prows of ships (*rostra*). Rome's orators great and small came here trying to draw a crowd and sway public opinion. Mark Antony rose to offer Caesar the laurel-leaf crown of kingship, which Caesar publicly (and hypocritically) refused while privately becoming a dictator. Men like Cicero railed against the corruption and decadence that came with the city's newfound wealth. In later years, daring citizens even spoke out against the emperors, reminding them that Rome was once free.

Picture the backdrop these speakers would have had—a mountain of marble buildings piling up on Capitol Hill. The impressive Temple of Saturn (eight remaining columns) stood to the left. And in imperial times, these voices of democracy would have been dwarfed by images of empire like the huge Arch of Septimius Severus (A.D. 203). The tall Column of Phocas nearby, one of the last great monuments erected in the Forum, was originally topped by a bronze statue.

In front of the Rostrum are trees bearing fruits that were sacred to the ancient Romans: olives (provided food, light, and preservatives), figs (tasty), and wine grapes (made a popular export product).

• *Return to the Temple of Julius Caesar and turn left up the exit ramp. From here you can look down at the remains of . . .*

6. Basilica Aemilia

A basilica was a Roman hall of justice. In a society that was as legal-minded as America is today, you needed a lot of lawyers and a big place to put them. Citizens came here to work out matters like inheritances and building permits, or to sue somebody.

Notice the layout. It was a long, rectangular building. The

stubby columns all in a row form one long, central hall flanked by two side aisles. Medieval Christian churches adopted this basilica floor plan.

• *Return again to the Temple of Julius Caesar. Notice the ruts in the stone street in front of the temple—carved by chariot wheels. To the right of the Temple are the three tall Corinthian columns of the Temple of Castor and Pollux—#7 on map. Beyond that is Palatine Hill.*

8. Caligula's Palace

Emperor Caligula (ruled A.D. 37–41) had a huge palace on Palatine Hill overlooking the Forum. It actually sprawled down the hill into the Forum (some supporting arches remain in the hillside), with an entrance by the Temple of Castor and Pollux.

Caligula was not a nice person. He tortured enemies, stole Senators' wives, crucified Christians, and parked his chariot in handicap spaces. But Rome's luxury-loving emperors only added to the glory of the Forum, with each one trying to make his mark on history.

• *To the left of the Temple of Castor and Pollux, find the remains of a small white circular temple...*

9. The Temple of Vesta

This was Rome's most sacred spot. Rome considered itself one big family, and this temple represented a circular hut like the kind Rome's first families lived in. Inside, a fire burned, just as in a Roman home. And back in the days before lighters and matches, you never wanted your fire to go out. As long as the sacred flame burned, Rome would stand. The flame was tended by priestesses known as Vestal Virgins.

• *Around the back of the Temple of Vesta you'll find two rectangular brick pools. These stood in the courtyard of...*

10. The House of the Vestal Virgins

The Vestal Virgins lived in a two-story building surrounding a central courtyard with these two pools at one end. Rows of statues to the left and right marked the long sides of the building. This place was the model—both architecturally and sexually—for medieval convents and monasteries.

The six Vestal Virgins, chosen from noble families before the age of 10, served a 30-year term. Honored and revered by the

Romans, the Vestals even had their own box opposite the emperor in the Colosseum.

As the name implies, a Vestal took a vow of chastity. If she served her term faithfully—abstaining for 30 years—she was given a huge dowry, honored with a statue (like the ones at left), and allowed to marry (life begins at 40?). But if they found any Virgin who wasn't, she was strapped to a funeral car, paraded through the streets of the Forum, taken to a crypt, given a loaf of bread and a lamp...and buried alive. Many women suffered the latter fate.

• *Return to the Via Sacra. Pause at the well-preserved Temple of Antoninus and Faustina.*

11. Temple of Antoninus and Faustina

These 50-foot Corinthian (leafy) columns must have been awe-inspiring to out-of-towners who grew up in thatched huts. Although the Temple has been reconstructed as a church, you can still see the

basic temple layout—a staircase led to a shaded porch (the columns), which admitted you to the main building (now a church) where the statue of the god sat. Originally, these columns supported a triangular pediment decorated with sculpture.

• *Now head uphill, back up the Via Sacra, in the direction of the Colosseum. Many of the large basalt stones under your feet were walked on by Caesar Augustus 2,000 years ago. Veer left on the path leading to the three enormous arches.*

12. Basilica Maxentius

Yes, these are big arches. But they represent only one-third of the original Basilica Maxentius, a mammoth hall of justice. The arches were matched by a similar set along the Via Sacra side (only a few squat brick piers remain). Between them ran the central hall, which was spanned by a roof 120 feet high—about 50 feet higher than the

side arches you see. (The stub of brick you see sticking up once spanned the central hall.) The hall itself was as long as a football field, lavishly furnished with colorful inlaid marble, fountains, and statues, and filled with strolling Romans. At the far (west) end was an enormous statue of Emperor Constantine on a throne.

This building was larger than Basilica Aemeilia but had the same general shape—rectangular, with a long central hall flanked by two side halls.

Rome Falls

This peak of Roman grandeur is a good place to talk about the Fall of Rome. Again, Rome lasted 1,000 years—500 years of growth, 200 years of peak power, and 300 years of gradual decay. The Fall had many causes, among them the barbarians that pecked away at Rome's borders. Christians blame the Fall on moral decay. Pagans blamed it on Christians. Marxists blame it on a shallow economy based on spoils of war. (Pat Buchanan blamed it on Marxists.) Whatever the reasons, the far-flung Empire could no longer keep its grip on conquered lands and pulled back. Barbarian tribes from Germany and Asia attacked the Italian peninsula and even looted Rome itself in A.D. 410, leveling many of the buildings in the Forum. In 476, when the last emperor checked out and switched off the lights, Europe plunged into centuries of ignorance, poverty, and weak government—the Dark Ages.

But Rome lived on in the Catholic Church—Catholicism was the state religion of Rome's last generations. Emperors became popes (both called themselves Pontifex Maximus), senators became bishops, orators became priests, and basilicas became churches. Christian worship services required a larger meeting hall than Roman temples provided, so they used the spacious Roman basilica (hall of justice) as the model for their churches. Cathedrals from France to Spain to England, from Romanesque to Gothic to

Renaissance, all have the same basic floor plan as a Roman basilica. And remember that the goal for the greatest church building project ever—that of St. Peter's—was to "put the dome of the Pantheon atop the Basilica Maxentius." The glory of Rome never quite died.

PALATINE HILL
TOUR

If you found the Forum absolutely enthralling, you'll be mildly
entertained by Palatine Hill. It's certainly jam-packed with history—
the "hut of Romulus and Remus," the huge Imperial Palace, a view
of the Circus Maximus—but there's only the barest skeleton of
rubble left to support all that history. Palatine Hill is highly recommended for serious sightseers with low expectations.

Orientation
Cost: L12,000
Hours: Daily 9:00–19:30 or an hour before darkness, off-season
9:00–15:00.
Getting there: Enter the Palatine Hill from within the Forum
(the side closest to the Colosseum). Buy your ticket at the booth
about 30 yards uphill from the Arch of Titus. (Metro: Colosseo.)
Tour length: Allow 90 minutes.
• *After you buy your ticket, follow the path the ancients walked straight
up the hill. At the top of the hill, keep heading to the grey, modern
building housing the museum ("Antaquario Palatino"). Orient with
your back to the museum, so you're facing the Forum (roughly north).*

THE IMPERIAL PALACE
You're standing at the center of a huge palace, the residence of
emperors for three centuries. Orgies, royal weddings, assassina-
tions, concerts, intrigues, births, funerals, banquets, and the
occasional Tupperware party took place within these walls.

What walls? The row of umbrella pines to the east (to your
right as you face the Forum) now marks one edge of the palace.
The reconstructed brick tower (at about 11 o'clock, as you face
the Forum) was the northwest corner. The palace also stretched
behind you (the area behind the museum) and beneath you, since

PALATINE HILL

some of the palace had a lower floor. The area to your left was the official wing of the palace; to your right were the private quarters. All in all, it made a cozy little 150,000-square-foot pad.

The palace was built by Emperor Domitian around A.D. 81, at about the same time he was finishing up the Colosseum. His family was trying to rid Rome of the bitter taste of Nero, and this palace was a way of one-upping Nero and his Golden House.

• *To your left (as you face the Forum) is a big rectangular field with an octagonal brick design in the center. Let's start with the Official Wing (Domus Flavia) of the palace: its main courtyard, throne room, and banquet hall.*

1. Main Courtyard (Peristilio)

The brick octagon was a sunken fountain in the middle of an open-air courtyard. Like even the humblest Roman homes, this palace was built around an oasis of peace where you could enjoy the sun, catch the precious rain, and listen to the babble of moving water. The courtyard was lined with columns (notice the fragments) supporting an arcade for shade. Originally the floor and walls of the courtyard were faced with shiny white marble.

• *Step between the big brick wall-stumps at the north (Forum) end of the courtyard, and you enter . . .*

2. Throne Room

The Throne Room was the official center of power, the nerve center of an empire that controlled some 50 million people from Scotland to Africa. The curved apse of the largest brick stump (there's now a plaque on it) marks the spot where the emperor sat on his throne for official business.

Imagine being a Roman citizen summoned by the emperor. You'd enter the palace through the main doorway (now a gap) at the far (Forum) end of the room, having climbed up three flights of a monumental staircase. The floor and walls dazzled with green, purple, red, white, and yellow marble. Along the walls were 12 colossal statues of Roman gods. The ceiling towered seven stories overhead. On either side were doorways leading to a basilica and the emperor's private temple. Ahead of you, in the apse, sat the emperor on a raised throne, dressed in royal purple, with a crown of laurel leaves on his head and a sceptre cradled in his arm. Big braziers burned on either side, throwing off a flickering light. As you approached, you'd raise your arm to greet him, saying, *"Ave, Cesare!"* The words would echo through the great hall.

• *From the Throne Room, return to the courtyard and walk to the far (south) end, to the square area with a sunken floor now covered with gravel.*

3. Banquet Hall (Triclinium)

The floor level of the banquet hall was a foot higher than the sunken level we see. It was raised on brick pillars (some of the raised floor still remains) and heated by air from underground stoves. At the far end of the room, the platform and curved apse mark the spot where the emperor ate while looking down on his subjects. On either side of the room are windows that the guests could look through to see oval-shaped fountains (these still remain) bubbling in an artificial cavern.

Here the wealthiest

Romans enjoyed the spoils that poured into Rome from their vast empire. Reclining on a couch, waited on by slaves, you'd order bowls of larks' tongues or a roast pig stuffed with live birds, then wash it down with wine. When you were stuffed but the waiters brought yet another delicacy, you could call for a feather, vomit, and start all over. Dancing, dark-skinned slave girls from Egypt or flute players from Greece entertained. If you fancied one, he or she was yours—the bedrooms were just down the hall.

Or so went the stories. In fact, many emperors were just and simple men, continuing the old Roman traditions of hard work and moderate tastes. But just as many were power-mad scoundrels who used their power to indulge their every urge.

• *The palace's stadium is 100 meters to the east. Belly up to the railing and look down on the elliptical track.*

4. Stadium (Hippodromo)

One hundred fifty yards long, this cigar-shaped, sunken stadium was the palace's rec room. It looks like a race track and may have been used for foot and horse races, but it also held gardens with strolling paths. The oval running-track at the south end was added later. The emperor had a raised box on the 50-yard line, in the curved apse across from you. At the

north end were changing rooms, and the marble fragments that litter the ground once held up an arcade.

5. Private Wing (Domus Augustana) of the Palace

The area between the stadium and official wing held the private rooms of the emperor and his extended family. Today a lone umbrella pine on a mound marks the courtyard of this wing. Wander through the maze of rooms (many of them reconstructed), noticing:

• The typical Roman building method: Build a brick shell, fill it

with concrete, then finish it with either plaster (you'll see an occasional faded fresco) or slabs of marble. The small round pockmarks on many walls show where the marble was fastened.

• Some brick walls have brick arches incorporated within them. These "blind arches" were structural elements that allowed the walls to be built higher. The iron bar clamps are recent additions and hold the crumbling walls together.

• Niches and apses once held statues. Every family had their own household gods and displayed small images of these guardian spirits, as well as busts of honored ancestors.

• The fragments of columns, reliefs, and sculpture scattered about suggest the wealth of this great palace.

• Finally, notice the floor plan—a complex, fantasyland maze of small, private, sometimes even curved rooms.

6. "Loggia Stati Mattei" Museum

This museum is located in one of the rooms of the Domus Augustana. From the balcony of this reconstructed room, look down on original frescoes dug out from the ancient Temple of Isis (located near where the Throne Room was later built).

• *In the south part of the Domus Augustana, you can look down on the ruins of the lower story.*

7. Lower Courtyard (Peristilio)

This open-air courtyard has the concave-convex remains of a large fountain that must have been a marvel. Try to mentally reconstruct the palace that surrounded this fountain. The emperors could look down on it from the upper story (where you're standing) or view it from the rooms around it on the lower story, where the emperor and his family ate their meals in private.

The lower story was built into the slope of the hill. The southern part of the palace was an extension of the hillside, supported beneath your feet by big arches.

• *Head to the southern edge of the hill, overlooking the Circus Maximus. Lean over the railing and you can see the concave shape of the palace's southern facade.*

8. Circus Maximus

If the gladiator show at the Colosseum was sold out, you could always get a seat at the Circus Max. In an early version of today's Demolition Derby, Ben Hur and his fellow charioteers once raced recklessly around this oblong course.

The chariots circled around the cigar-shaped mound in the center (notice the lone cypress tree that now marks one end of the mound). Bleachers (now grassy banks) originally surrounded the track.

The track was 400 yards long, while the whole stadium measured 650 by 220 yards and seated—get this—250,000 people. The wooden bleachers once collapsed during a race, killing 13,000.

The horses started from a starting gate at the west end (to your right), while the public entered at the other end. Races consisted of seven laps (about a mile total). In such a small space collisions and
overturned chariots were common. The charioteers were usually poor low-borns who used this dangerous sport to get rich and famous. Many succeeded.

The public was crazy about the races. There were 12 a day, 240 days a year. Four teams dominated the competition—Reds, Whites, Blues, and Greens—and every citizen was fanatically devoted to one of them. Obviously, the emperors had the best seats in the house; built into the palace's curved facade was a box overlooking the track. For their pleasure, emperors occasionally had the circus floor carpeted with designs in colored powders. Picture the scene: intact palace; emperor watching; a quarter of a million Romans cheering, jeering, and furiously betting.

Horses raced here for over a thousand years. The track was originally built by Rome's Etruscan kings (c. 600 B.C.), and the spectacles continued into the Christian era, until 549, despite church disapproval.

From this viewpoint, looking to the left, you can see the ruins of the Baths of Caracalla rising above the trees a half-mile away. About a mile beyond that, the Appian Way led from a grand gate in the ancient wall, past the catacombs, to Brindisi.

9. Museum (Antaquario Palatino)

The museum contains statues and frescoes that help you imagine the luxury of the Imperial Palatine. Upstairs, pause at the statue of "Magna Mater" on her throne. This Great Mother brought life and fertility to the Roman people, who worshiped her at the Temple of Cybele (which we'll see later). Her arms and foot were destroyed by time, but there was always a cavity where her head should be—this was a standard Roman device in which inter-changeable heads could be inserted. In this case, the Magna Mater's "head" was actually a sacred black, cone-shaped meteorite that caused astonishment when it fell from the sky.

Downstairs, there's a helpful model of the Iron Age huts of Romulus (and a WC).

• *From the museum, head west, crossing the octagonal-brick courtyard and continuing through ruins. As you exit the ruins of the Imperial*

Palace, you'll run into a railing overlooking the sunken remains (with modern corrugated roof) of . . .

10. House of Livia and Augustus (Casa di Livia)

Augustus, the first emperor, lived in this house (and the neighboring house to the left) with his wife, Livia. Peer down the hallways at the small rooms with honeycomb brick walls that surrounded a small courtyard. This relatively humble dwelling is a far cry from the later Imperial Palace. There are some fine frescoes inside (usually closed for restoration), but Casa di Livia had little of the lavish marble found in most homes of the wealthy.

Augustus was a modest man who believed in traditional Roman values. His wife and daughter wove the clothes he wore. He slept in the same small bedroom for 40 years. He burned the midnight oil in his study, reading and writing his memoirs. Augustus set a standard for emperors' conduct that would last . . . until his death.

• *To the right of Casa di Livia are the Farnese Gardens. These grow over the remains of what was the . . .*

11. Palace of Tiberius and Caligula (and the Cryptoporticus Tunnel)

Augustus' successors started the trend of fancy imperial homes with a palace that sprawled all the way from here to the Forum. Virtually nothing is visible today. One feature that remains is the underground passageway (Cripto Portico) that runs from near Casa di Livia towards the Forum—425 feet long. Look down and see some of the mosaic floor of this once-marbled and -stuccoed passageway, which is lit by windows along the side. Emperors used it as a private, convenient way to get around the hill. Caligula may have been murdered in it.

• *Circle clockwise around Casa di Livia to an area with several archaeological sites. Head for the far, southwest corner. Under a corrugated roof are the scant outlines of . . .*

12. Iron Age Huts— "The Huts of Romulus and Remus"

Looking down into the pit from the railing (stand at the far right), you can make out some elliptical and rectangular shapes carved into the stony ground—the partial outlines of huts from around 850 B.C. Some have holes that once held the wooden posts of round, thatched huts.

Romulus and Remus were babies orphaned when their mother, a disgraced Vestal Virgin, was executed. (She claimed she was raped by Mars, the War God.) Set adrift on the flooding Tiber, the babes washed ashore at the foot of Palatine Hill.

A shepherd discovered them in a cave just downhill from here, being suckled by a mother wolf. He took them home—maybe right here— and raised them as his own. When Romulus grew up, he killed his brother and built a square wall (Roma Quadrata) around the tiny hill town, founding the city of Rome. (The dusty-orange blocks of volcanic tufa stone may be part of that wall.)

For centuries, the Romans believed this legend. They honored the wolf's cave—called the "Lupercal," where every February 15th men dressed up in animal skins and whipped women—as well as the spot where Romulus lived. Lo and behold, in the 1940s, these huts were unearthed, and the legend became history.

• *Over your right shoulder are the rectangular walls of the...*

13. Temple of Cybele (Templo di Cibele), or Temple of the Magna Mater

The statue of the Mother of the Gods, built to thank her for saving Rome from Hannibal and his elephants (c. 200 B.C.), once sat at the far end of this temple. (It's now in the museum.)

March 22 was a festive day at the temple as new priests joined the Magna Mater's cult by castrating themselves and draping their testicles over the altar, helping the goddess fertilize the world.

From here at Rome's birthplace, reflect on the rise of this great culture—from thatched hut to the modest house of Augustus to the massive Imperial Palace of Domitian with its stadium and view over the Circus Maximus. It's no wonder that the hill's name gave us our English word "palace."

• *A good way to complete your Palatine visit is to stroll through the Farnese Gardens (Horti Farnesini), admiring its exotic plants, fountains, underground grotto, and pavilions. When you see the view of the Forum from here, you'll know why the Palatine was Rome's best address.*

TRAJAN'S COLUMN & FORUM

Rome's expansion peaked under Emperor Trajan (ruled A.D. 98–117)—the empire stretched from Scotland to the Sahara, from Spain to Asia. A triumphant Trajan returned to Rome with his booty and shook it all over the city. He extended the Forum by building his own commercial, political, and religious center nearby, complete with temples, law courts, squares lined with shops, and a monumental column.

Orientation

Trajan's Column is just a few steps off Piazza Venezia, on Via dei Fori Imperiali, across the street from the Victor Emmanuel Monument (free). It's always viewable, as is Trajan's Forum, which stretches southeast of the Column. You can pay to go down into the Forum ruins (L4,000, entrance near Column), but unless that also includes admission inside the more-interesting Market buildings (closed in '99), it's probably not worth it.

Trajan's Column

Rising 125 feet and decorated with a spiral relief of 2,500 figures trumpeting Trajan's exploits, this is the world's grandest column from antiquity. The ashes of Trajan and his wife (which were last seen in the Middle Ages) were once held in the base, and the sun once glinted off a polished bronze statue of Trajan at the top. (Today St. Peter is on top.) Built as a stack of 17 marble dough-nuts, the column is hollow (note the small window-slots) with a spiral staircase inside leading up to the balcony.

The relief unfolds like a scroll, telling the story of Trajan's conquest of Dacia (modern-day Romania). It starts at the bottom with a trickle of water that becomes a river and soon picks up boats full of supplies. Then come the soldiers themselves, who spill out from the gates of the city. A river god (bottom band, south side) surfaces to bless the journey. Along the way (second band), they build roads and forts to sustain the vast enterprise, including (third band, south side) Trajan's half-mile-long bridge over the Danube, the longest for a thousand years. (Find the three tiny crisscross rectangles representing the wooden span.) Trajan himself (fourth band, in military skirt with toga over his arm) mounts a podium to fire up the troops. They hop into a Roman galley ship (fifth band) and head off to fight the valiant Dacians in the middle of a forest (eighth

band). Finally, at the very top, the Romans hold a sacrifice to give thanks for the victory while the captured armour is displayed on the pedestal. Originally, the entire story was painted in bright colors. If you unwound the scroll, it would stretch over two football fields—it's far longer than the frieze around the Greek Parthenon. (An unscrolled copy is in E.U.R.'s Museum of Roman Civilization.)

Trajan's Forum

The best place to view the ruins of the Forum is on the pedestrian-only Via Alessandrina, which cuts right through the heart of the Forum.

Trajan's Forum starts at Trajan's Column and runs about 100 yards southeast toward the Colosseum. It's mostly rubble today. The highlight of the Forum then and now is Trajan's Market—the big, crescent-shaped brick structure that rises up the flank of Quirinal Hill.

Trajan's Forum was a crucial expansion of the old Roman Forum, which was too small and ceremonial to fill the commercial needs of a booming city of over a million people. Built with the staggering haul of gold plundered from Dacia (Romania), this was the largest Forum ever—its opulence astounded even the jaded Romans. You entered at the Colosseum end through a triumphal arch and were greeted in the main square by a large statue of the soldier-king on a horse. Continuing on, you'd enter the Basilica Ulpia (the grey granite columns near Trajan's Column), the largest law court of its day. Finally, at the far end was Trajan's Column, flanked by two libraries that contained the world's knowledge in Greek and Latin. Balconies on the libraries gave close-up looks at the upper reliefs of the Column, in case anyone doubted the outcome of Trajan's war.

TRAJAN'S FORUM

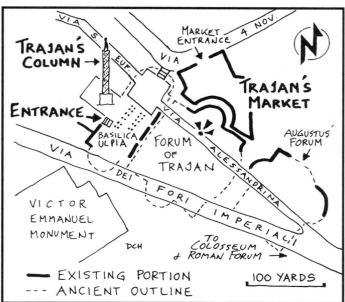

To build his Forum, Trajan literally moved mountains. He cut away a ridge that once connected the Quirinal and Capitol Hills, creating this artificial valley. Trajan's Column marks the hill's original height—125 feet.

Trajan's Market

Nestled into the cut-away curve of the hill is the semicircular brick complex of Trajan's Market. Part shopping center, part warehouse, part administration office, it was a place Romans gravitated to and a popular spot to bring out-of-town guests.

At ground level, the 11 tall arches housed (shallow) shops selling fresh fruit, vegetables, and flowers to shoppers who passed by on the street. The 26 windows (above) lighted a covered walkway lined with shops that sold wine and olive oil. On the roof runs a street that held still more shops, making about 150 in all. Shoppers could browse through goods from every corner of Rome's vast empire—exotic fruits from Africa, spices from Asia, fish and chips from Britain.

Above the semicricle, the upper floors of the complex housed bureaucrats in charge of a crucial element of city life—doling out free grain to unemployed citizens, who lived off the wealth plundered from distant lands. Better to pacify them than risk a riot. Above the offices, at the very top, rises a tower added in the Middle Ages.

The Market was beautiful and functional, filling the space of the curved hill perfectly and echoing the curved side of the Forum's main courtyard. (The wall of rough tufa stones in the left-foreground once extended into a semicircle.) Unlike most Roman buildings, the brick facade was never covered with plaster or marble. The architect liked the simple contrast between warm brick and the white stone lining the arches and windows.

Trajan's conquest of the Dacians was Rome's last and greatest foreign conquest. It produced this Forum, which stood for centuries as a symbol of a truly cosmopolitan civilization.

PANTHEON
TOUR

The Pantheon was a Roman temple dedicated to all *(pan)* the gods *(theos)*. First built in 27 B.C., it was completely rebuilt around A.D. 120 by the Emperor Hadrian. In a gesture of modesty admirable in anyone but astounding in a Roman emperor, Hadrian left his own name off of it, putting the name of the original builder on the front—"M. Agrippa."

Several interesting churches are clustered near the Pantheon. These are described below, after the Pantheon Tour.

Orientation

Cost: Free
Hours: Mon–Sat 9:00–18:30, Sun 9:00–13:00.
Getting there: Walk (it's a 10- to 15-minute walk from the Forum), take a taxi, or catch a bus (#64, which runs between the train station and Vatican, stops at Largo Argentina, a few blocks south of the Pantheon; or try *electrico minibus* #116, which runs between Campo de' Fiori and Piazza Barberini via the Pantheon).
Information: Tel. 06-6830-0230. Small gift shop inside entrance. Nearest WCs at bars and McDonald's on the square.
Tour length: Allow 45 minutes.

Exterior

The Parthenon doesn't look like much from the outside, but this is perhaps the most influential building in art history. Its dome was the model for the Florence cathedral dome, which launched the Renaissance, and for Michelangelo's dome of St. Peter's, which capped it all off. Even Washington, D.C.'s Capitol was inspired by this dome.

• *Pass between the enormous one-piece granite columns and through the enormous original bronze door. Stand awestruck for a moment, then take a seat on the bench to your right.*

Interior

The dome, which was the largest made until the Renaissance, is set on a circular base. The mathematical perfection of this dome-on-a-base design is a testament to Roman engineering. The dome is as high as it is wide—142 feet. (To picture it, imagine a basketball set inside a wastebasket so that it just touches bottom.)

The dome is made from concrete that gets lighter and thinner as it reaches the top. The walls at the base are 20 feet thick and made from heavy travertine concrete, while near the top they're only five feet thick and made of a light volcanic rock. Both Brunelleschi and Michelangelo studied this dome before building their own (in Florence and in the Vatican). Remember, St. Peter's Cathedral is really only "the dome of the Pantheon atop the Basilica Maxentius."

The oculus, or eye-in-the-sky, at the top, the building's only light source, is almost 30 feet across. The 1,800-year-old floor has holes in it and slants towards the edges to let the rainwater drain. The marble floor is largely restored though the designs are close to the originals.

In ancient times, this was a one-stop-shopping temple where you could worship any of the gods whose statues decorated the niches. If you needed a favor, you might buy a live animal outside in the square then have the priests sacrifice it on the altar placed in the center. The fumes would rise up through the oculus to heaven, where the gods could smell it and—if they were pleased—grant you a blessing.

The barbarians passed the Pantheon by when they sacked Rome. Early in the Middle Ages it became a Christian church (from "all the gods" to "all the martyrs"), which saved it from architectural cannibalism and ensured its upkeep through the Dark Ages. The only major destruction came in the 17th century, when the pope stole the bronze plating and melted it down to build the huge bronze canopy over the altar at St. Peter's. About the only new things in the interior are the decorative statues and the tombs of famous people, like the artist Raphael (to the left of the main altar, in the glass case) and modern Italy's first two kings, Victor Emmanuel II and Umberto I (to the right).

The Pantheon is the only continuously used ancient building in Rome. When you leave you'll notice how the rest of the city has risen on 20 centuries of rubble.

The Pantheon also contains the world's greatest Roman column. There it is, spanning the entire 142 feet from heaven to earth—the pillar of light from the oculus.

CHURCHES NEAR THE PANTHEON:
Francesi, Gesu, Sopra Minerva, and St. Ignazio

Church of San Luigi dei Francesi

The one truly *magnifique* sight in the French national church is
the chapel in the far left corner that was decorated by Caravaggio
(free, but bring L500 coins to buy light, Fri–Wed 7:30–12:30,
15:30–19:00, Thu 7:30–12:30, sightseers should avoid Mass at 7:30
and 19:00, modest dress recommended).

The Calling of St. Matthew (left wall)
Matthew and his well-dressed tax-collecting cronies sit in a dingy
bar and count the money they've extorted. Suddenly, two men in
robes and bare feet enter from the right—Jesus and Peter. Jesus'
"Creation-of-Adam" hand emerges from the darkness to point at
Matthew. A shaft of light extends the gesture, lighting up the face
of bearded Matthew, who points to himself Last-Supper-style to
ask, "You talking to me?" Jesus came to convince Matthew to
leave his sleazy job and preach Love. Matthew did.

In this, his first large-scale work, 29-year-old Caravaggio
(1571–1610) shocked critics and clerics by showing a holy scene in
a down-to-earth location. Lower-class people in everyday clothes
were his models; his setting was a dive bar (which he knew well).
Christ's teeny gold halo is the only hint of the supernatural, as
Caravaggio makes a bold proclamation—that miracles are natural
events experienced in a profound way.

St. Matthew and the Angel (center wall)
Matthew followed Christ's call, traveled with Him, and (supposedly) wrote His life's story (The Gospel of Matthew). Here,
Matthew is hard at work when he's interrupted by an angel with a
few suggestions. Matthew's bald head, wrinkled face, and grizzled
beard make him an all-too-human saint. Even the teen angel lacks
a holy glow—he just hangs there. Caravaggio paints a dark background, then shines a dramatic spotlight on the few things that
tell the story.

The Martyrdom of St. Matthew (right wall)
Matthew lies prone while a truly scary man straddles him and bran-
dishes a sword. The bystanders shrink away from this angry executioner. Caravaggio shines his harsh third-degree spotlight on
Matthew and the killer, who are the focus of the painting. The
other figures swirl around them in a circle (with the executioner's
arm as the radius). Matthew, who thought he had given up
everything to follow Christ, now gives up his life as well.

When the chapel was unveiled in 1600, Caravaggio's ultra-realism shocked Rome. (Find his bearded self-portrait in the background.) Although he died only 10 years later, his uncompromising details, emotional subjects, odd compositions, and dramatic lighting set the tone for later Baroque painters.

Il Gesu Church

The center of the Jesuit order and the best symbol of the Catholic Counter-Reformation, the Gesu Church is packed with overblown art and underappreciated history (free, daily 6:00–12:30, 16:00–19:15, modest dress recommended).

Exterior

The facade looks ho-hum, like a thousand no-name Catholic churches scattered from Europe to Southern California... until you realize that this was the first, the model for the others. Its scroll-like shoulders were revolutionary, breaking up the rigid rectangles of Renaissance architecture, and signaling the coming of Baroque.

The building to the right of the church is where Ignatius of Loyola, the founder of the Jesuits, lived, worked, and died.

• *Step inside the church and look up at the huge painting on the ceiling.*

1. Ceiling Fresco and Stucco —
The Triumph of the Name of Jesus (by Il Baciccia)

A twisted tangle of bodies—the Damned—spills over the edge of the ceiling, plunging downward on the way to Hell. Notice how the painted bodies become 3-D stucco bodies in a classic example of Baroque multimedia.

During the Counter-Reformation, when Catholics fought Protestants for the hearts and minds of the world's Christians, art became propaganda. The moral here is clear—this is the fate of Protestant heretics who dared pervert the true teachings of Jesus.

2. The Nave

When the church was originally built (1568), the walls were white, the decor was simple; it was designed for what the Jesuits did best—teaching. The Jesuits wanted to educate Catholics to prepare them for the onslaught of probing Protestant questions. The church's nave is like one big lecture hall, with no traditional side-aisles. Acoustics were great and the light was bright so worshipers could read along. Catholics had nothing to hide.

In the 1500s, the best way to keep Protestants from stealing your church members was to reason with them. By the 1600s, it was easier to kill them, and the Thirty Years' War raged across Europe. The church became crusted over with the colorful, bombastic, jingoistic Baroque you see today.

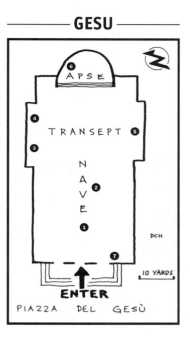

3. Tomb and Altarpiece of St. Ignatius of Loyola
(in left transept)

The gleaming statue of Ignatius spreads his arms wide and gazes up, receiving a vision from on high. Ignatius (1491–1556) was a Spanish soldier during the era of conquistadors. Then, at age 30, he was struck down by a cannonball. While convalescing, he was seized by the burning desire to change his life. He wandered Europe and traveled to Jerusalem. He meditated with monks. He lived in a cave. At 33 he enrolled in a school for boys to pick up the knowledge he'd missed. He studied in Paris and in Rome. Finally, after almost two decades of learning and seeking, he found a way to combine his military training with his spiritual aspirations.

In 1540 the pope gave approval to Ignatius and his small band of followers—the Society of Jesus (Jesuits). These monks, organized like a military company, vowed complete obedience to their "General," and placed themselves at the service of the pope. Their mission? To be the intellectual warriors doing battle with heretics. They were in the right place at the right time—Ignatius and Luther were almost exact contemporaries.

Ignatius' body lies in the small coffin beneath the statue (near ground level). This simple, intense man might have been embarrassed by the lavish memorial to him, with its silver, gold, green marble, and lapis lazuli columns. Above Ignatius, a statue of God stands near a lapis lazuli globe (the biggest in the world) and gestures as though to say, "Go and spread the Word to every land"... which the Jesuits tried to do.

4. "Religion Vanquishing Untruth"
(marble statue-group to the right of Ignatius)
This statue (and a similar one to the left of Ignatius) shows the Church as a woman hauling back and just wailing on a bunch of

miserable Protestants. Not too subtle.

Yes, the Jesuits got a reputation for unfeeling dedication to truth above all else, but their weapons were words, ideas, and critical reasoning. They taught and defended the recently revamped doctrines of the Council of Trent (1545–1563).

5. Tomb and Altarpiece of St. Francis Xavier
(right transept)
This was also the Age of Discovery, when Spain and Portugal were colonizing and Christianizing the world, using force if necessary. Francis Xavier joined a Portuguese expedition and headed out to convert the heathen. He touched down in Africa, India, Indonesia, China, and Japan. Along the way he learned new languages and customs as he tried to communicate a strange monotheistic religion to puzzled polytheists.

He was on the road more than a decade (1552) when he died on an island off China (see the painting over the altar). Thanks largely to zealous Jesuits like Francis, Catholicism became a truly worldwide religion.

6. Bust of Cardinal Roberto Bellarmine —
by Gian Lorenzo Bernini (in apse, left side)
The great sculptor Bernini attended this church and honored Bellarmine with a bust. The Jesuits produced some great, open-minded thinkers, from the poet Gerard Manley Hopkins to modern mystic Teilhard de Chardin. But they also caught flak for being closed-minded to new ideas. In the 1700s, several countries expelled them, and finally (1773) the pope even banned the Society. Chastened, they were brought back (1814) and today fill the staff of many a Catholic college.

7. Manger Scene

Don't leave before pressing the button to see water run, comets shoot, and angels fly. It's cheesy, but it carries on the Baroque use of whiz-bang effects to make the supernatural seem tangible to the masses.

Church of Santa Maria sopra Minerva

This is the only Gothic church you'll see in Rome (free, 7:00–12:00, 15:30–19:00, modest dress recommended). On a little square behind the Pantheon to the east, past the Bernini statue of an elephant carrying an Egyptian obelisk, this Dominican church was built in the eighth century *sopra* (over) a pre-Christian temple of Minerva. Before stepping in, notice the high-water marks on the wall (right of the door). Inside you'll see that the lower parts of the frescoes were lost to floods. (After the last great flood, in 1870, Rome built the present embankments, finally breaking the spirit of the Tiber River.)

When this Gothic-style church was built, Rome was at its low ebb, almost a ghost town. Little was built during this time. And, considering what the Goths had done to Rome, the Gothic style was unpopular. Much of what was built was redone in the Baroque style. This church is a refreshing exception.

St. Catherine's body lies under the altar (her head is in Siena). In the 1300s, she convinced the pope to return from France to Rome, thus saving Italy from untold chaos.

Left of the altar stands a little-known Michelangelo statue, *Christ Bearing the Cross*. Michelangelo gave Jesus an athlete's or warrior's body (a striking contrast to the more docile Christ of medieval art) but left the face to one of his pupils. Fra Angelico's simple tomb is farther to the left, on the way to the back door. Before leaving, head over to the right (south transept), pop in a L500 coin for light, and enjoy a fine Filippo Lippi fresco showing scenes from the life of St. Thomas Aquinas (the big man in black and white).

Exit the church via its rear door (behind the Michelangelo statue), walk down Fra Angelico lane (spy any artisans at work), turn left, and walk to the next square. On your right you'll find the...

Church of St. Ignazio

This church is a riot of Baroque illusions (free, 7:00–12:30, 15:30–19:00, modest dress recommended). Study the fresco over the door and the ceiling in the back of the nave. Then stand on the yellow disk on the floor, between the two stars. Look at the central (black) dome. Keeping your eyes on the dome, walk under and past it. Church building project runs out of money? Hire a painter to paint a fake, flat dome.

Back outside, the church faces the yellow headquarters of the Carabinieri police force, forming a square that has been compared to a stage set, with several converging streets. Sit on the church steps, admire the theatrical yellow backdrop, and watch the "actors" enter one way and exit another, in the human opera that is modern Rome.

BATHS OF DIOCLETIAN
TOUR

⑩

rome

Of all the marvelous structures built by the Romans, their public baths were the grandest, and the Baths of Diocletian were the granddaddy of them all. The baths sprawled over 10 acres—roughly twice the area of the entire Forum—and could cleanse 3,000 Romans at once. Today, there are several sections you can visit:

The **Church of Santa Maria degli Angeli**, housed in the former main hall of the baths, is the single most impressive place. The entrance is on Piazza Repubblica (free).

The **Octagonal Hall**, also facing Piazza Repubblica, is a well-preserved rotunda that now displays sculpture from the baths. As you face the church entrance, the Octagonal Hall is 100 meters to your left (free, Tue–Sat 9:00–14:00, Sun 9:00–13:00, closed Mon, borrow the English description booklet, handy WC hidden in the back corner through an unmarked door).

The **National Baths Museum** (Museo Nazionale Romano, Terme di Diocleziano), which is supposed to open sometime in 2000, shows several rooms of the baths with mosaics and statues. The entrance faces the Termini train station.

Energetic architecture wonks can even walk the perimeter of the baths: from Via Torino to Piazza dei Cinquecento to Via Volturno to Via XX Settembre.

SANTA MARIA DEGLI ANGELI

From Piazza Repubblica, step through the curved brick wall of the ancient baths and into a church housed in the main part of the former baths.

The Church's Entry Hall — The Baths' Tepidarium

This round-domed room with an oculus (open skylight) was once the cooling-off room of the baths where medium, "tepid"

——— BATHS OF DIOCLETIAN ———

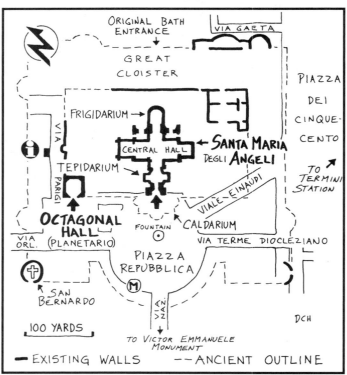

ORIGINAL BATH ENTRANCE

VIA GAETA

GREAT CLOISTER

PIAZZA DEI CINQUE-CENTO

FRIGIDARIUM →

VIA

CENTRAL HALL ← **SANTA MARIA** DEGLI **ANGELI**

TEPIDARIUM →

VIA PARIGI

TO TERMINI STATION

OCTAGONAL HALL (PLANETARIO)

FOUNTAIN

VIALE EINAUDI

CALDARIUM

VIA ORL.

VIA TERME DIOCLEZIANO

PIAZZA REPUBBLICA

SAN BERNARDO

M

100 YARDS

>N<
>A<
>Z>

DCH

TO VICTOR EMMANUELE MONUMENT

— EXISTING WALLS   — — ANCIENT OUTLINE

temperatures were maintained. Romans loved to sweat out last night's indulgences at the baths. After stripping in the locker rooms, they'd enter the steam baths of the *caldarium*, located where Piazza Repubblica is today. The *caldarium* had wood furnaces, stoked by slaves, under the raised floors to heat the floors and hot tubs. The ceiling was low to keep the room steamy.

Next you'd pass into this *tepidarium*, where masseuses would rub you down and scrape you off with a stick (Romans didn't use soap). Finally, you'd continue on to the central area of the baths...

The Church's Large Transept —
The Baths' Central Hall

This hall retains the grandeur of the ancient baths. It's the size of a football field and seven stories high—originally higher, since the old floor was 15 feet below its present level. The ceiling's criss-cross arches were an architectural feat unmatched for a thousand years. The eight red granite columns are original—stand next to one and feel its five-foot-wide girth. (Only the eight in the transept proper are original. The others are made of plastered-over brick.) The original hall was covered with mosaics, marble, and gold, and lined with statues.

From here, Romans could continue on (through what is now the apse, near altar) into a large, open-air courtyard to take a dip in the huge swimming pool (in the *frigidarium*) that paralleled this huge hall. Many other rooms, gardens, and courtyards extended beyond what we see here. The baths were built in only 10 years (around A.D. 300), amazing when you think of the centuries it took builders of puny medieval cathedrals like Paris' Notre-Dame.

Mentally undress your fellow tourists and church-goers and imagine hundreds of naked or togaed Romans wrestling, doing jumping jacks, singing in the baths, shouting, networking, or just milling about.

The baths were more than washrooms. They were health clubs with exercising areas, equipment, and swimming pools. They had gardens for socializing. Libraries, shops, bars, fast-food vendors, pedicurists, depilators, and brothels catered to every Roman need. Most importantly, perhaps, the baths offered a spacious, cool-in-summer/warm-in-winter place for Romans to get out of their stuffy apartments, schmooze, or simply hang out.

Admission was virtually free, requiring only the smallest coin. Baths were open to men and women—and during Nero's reign, co-ed bathing was popular—but generally there were either separate rooms or separate entry times. Most Romans went daily.

The church we see today was designed by Michelangelo (1561), who placed the entry at the right end of the transept and used the long hall as the nave. Later, when Piazza Repubblica became an important Roman intersection, another architect reoriented it, turning Michelangelo's nave into a long transept so people could enter from the piazza.

Step into the sacristy (free, left of main altar) for an explanation of the church's architectural history and copies of Michelangelo's drawings.

Notice the immensity and power of the Roman brickwork in this room. Large building projects like this were political security: They provided employment and fed the masses.

Diocletian (ruled A.D. 285–305) struggled with a system to rule his unwieldy empire. He broke it into zones ruled by four "tetrarchs." Later, Constantine divided the empire into east and west halves. During Diocletian's "tetrarchs" period, architecture and art was grandiose but almost a caricature of greatness—meant to proclaim to Romans that their city was still the power it no longer was.

The baths were one of the last great structures built before Rome's 200-year Fall. They functioned until A.D. 537, when barbarians cut the city's aqueducts, plunging Rome into a thousand years of B.O.

OCTAGONAL HALL (AULA OTTAGONA)

This octagonal building, capped by a dome with a hole in the top, may have served as a cool room *(frigidarium)*, with small pools of cold water for plunging into. Or, because of its many doors, it may simply have been a large intersection, connecting other parts of the baths. Whatever, it's one of the best-preserved rooms. Originally, the floor was 20 feet lower— as you can see through the glass-covered hole in the floor. The graceful iron grid supported the canopy of a 1928 planetarium. Today the hall's a free gallery showing off fine bronze and marble statues. Of the statues (mostly Roman copies of Greek originals—athletes, gods, Hercules, satyrs, and portraits) two merit a close look:

The Boxer at Rest—Pugilatore, 1st century B.C.

An exhausted boxer sits between rounds and gasps for air. See the brass-knuckle-type Roman boxing gloves. Textbook Hellenistic, this bronze statue is realistic and full of emotion. His face is scarred, his back muscles are knotted, and he's got cauliflower ears. He's losing. Slumped over, he turns with a questioning look ("Why am I losing again?"), and eyes that once held glass now make him look empty indeed. I coulda been a contender.

Roman Aristocrat

The aristocrat's face is older than his body. This bronze-casted statue is typical of the day: Take a body of Alexander the Great and pop on a portrait bust.

* *Exit onto Piazza Repubblica.*

PIAZZA REPUBBLICA

The piazza, shaped like an exedra (a semicircular recess in a wall or building), echoes a wall of the original baths. It was called Piazza Exedra until Italian unification. The thundering Via Nazionale starts at what was an ancient door. Look down it (past the almost erotic nymphs of the Naiad fountain) to the Victor Emmanuel Monument. The Art Nouveau fountain of the four water nymphs created quite a stir when unveiled in 1911. The nymphs were modeled after a set of twins who used to visit as late as the 1960s for a reminder of their nubile youth.

NATIONAL MUSEUM OF ROME TOUR

Museo Nazionale Romano
Palazzo Massimo alla Terme

rome ⑪

Rome lasted a thousand years, and so do most Roman history courses. But if you want a breezy overview of this fascinating society, there's no better place than the Palazzo Massimo.

Rome took Greek culture and wrote it in capital letters. Thanks to this lack of originality, ancient Greek statues were preserved for our enjoyment today. But the Romans also pioneered an unheard-of path in art—sculpting painfully realistic portraits of emperors and important citizens.

Think of this museum as a walk back in time. As you gaze at the same statues the Romans swooned over, Rome comes alive—from Romulus sucking a wolf's teat to Julius Caesar's murder to Caligula's incest to the coming of Christianity.

Orientation

Cost: L12,000

Hours: Tue–Sun 9:00–19:45 (last admission at 19:00), closed Mon. To see the fresco collection, you must reserve an entry time for a free, 45-minute tour led by an Italian-speaking guide. If interested, book the next available tour when you buy your ticket. Information: tel. 06-481-5576.

Getting there: The museum is about 100 yards from the Termini train station. As you leave the station, it's the sandstone-brick building on your left. Enter at the far end, at Largo di Villa Peretti.

Tour length: Allow two hours.

Starring: The Discus Thrower, Roman emperor busts, original Greek statues, and fine Roman copies.

THE MUSEUM

The Palazzo Massimo is now the permanent home of the major Greek and Roman statues that were formerly scattered in other museums. However, some famous statues once in the collection (*The Boxer at Rest, Gaul Killing His Wife,* and *Ludovisi Throne*) are still located elsewhere. The Palazzo Massimo seems to be searching for a convenient nickname to distinguish it from other "Museo Nazionales" around town.

The museum is rectangular, with rooms and hallways built around a central courtyard. The ground-floor displays follow Rome's history as it changes from democratic republic to dictatorial empire. The first floor exhibits take Rome from its peak to its slow fall. The second floor houses rare frescoes and fine mosaics (reservation for a free tour required), and the basement displays coins and everyday objects. As you follow this tour, note that "room" is *sala* in Italian and "gallery" is *galleria.*

GROUND FLOOR—FROM SENATORS TO CAESARS

• *Buy your ticket and pass through the turnstile, where you'll find . . .*

Minerva

It's big, it's gaudy, it's a weird goddess from a pagan cult. Welcome to the Roman world. The statue is also a good reminder that all the statues in this museum—now missing limbs or scarred by erosion or weathered down to the bare stone—were once whole and painted to look as lifelike as possible.

• *Continuing to the right, you'll stand at the head of . . .*

Gallery I — Portrait Heads from the Republic, 500–501 B.C.

Stare into the eyes of these stern, hardy, no-nonsense farmer-stock people who founded Rome. The wrinkles and crags of these original "ugly Republicans" tell the story of Rome's roots as a small agricultural tribe that fought neighboring tribes for survival.

These faces are brutally realistic, unlike more idealized Greek statues. Romans honored their ancestors and worthy citizens in the "family" *(gens)* of Rome. They wanted lifelike statues to remember them by, and to instruct the young with their air of moral rectitude.

In its first 500 years, Rome was a republic ruled by a Senate of wealthy landowners. But as Rome expanded throughout Italy and the economy shifted from farming to booty, changes were needed.

• *Enter Room I (Sala I) and find the bust of . . .*

Julius Caesar (Rilievo con Ritratto c.d. Cesare), c. 100–44 B.C.

The prominent brow, the strong nose, the male-pattern baldness with the forward comb-over—these features identify the man who changed Rome forever. (Or some think it may be a lookalike.)

——NATIONAL MUSEUM, GROUND FLOOR——

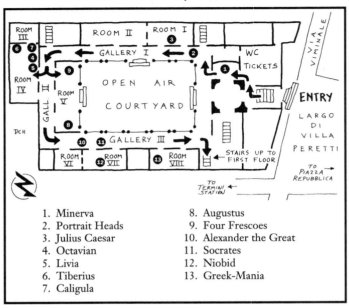

1. Minerva
2. Portrait Heads
3. Julius Caesar
4. Octavian
5. Livia
6. Tiberius
7. Caligula

8. Augustus
9. Four Frescoes
10. Alexander the Great
11. Socrates
12. Niobid
13. Greek-Mania

When this charismatic general swept onto the scene, Rome was in chaos. Rich landowners were fighting middle-class plebs, who wanted their slice of the plunder. Slaves like Spartacus were picking up hoes and hacking up masters. And renegade generals—the new providers of wealth and security in a booty economy—were becoming dictators. (Notice the life-size statue of an unknown but obviously once-renowned general.)

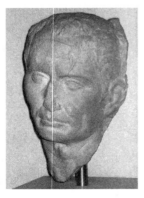

Caesar was a people's favorite. He conquered Gaul (France), then sacked Egypt, then impregnated Cleopatra. He defeated rivals and made them his allies. He gave great speeches. Chicks dug him.

With the army at his back and the people in awe, he took the reins of government, instituted sweeping changes, made himself the center of power . . . and antagonized lovers of freedom everywhere.

A band of Republican assassins surrounded him in a Senate meeting. He called out for help as one by one they stepped up to take turns stabbing him. The Senators sat and watched in silence. One of the killers was his adopted son, Brutus, and Caesar died saying, *"E tu, Brute?"*

• *At the end of the hall, enter into . . .*

Room IV — The Julio-Claudian Family: Rome's First Emperors, c. 50 B.C.– A.D. 68

Julius Caesar died, but his family name, his politics, and his flamboyance lived on, turning Rome into a dictatorship ruled by an emperor.

Octavian, later called Augustus (Ritratto di Ottaviano), ruled 27 B.C.–A.D. 14

Julius Caesar adopted his grandnephew Octavian. After the assassination, 18-year-old Octavian got revenge against Brutus and the others, then eliminated his own rivals, Mark Antony and wife Cleopatra. For the first time in almost a century of fighting, one general reigned supreme. Octavian took the title "Augustus" ("He who just keeps getting bigger"), becoming the first of the emperors who would rule Rome for the next 500 years. (More on Augustus later.)

Livia

Augustus/Octavian's wife, Livia, was a major power behind the throne. Her stern, thin-lipped gaze withered rivals at court. Her hairstyle—bunched up in a peak, braided down the center, and tied in back—became the rage of Europe as her face appeared everywhere in statues and on coins. Notice that by the next generation (Antonia Minore, Livia's daughter-in-law), a simpler bun was chic. And by the following generation, it was tight curls. Empresses dictated fashion like emperors dictated policy.

Livia bore Augustus no sons. She lobbied hard for her own son (by a first marriage) to succeed as emperor. Augustus didn't like him, but Livia was persuasive. He relented, ate some bad figs, and died— the gossip was that Livia poisoned him to seal the bargain. The pattern of succession was established—adopt a son from within the extended family—and Tiberius was proclaimed emperor.

Tiberius (ruled A.D. 14–37)

Acne may have soured Tiberius to the world. Shy and sullen but diligent, he worked hard to be the easygoing leader of men

Augustus had been. Early on he was wise and patient, but he suffered personal setbacks. Politics forced him to divorce his only beloved and marry a slut. His favorite brother died, then his son. Embittered, he let subordinates run things and retired to Capri where he built a villa with underground dungeons. There he hosted orgies of sex, drugs, torture, really loud music, and execution. At his side was his young grandnephew whom he adopted as next emperor.

Caligula (Caligola; in the glass case), ruled A.D. 37–41

This emperor had sex with his sisters, tortured his enemies, stole friends' wives during dinner then returned to rate their performance in bed, crucified Christians, tore up parking tickets, and had men kneel before him as a god. Caligula has become the archetype of a man with enough power to act out his basest fantasies.

Politically, he squandered Rome's money then taxed and extorted from the citizens. Perhaps he was made mad by illness, perhaps he was the victim of vindictive historians, but still, no one mourned when assassins ambushed him and ran a sword through his privates. Rome was tiring of this family dynasty's dysfunction. Augustus must have been rolling in his grave...and they hadn't even seen Nero yet.

Before leaving the room, look around and see if you can spot a family resemblance. Livia's thin lips and Augustus' strong nose? Maybe.

Room V — Augustus and Rome's Legendary Birth

Statue of Augustus as Pontifex Maximus (Ritratto di Augusto in Vesta di Offerente)

Here 50-year-old Emperor Augustus takes off his armor and laurel-leaf crown and dons the simple hooded robes of a priest. In fact, Augustus was a down-to-earth man who lived simply, worked hard, read books, listened to underlings, and tried to restore traditional Roman values after the turbulence of Julius Caesar's time. He outwardly praised and defended the Senate and the  Republic while actually becoming its emperor. Despite the excesses of his descendants, Augustus' reign marked the start of 200 years of peace and prosperity, the "Pax Romana."

See if the statue matches a description of Augustus by a contemporary—the historian Seutonius: "He was unusually handsome. His expression was calm and mild. He had clear, bright eyes, in which was a kind of divine power. His eyebrows met. His hair was slightly curly and somewhat golden." Any variations were made by sculptors who idealized features to make him almost godlike.

Augustus proclaimed himself a god—not arrogantly or blasphemously as Caligula later did, but as the honored "father" of the "family" of Rome. As the empire expanded, the vanquished had to worship the emperor's statue as a show of loyalty. Augustus even claimed he was descended from Romulus and Remus. Such propaganda solidified the emperor's hold over Rome as both political and spiritual head.

Four Frescoes of Rome's Mythical Origins (Fregio Pittorico, etc.)

These cartoon-strip frescoes (read right to left) tell the story of Augustus' legendary forebears.

1. Upper right fresco: Aeneas (red skin) arrives in Italy from Troy and fights the locals for a place to live.

2. Upper left: His wife (far left, seated, in purple) and son build a city wall around Rome. The women-folk are safe and the city prospers.

3. Lower right: Several generations later, the God of War (in center, with red skin) lies in wait to rape and impregnate a Vestal Virgin.

4. Lower left: Her disgraced babies, Romulus and Remus, are placed in a basket (center) and set adrift on the Tiber River. They wash ashore, are suckled by a wolf, and finally (far left) taken in by a shepherd. These legendary babies, of course, grow up to found the city which makes real history.

• *Exit the room and go round the corner to busts of . . .*

Gallery III — Rome's Greek Mentors

Alexander the Great (Alessandro Magno)

Alexander the Great (356–323 B.C.) single-handedly created an empire by conquering, in just a few short years, lands from Greece to Egypt to Persia, spreading Greek culture and language along the way. Later, when the Romans conquered Greece (c. 200 B.C.), they inherited this pre-existing collection of cultured, Greek-speaking cities ringing the Mediterranean.

Alexander's handsome statues set the standard for those of later Roman emperors. His features were chiseled and youthful, and he was adorned with pompous decorations like a golden sunburst aura (which was fitted into holes). The greatest man of his day, he ruled the known world by the age of 30.

Alexander, a Macedonian, had learned Greek culture from his teacher, none other than the philosopher Aristotle. Aristotle's teacher was Plato, whose mentor was...

Socrates (Socrate)

This nonconformist critic of complacent thinking is the father of philosophy. The Greeks were an intellectual, introspective, sensitive, and artistic people. The Romans were practical, no-nonsense soldiers, salesmen, and bureaucrats. Many a Greek slave—warning a Roman Senator not to wear a plaid toga with a polka-dot robe—was more cultured than his master.

Room VII — Pure Greek Beauty in Greek Originals

Niobid (Niobide Ferita), 440 B.C.

The Romans were astonished by the beauty of Greek statues. This woman's smooth skin contrasts with the rough folds of her clothing. Her pose is angular but still balanced—notice how she twists naturally around an axis running straight up and down. She looks like a classical goddess awakening from a beautiful dream. But...

Circle around back. The hole bored in her back, right in that itchy place you can't quite reach, once held a golden arrow. The woman has been shot by Artemis, goddess of hunting, because her mother dared to boast to the gods about her kids. The Niobid reaches back in vain, trying to remove the arrow before it drains her of life.

Romans ate this stuff up: the sensual beauty, the underplayed pathos, the very Greekness of it. They crated up centuries-old statues like this and brought them home to their gardens and palaces. Appreciate the beauty in this room, since these are some of the world's rare, surviving Greek originals.

Room VIII — Greek Mania

By Julius Caesar's time, Rome was in the grip of a "Neo-Attic" craze, and there weren't enough old statues to fill the demand. Crafty Greeks began cranking out knock-offs of Greek originals for mass consumption. The works in this room were of extremely high quality, while others were more like cheesy fake "*Davids*" in a garden store.

To the Romans, this "art" was just furniture for their homes. An altar from a Greek temple became a place to set your wine, a sacred basin was a rain catcher, a statue of Athena took your olive pits. Different styles from different historical periods were mixed and matched to suit Roman tastes. The rich Roman who bought *Afrodite Pudica*, signed along the base by "Menophantos," would not have known or cared that the artist was copying a one-of-a-kind original done by the great Praxiteles 400 years before, back when Greece was Golden.

Julius, Augustus, and their descendants certainly conquered the world, but the Greeks conquered Rome.

• *Take a break, then head upstairs to the first floor.*

FIRST FLOOR

As we saw, Augustus' family did not always rule wisely. Under Nero (ruled A.D. 54–68), the debauchery, violence, and paranoia typical of the Julio-Claudians festered to a head. When the city burned in the great fire of 64, the Romans suspected Nero of torching it himself to clear land for his enormous luxury palace.

Enough. Nero was assassinated, and an outsider was brought in to rule.

Room I — The Flavian Family

Vespasian (Vespasianus), ruled A.D. 69–79

Balding and wrinkled, with a big head, a double chin, and a shy smile, Vespasian was a common man. The son of a tax collector, he rose through the military ranks with a reputation as a competent drudge. As emperor, he restored integrity, raised taxes, built the Colosseum, and suppressed the Jewish rebellion in Palestine.

Domitian (Domitianus)

Vespasian's son Domitian (emperor A.D. 81–96) used his father's tax revenues to construct the massive Imperial Palace on Palatine Hill, home to emperors for the next three centuries. Shown with his lips curled in a sneering smile, he was a moralistic prude who executed several Vestal ex-Virgins, while in private he took one mistress after another. Until...

Domitia

... until his stern wife found out and hired a servant to stab him in the groin. Domitia's hairstyle is a far cry from the "Livia" cut, with a high crown of tight curls.

NATIONAL MUSEUM, FIRST FLOOR

1. Vespasian
2. Domitian
3. Domitia
4. Nerva
5. Trajan
6. Hadrian
7. Aphrodite Crouching
8. Apollo
9. Discus Thrower
10. Hermaphrodite
11. Septimius Severus
12. Caracalla
13. Balbinus
14. Gordianus III
15. Sarcophagus
16. Christ Teaching

Nerva

The Flavian dynasty was no better than its predecessors. Nerva, old and childless, made a bold, far-sighted move—he adopted a son from outside of Rome's corrupting influence.

Room II — A Cosmopolitan Culture

Trajan (Traianus-Hercules), ruled A.D. 98–117

Born in Spain, this conquering hero pushed Rome's borders to their greatest extent, creating a truly worldwide empire. The spoils of three continents funneled into a city of a million-plus people. Trajan could present himself as a "new Hercules" and no one found it funny. Romans felt a spirit of Manifest Destiny: "The gods desire that the City of Rome shall be the capital of all the countries of the world." (Livy)

Hadrian (Hadrianus), ruled A.D. 117–138

Hadrian was a fully cosmopolitan man. His beard—the first we've seen—shows his taste for foreign things; he poses like the Greek philosopher he imagined himself to be.

Hadrian was a voracious tourist, personally visiting almost every corner of the vast empire, from Britain (where he built Hadrian's Wall) to Egypt (where he sailed the Nile), from Jerusalem (where he suppressed another Jewish revolt) to Athens (where he soaked up classical culture). An omnivorous learner, he scaled Mount Etna just to see what made a volcano tick. Back home, he beautified Rome with the Pantheon and his Villa at Tivoli, a microcosm of places he'd visited.

Hadrian is flanked here by the two loves of his life. His wife, Sabina, with modest hairstyle and scarf, kept the home fires burning for her traveling husband. Hadrian was 50 years old when he became captivated by the teen-age boy, Antinous, with his curly hair and full, sensual lips. Together they traveled the Nile, where Antinous drowned. Hadrian wept. This public display of emotion, somewhat embarrassing to the stoic Romans, became a legend among Greeks, who erected Antinous statues everywhere.

Hadrian spent his last years at his lavish villa outside Rome, surrounded by buildings and souvenirs that reminded him of his traveling days.

Rooms V and VI — Rome's Grandeur

Pause at Rome's peak to admire the things they found beautiful. Imagine these statues in their original locations, in the pleasure gardens of the Roman rich—surrounded by greenery, with the splashing sound of fountains, the statues all painted in bright, life-like colors. Though executed by Romans, the themes are mostly Greek, with godlike humans and human-looking gods.

Aphrodite Crouching (Afrodite Accovacciata)

Hadrian had good taste—he ordered a copy of this Greek classic for his bath room. The goddess of beauty crouches while bathing, then turns to admire herself. This sets her whole body in motion—one thigh goes down, one up; her head turns clockwise while her body goes reverse—yet she's perfectly still. The crouch creates a series of symmetrical love-handles, molded by the sculptor into the marble like wax.

Apollo

The god of light appears as a slender youth, not some burly, powerful, autocratic god. He stands *contrapposto*—originally he was leaning against the tree—in a relaxed and very human way. His curled hair is tied with a headband, with strands that tumble down his neck. His muscles and skin are smooth. (The rusty stains come from

the centuries Apollo spent submerged in the Tiber.) Apollo is in a reflective mood, and the serenity and intelligence in his face shows off classical Greece as a nation of thinkers.

The Discus Thrower (Discobolo)

An athlete winds up, about to unleash his pent-up energy and hurl the discus. The sculptor has frozen the moment for us, so we can examine the inner workings of the wonder called man. The perfect pecs and washboard abs make this human godlike. Geometrically, you could draw a perfect circle around him, with his hipbone at the center. He's natural yet ideal, twisting yet balanced, moving while at rest. For the Greeks, the universe was a rational place, and the human body was the perfect em-bodi-ment of the order found in nature.

This statue is the best-preserved Roman copy (not one member is missing—I checked) of the original Greek work by Myron (450 B.C.). Statues of athletes like this commonly stood in the baths, where Romans cultivated healthy bodies, minds, and social skills, hoping to live well-rounded lives. The *Discus Thrower*, with his geometrical perfection and godlike air, sums up all that is best in the classical world.

Room VII

Hermaphrodite Sleeping (Ermafrodito Dormiente)

After leaving the baths, a well-rounded Roman may head posthaste to an orgy, where he might see a reclining nude like this, be titillated, circle around for a closer look, and say, "Hey! (Insert your reaction here)!"

Room XIII — Beginning of the End

Septimius Severus, ruled A.D. 193–211

Rome's sprawling empire was starting to unravel, and it took a disciplined emperor-general like this African to keep it together. Severus' victories on the frontier earned him a grand triumphal arch in the Forum, but here he seems to be rolling his eyes at the chaos growing around him.

Caracalla, ruled A.D. 211–217

The stubbly beard, cruel frown, and glaring eyes tell us that Severus' son was bad news. He murdered his little brother, Geta, to seize power, then proceeded to massacre thousands of loyal citizens on a whim. The army came to distrust rulers whose personal agenda got in their way, and Caracalla was stabbed in the back by a man whose brother had just been executed.

Room XIV — The Fall

There's a lot of scared faces in this room. People who grew up in the lap of luxury and security were witnessing the unthinkable— the disintegration of a thousand years of tradition. Rome never recovered from the chaos of the third century. Disease, corruption, revolts from within, and "barbarians" pecking away at the borders were body blows that sapped Rome's strength.

Balbinus, ruled A.D. 238

This old man was appointed emperor by the Senate, but he was no soldier, and the army didn't like him. He was one of some twenty emperors in the space of forty years who was saluted, then murdered at the whim of soldiers of fortune. At one point, the office of emperor was literally auctioned to the highest bidder. Balbinus, with his stubbly beard and forlorn look, knows he's lost the army's confidence, and he waits for the axe to fall. Next.

Gordianus III, ruled A.D. 238–244

The 13-year-old Gordianus, with barely a whisp of facial hair, was naive and pliable, the perfect choice—until he got old enough to question the generals. His assassins had no problem sneaking up on him because, as you can see, he had no ears.

Sarcophagus of a Procession (Sarcofago con Corteo, etc.), A.D. 270

This coffin shows a parade of dignitaries accompanying a new Roman leader. As they march up Capitol Hill, they huddle together, their backs to the wall, looking around suspiciously for assassins. Their faces reflect the fear of the age. Rome would stagger on for another 200 years, but the glory of old Rome was gone. The city was becoming a den of thugs, thieves, prostitutes, barbarians... and Christians.

Small Statuette of Christ Teaching (Cristo Docente), A.D. 350

Christ sits like a Roman senator—in a toga, holding a scroll, dispensing wisdom like the law of the land. The statue comes from those delirious days when formerly persecuted Christians could now "come out" and worship in public. Emperor Constantine (ruled 306–337) legalized the religion, and within two generations it was Rome's official religion.

Whether Christianity invigorated or ruined Rome is debated, but the Fall was inevitable. Rome's once-great legions backpedaled until even the city itself was raped and plundered by foreigners (410). In 476, the last emperor sold his title for a comfy pension plan, and "Rome" was just another dirty city with a big history. The barely-flickering torch of ancient Rome was passed on to medieval Christians: senators became bishops, basilicas became churches, and the Pontifex Maximus (Emperor) became the Pontifex Maximus (Pope).

THE REST OF THE MUSEUM

The second floor contains frescoes and mosaics that once decorated the walls and floors of Roman villas. The frescoes (in black, red, yellow, and blue) show a few scenes of people and animals but
are mostly architectural designs, with fake columns and "windows" that "look out" on landscape scenes. Granted, the collection is impressive, but the required tour can be a pain to schedule, the guides speak limited English, and it's a 45-minute commitment.

More interesting stuff is in the basement, housing coins and everyday objects from ancient Rome. In A.D. 300 one *denar* bought one egg. Evaluate Roman life by studying Diocletian's wage and price controls. Find your favorite emperor or empress on the coins using remote-control magnifying glasses. A free audioguide (slow and moody) and English explanations help bring it alive.

BORGHESE GALLERY TOUR

Galleria Borghese

More than just a great museum, Galleria Borghese is a beautiful villa set in the greenery of surrounding gardens. You get to see art commissioned by the luxury-loving Borghese family displayed in the very rooms they were created for. Frescoes, marble, stucco, and interior design enhance the masterpieces. This is a place where—regardless of whether you learn a darn thing—you can sit back and enjoy the sheer beauty of the palace and its art.

Orientation

Cost: L10,000 plus L2,000 for the required reservation.

Hours: Tue–Fri 9:00–21:00, Sat 9:00–23:30, Sun 9:00–20:00, closed Mon.

Getting there: A taxi can get you within 100 meters of the entrance. Otherwise, Metro to Spagna and take a 15-minute walk through the park.

Reservations: Reservations are mandatory and easy to get in English over the Internet (www.ticketeria.it) or by phone: call 06-32810 (Mon–Fri 9:00–19:00, Sat 9:00–13:00). Every two hours, 360 people are allowed to enter the museum. Entry times are: 9:00, 11:00, 13:00, 15:00, 17:00, 19:00 (June–mid-Sept the museum is likely open until 23:30). When you reserve, you'll be given the time you choose and a claim number. While you'll be advised to come 30 minutes early, you can arrive a few minutes beforehand, but don't be late as no-show tickets are given to stand-bys.

Remember, visits are strictly limited to two hours. Concentrate on the first floor but leave yourself 30 minutes (maximum time allowed) for the paintings of the Pinacoteca; highlights are marked by the acoustic guide icons. The fine bookshop and cafeteria are best visited outside your two-hour entry window.

If you don't have a reservation, show up and get on the waiting

list. Reservations are tightest at 11:00 and on weekends. No-shows are released a few minutes after the top of the hour. Generally, out of 360 reservations a few will fail to show (but more than a few may be waiting to grab them). **Tours:** Guided English tours at 11:10 and 15:10 for L8,000, reserve with entry reservation. L8,000 for excellent CD-wand audio tour.

Tour Length: Two hours maximum.

Photography: No photos are allowed.

Portico

Ancient Roman reliefs (at either end) topped by Michelangelo-designed panels capture the essence of the collection—a gathering of beautiful objects from every age and culture inside a lavish 17th-century villa. Cardinal Borghese built the villa, collected ancient works, and hired the best artists of his day. In pursing the optimistic spirit of the Renaissance, they invented Baroque.

Main Entry Hall

Five Roman mosaics decorate the floor with colorful, festive scenes of slaughter. Gladiators fight animals and each other with swords, whips, and tridents. The Greek letter θ (theta) marks the dead. Notice some of the gladiators' pro-wrestler nicknames: "Cupid," "Serpent," "Licentious."

On the wall is a thrilling first-century Greek sculpture of a horse falling. The Renaissance-era rider was added by Pietro Bernini, father of the famous Bernini.

Room I

Statue of Pauline Bonaparte as Venus (Paolina Borghese Bonaparte) — Antonio Canova (1808)

Napoleon's sister went the full monty for the sculptor Canova, scandalizing Europe. ("How could you have done such a thing?!" she was asked. She replied, "The room wasn't cold.") With the famous nose of her conqueror brother, she strikes the pose of Venus as conqueror of men's hearts. Her relaxed afterglow and

slight smirk say she's already had her man. The light dent she puts in the mattress makes this goddess human.

Notice the contrasting textures that Canova gets out of the pure-white marble: the rumpled sheet versus her smooth skin. The satiny-smooth pillows and mattress versus the creases in them. Her porcelain skin versus the hint of a love-handle. Canova polished and waxed the marble until it looks as soft and pliable as cloth.

The mythological pose, the Roman couch, the ancient hairdo, and the calm harmony make Pauline the epitome of the neoclassical style.

Room II

David — Gian Lorenzo Bernini (1624)

Duck! David twists around to put a big rock in his sling. He purses his lips, knits his brow, and winds his body like a spring as his eyes lock onto the target— Goliath, who's somewhere behind us, putting us right in the line of fire.

In this self-portrait, 25-year-old Bernini is ready to take on the world. He's charged with the same fighting energy that fueled the missionaries and conquistadors of the Counter-Reformation.

Compared with Michelangelo's *David*, this is gritty realism—an unbalanced pose, bulging veins, unflattering face, and armpit hair. Bernini slays the pretty-boy Davids of the Renaissance and prepares to invent Baroque.

The sarcophagus on the wall on David's left shows the Hellenistic inspiration for Baroque. Look at the Labors of Hercules (A.D 160, at chest level).

Room III

Apollo and Daphne (Apollo e Dafne) — Bernini (1625)

Apollo—made stupid by Cupid's arrow of love—chases after Daphne, who has been turned off by the "arrow of disgust." Just as he's about to catch her, she calls to her father to save her. Magically, her fingers begin to sprout leaves, her toes become roots, her skin turns to bark, and she transforms into a tree.

Frustrated Apollo ends up with a handful of leaves.

Stand behind the statue to experience it as Bernini originally intended. It's only when you circle around to the front that he reveals the story's surprise ending.

Walk slowly around. It's as much air as stone. The back leg defies gravity. It was two years in restoration (described to me as being something like dental work). The marble leaves at the top ring like crystal when struck. Notice the same scene, colorized, painted on the ceiling above.

Bernini carves out some of the chief features of Baroque art: He makes a super-natural event seem realistic. He freezes it at the most dramatic, emotional moment. The figures move and twist in unusual poses. He turns the wind machine on, sending Apollo's cape billowing behind him. It's a sculpture group of two, forming a scene, rather than a stand-alone portrait. And the subject is classical. Even in strict Counter-Reformation times, there was always a place for groping, if the subject matter had a moral—this one taught you not to pursue fleeting earthly pleasures. And besides, Bernini tends to show a lot of skin but no genitals.

Room IV

The Rape of Proserpine (Il Ratto di Proserpina) — Bernini (1622)

Pluto strides into the Underworld and shows off his catch—the beautiful daughter of the earth goddess. His three-headed guard dog, Cerberus, barks triumphantly. Pluto is squat, thick, and uncouth, with knotted muscles and untrimmed beard. He's trying not to hurt her, but she pushes her divine molester away and twists to call out for help. Tears roll down her cheeks. She wishes she could turn into a tree.

Bernini was the master of marble. Look how Pluto's fingers dig into her thigh like it was real flesh. Bernini picked out this Carrara marble knowing that its relative suppleness and ivory hue would lend itself to a fleshy statue.

Diana the Hunter (Artemis) — Artist Unknown

The statues in the niches are classical originals. *Diana the Hunter* is a rare Greek original from the second century B.C. The traditional *contrapposto* pose (weight on one leg) and idealized grace

were an inspiration for artists like Canova who grew tired of
Bernini's Baroque bombast.

The Marbles in Room IV

Appreciate the beauty of the different types of marble in the
room: Bernini's ivory Carrara, Diana's translucent white, purple
porphyry emperors, granite-like columns that support them,
wood-grained pilasters on the walls, and the different colors on
the floor—green, red, grey, lavender, and yellow, some grainy,
some "marbled" like a steak. Some of the world's most beautiful
and durable things have been made from the shells of sea creatures
layered in sediment, fossilized into limestone, then heated and
crystallized by the pressure of the earth: marble.

Room VI

Aeneas ("Enea" etc.) — Bernini (1620)

Aeneas' home in Troy is in flames, and he escapes with the three
most important things: his family (decrepit father on his shoulder
and baby boy), his household gods (the statues in dad's hands), and
the Eternal Flame (carried by son). They're all in shock, lost in
thought, facing an uncertain future. Aeneas isn't even looking
where he's going, he just puts one foot in front of the other. Little
do they know that eventually they'll wind up in Italy, where
Aeneas will found the city of Rome and house the flame in the
Temple of Vesta.

Bernini was still a teenager when he started this, his first
life-size work. He was probably helped by his dad, who nurtured
the child prodigy much like Leopold mentored Mozart, but without the rivalry. Bernini's portrayal of human flesh—from baby fat
to middle-age muscle to sagging decrepitude—is astonishing. Still,
the composition is static—not nearly as interesting as the reliefs
up at the ceiling, with their dancing, light-footed soldiers with
do-si-do shields.

Room VII

"The Theater of the Universe"

The room's decor sums up the eclectic nature of the villa. There
are Greek statues and Roman mosaics. There are fake "Egyptian"
hieroglyphs (perfectly symmetrical in good neoclassical style). Look
out the window past the sculpted gardens, at the mesh domes of
the aviary once filled with exotic birds. Cardinal Borghese's vision
was to make a place where art, history, music, nature, and science
would come together ... "a theater of the universe."

Room VIII

Caravaggio

The paintings in this room change often, but you'll likely find one or two by the Baroque innovator Caravaggio (1571–1610).

 Caravaggio brought Christian saints and Greek gods down to earth with gritty realism. His saints are balding and wrinkled. His Bacchus (a self-portrait) is pale and puffy-faced. David sticks Goliath's severed head (a self-portrait) right in your face. The Madonnas scarcely glow. Baby Jesus is buck naked. Ordinary people were his models. Caravaggio's straightforwardness can be a refreshing change in a museum full of (sometimes overly) refined beauty.

Pinacoteca — Painting Gallery

To reach the Pinacoteca, go outside and return to the basement where you got your ticket, follow signs to the Pinacoteca, show your ticket to the guard, and climb the long spiral stairway. Remember, you're limited to only 30 minutes in the Pinacoteca, and you must visit it within the two-hour window of time printed on your ticket. Most visitors wait until the last half-hour to see the Pinacoteca, so that's when it's most crowded (and the ground floor is less crowded). If you see the paintings first, remember that given a two-hour visit, the ground floor with the sculpture is worth most of that time.

Room XIV

Bust of Cardinal Borghese (Ritr. del Card. Scipione Borghese) — Bernini (1632)

Say *grazie* to the man who built this villa, assembled the collection, and hired Bernini to sculpt masterpieces. The cardinal is caught turning as though to greet someone at a party. There's a twinkle in his eye and he opens his mouth to make a witty comment. This man of the cloth was, in fact, a sophisticated hedonist.
• *On the table nearby, find the smaller . . .*

Bust of Pope Paul V

The cardinal's uncle was a more sober man but also a patron of the arts who hired Bernini's father. When Pope Paul saw sketches made by little Lorenzo, he announced: "This boy will be the Michelangelo of his age."
• *On the wall above the table, find these paintings . . .*

Two Bernini Self-Portraits (Autoritratto giovanile, 1623 and Autoritratto in eta matura, 1630/35)

Bernini was a master of many media, including painting. The younger Bernini looks out a bit hesitantly, as if he's still finding his way in high-class society. But with a few masterpieces under his belt, his next self-portrait shows Bernini with more confidence and facial hair—the dashing and passionate man who would rebuild Rome in Baroque style, from St. Peter's Square to the fountains that dot the piazzas.

Room IX

Deposition (Raffaelo Sanzio — Deposizione di Cristo) — Raphael

Jesus is being taken from the cross. The men support him while the women support Mary, who has fainted. The woman who commissioned the painting had recently lost her son. She wanted to show the death of a son and the grief of a mother.

In true Renaissance style, Raphael orders the scene with geometrical perfection. The curve of Jesus' body is echoed by the swirl of Mary Magdalene's hair and then by the curve of Calvary Hill, where he met his fate.

Room X

Danae — Correggio

Cupid strips Danae as she spreads her legs most unlady-like to receive a trickle of gold from the smudgy cloud overhead—this was Zeus' idea of intercourse with a human. The sheets are rumpled and Danae looks right where the action is with a smile on her face. It's hard to believe that a supposedly religious family would display such an erotic work. But the Borgheses felt that the Church was truly "catholic" (universal), and that all forms of human expression—including physical passion—glorified God.

Room XX

Sacred and Profane Love (Tiziano Vecello — Amor Sacrae, Amor Profane) — Titian

The clothed woman at left was recently married, and she cradles a vase filled with jewels representing the riches of earthly love. Her naked twin on the right holds the burning flame of eternal,

heavenly love. Baby Cupid, between them, playfully stirs the waters.

This exquisite painting expresses the spirit of the Renaissance—that earth and heaven are two sides of the same coin. And here in the Borghese Gallery, that love of earthly beauty can be spiritually uplifting—as long as you do it within two hours.

VATICAN MUSEUM TOUR

The glories of the ancient world displayed in a lavish papal palace, decorated by the likes of Michelangelo and Raphael...the Musei Vaticani. Unfortunately, many tourists see the Vatican Museum only an obstacle between them and its grand finale, the Sistine Chapel. True, this huge, confusing, and crowded mega-museum can be a jungle, but with this book as your vine, you should swing through with ease, enjoying the highlights and getting to the Sistine just before you collapse. On the way, you'll enjoy some of the less appreciated but equally important sections of this warehouse of Western civilization.

Orientation

Cost: L18,000, free on last Sunday of each month.
Hours: April–mid-June and Sept and Oct Mon–Fri 8:45–16:45, Sat 8:45–13:45, usually closed Sun except last Sun of the month (when it's free and open 8:45–13:45). Rest of the year Mon–Sat 8:45–13:45. Last entry an hour before closing time. Sistine closes 30 minutes early.

Closed on 13 religious holidays, including Corpus Christi and St. Peter and Paul Day (June 29) and Assumption Day (August 15). Some individual rooms close at odd hours, especially after 13:00. A lighted board inside the entrance lists closures. The rooms described here are usually open.

Modest dress (no short shorts) is appropriate, and often required. It's generally hot and crowded. Saturday, the last Sunday of the month, and Monday are the worst; late afternoons are best.
Getting there: From the nearest Metro stop, Cipro–Musei Vaticani, it's a 10-minute walk. From St. Peter's Square, it's about a 15-minute walk. Taxis are reasonable (hop in and say "moo-ZAY-ee vah-tee-KAHN-ee").

THE VATICAN

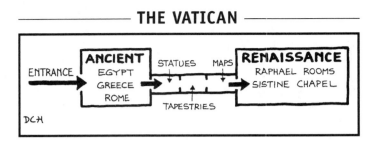

Information: An information booth is on the ground floor at the entry (English spoken). The museum has signs to four color-coded, self-guided tours (A—the Sistine blitz, C—a good tour, D—everything). Some exhibits have English explanations. You can rent a CD audioguide at the entrance. Post office, writing room, stingy exchange bank, and a bookshop are next to the ticket booth. Tel. 06-6988-3333.

Tour length: Until you expire, or 2.5 hours, whichever comes first.

Cuisine art: An expensive cafeteria with a long, slow line is just inside the entry. Better choices: The great Via Andrea Doria produce market is three blocks north of the entrance (head across the street, down the stairs, and continue straight), cheap Pizza Rustica shops line Viale Giulio Cesare, and good restaurants are nearby (see Eating chapter).

Photography: No photos are allowed in the Sistine Chapel. Elsewhere in the museum, photos without a flash are permitted.

Starring: World history, Michelangelo, Raphael, *Laocoön*, the Greek masters, and their Roman copyists.

The Pope's Collection

With the fall of Rome, the Catholic (or "universal") Church became the great preserver of civilization, collecting artifacts from cultures dead and dying. Renaissance popes (15th and 16th centuries) collected most of what we'll see. Those lusty priests-as-Roman-emperors loved the ancient world. They built these palaces and decorated them with classical statues and Renaissance paintings. They combined the classical and Christian worlds, finding the divine in the creations of man.

We'll concentrate on classical sculpture and Renaissance painting. But along the way (and there's a lot of along-the-way here), we'll stop to leaf through a few yellowed pages from this 5,000-year-old scrapbook of mankind.

This heavyweight museum is shaped like a barbell—two buildings connected by a long hall. The entrance building covers the ancient world (Egypt, Greece, Rome). The one at the far end covers its "rebirth" in the Renaissance (including the Sistine Chapel). The halls there and back are a mix of old and new. Move quickly—don't burn out before the Sistine Chapel at the end—and see how each civilization borrows from and builds on the previous one.

• *Leave Italy by entering the doors. Buy your ticket, show it at the turnstiles, and follow the crowds. Then turn left and head up the stairs to the first-floor Egyptian Rooms (Musei Egizio). Don't stop until you find your mummy.*

EGYPT (3000–1000 B.C.)

Egyptian art was for religion, not decoration. A statue or painting preserved the likeness of someone, giving him a form of eternal life. Most of the art was for tombs, where they put the mummies. Notice that the art is only realistic enough to get the job done. You can recognize that it's a man, a bird, or whatever, but these are stiff, two-dimensional, schematic figures—functional rather than beautiful.

Mummies

This woman died three millennia ago. Her corpse was disemboweled, and her organs were placed in a jar like those you see nearby.

Then the body was refilled with pitch, dried with natron (a natural sodium carbonate), wrapped in linen, and placed in a wood coffin, which went inside a stone coffin, which was placed in a tomb. (Remember that the pyramids were just big tombs.) In the next life, the spirit was homeless without its body, and you wanted to look your best—notice the henna job on her hair.

Notice, painted inside the coffins, what the deceased "packed" for the journey to eternity. The coffins were decorated with magical spells to protect the body from evil and to act as crib notes for the confused soul in the netherworld.

Egyptian Statues

Even in the Romanized versions, it's clear that Egyptian statues are stiff and unnatural. They step out awkwardly with arms straight down at their sides. Each was made according to an established set of proportions. Little changed over the centuries. These had a function and

they worked. In Egyptian belief, a statue like this could be a place of refuge for the wandering soul of a dead man.

Various Egyptian Gods as Animals
Before technology made humans top dogs on earth, it was easier to appreciate our fellow creatures. The Egyptians saw the superiority of animals and worshiped them as incarnations of the gods. Wander through a pet store of Egyptian animal gods. The lioness portrays the fierce goddess Sekhmet; the clever baboon is the god of wisdom, Thot, and Horus has a falcon's head.

• *Continue through a curved corridor of animal gods, then through three more rooms, pausing at the glass case in the third room, which contains brown clay tablets.*

Sumerian Writing
Even before Egypt, civilizations flourished in the Middle East. The Sumerian culture in Mesopotamia (modern Iraq) invented writing around 3000 B.C. You can see the clay tablets with this cuneiform (wedge-shaped) script. Also notice the ingenious cylindrical seals, with which they made impressions in soft clay to seal documents and mark property.

• *Go with the flow past a view of Rome out the window, then turn left into the octagonal courtyard of the "Pio-Clementino" section.*

SCULPTURE — GREECE AND ROME (500 B.C.–A.D. 500)
This palace wouldn't be here, this sculpture wouldn't be here, and you'd be spending your vacation in South Dakota at Reptile Gardens if it weren't for a few thousand Greeks in a small city about 450 years before Christ. Athens set the tone for the rest of the West. Democracy, theater, economics, literature, and art all got their start in Athens during a 50-year "Golden Age." Greek culture was then appropriated by Rome and revived again 1,500 years later, during the Renaissance. The Renaissance popes built and decorated these palaces, recreating the glory of the classical world.

Apollo Belvedere
Apollo, the god of the sun and also of music, is hunting. He has spotted his prey and is about to go after it with his (missing) bow and arrows. The optimistic Greeks conceived of their gods in human form...and buck naked.

The great Greek sculptor Praxiteles has fully captured the beauty of the human form. The anatomy is perfect, the pose is natural. Instead of standing at attention, face forward with his

arms at his sides (Egyptian style), Apollo is on the move, stepping forward slightly with his weight on one leg.

The Greeks loved balance. A well-rounded man was both a thinker and an athlete, a poet and a warrior. In art, the *Apollo Belvedere* balances several opposites. Apollo eyes his target, but hasn't attacked yet. He's moving, but not out of control. He's also a balance between a real person and an ideal god. And the smoothness of his muscles is balanced by the rough folds of his cloak. The only sour note: his recently added left hand. Could we try a size smaller?

During the Renaissance, when this Roman copy of the original Greek work was discovered, it was considered the most perfect work of art in the world. The handsome face, eternal youth, and the body that seems to float a half-inch off the pedestal made *Apollo Belvedere* an object of wonder and almost worship. Apollo's grace was something superhuman, divine, and godlike, even for devout Christians.

• *In the neighboring niche to the right, a bearded old Roman river god lounges in the shade. This pose inspired Michelangelo's Adam in the Sistine Chapel (coming soon). While there are a few fancy bathtubs in this courtyard, most of the carved boxes you see are sarcophagi—Roman coffins and relic-holders, carved with the deceased's epitaph in picture form.*

Laocoön

Laocoön (lay-AWK-oh-wahn) was a pagan high priest of Troy, the ancient city attacked by the Greeks. When the Greeks brought the Trojan Horse to the gates as a ploy to get inside the city walls, Laocoön tried to warn his people not to bring it inside. But the gods wanted the Greeks to win, so they sent huge snakes to crush him and his two sons to death. We see them at the height of their terror, when they realize that, no matter how hard they struggle, they—and their entire race—are doomed.

The *Laocoön* is Hellenistic, done four centuries after the Golden Age, after the scales of "balance" had been tipped. Where *Apollo* is a balance between stillness and motion, this is unbridled motion. Where *Apollo* is serene, this is emotional. Where *Apollo* is idealized grace, this is powerful and gritty realism. The figures (carved from four blocks of marble pieced together seamlessly) are powerful, not light and graceful. The poses are as twisted as possible, accentuating every rippling muscle and bulging vein. Follow the line of motion from *Laocoön*'s left foot, up his leg, through his body and out his

right arm (which some historians used to think extended straight out—until the elbow was unearthed early in the 1900s). Goethe used to stand here and blink his eyes rapidly, watching the statue flicker to life.

Laocoön was the most famous Greek statue in ancient Rome and considered "superior to all other sculpture or painting." It was famous in the Renaissance, too—though no one had seen it, only read about it in ancient accounts. Then, in 1506, it was unexpectedly unearthed in the ruins of Nero's Golden House near the Colosseum. The discovery caused a sensation. They cleaned it off and paraded it through the streets before an awestruck populace. No one had ever seen anything like its motion and emotion, having been raised on a white-bread diet of pretty, serene, and balanced *Apollo*s. One of those who saw it was the young Michelangelo, and it was a revelation to him. Two years later, he started work on the Sistine Chapel, and the Renaissance was about to take another turn.

• *Leave the courtyard. Swing around the Hall of Animals, a jungle of beasts real and not so real, to the limbless* Torso *in the middle of the next large hall.*

Belvedere Torso

My entire experience with statues consists of making snowmen. But standing face to face with this hunk of shaped rock makes you appreciate the sheer physical labor involved in chipping a figure out of solid rock. It takes great strength, but at the same time, great delicacy.

This is all that remains of an ancient statue of Hercules seated on a lion skin. Michelangelo loved this old rock. He knew he was the best sculptor of his day. The ancients were his only peers—and his rivals. He'd caress this statue lovingly and tell people, "I am the pupil of the *Torso*." To him, it contained all the beauty of classical sculpture. But it's not beautiful. It's ugly. Compared with the pure grace of the *Apollo*, it's downright hideous.

But Michelangelo, an ugly man himself, was looking for a new kind of beauty—not the beauty of idealized gods, but the innate beauty of every person, even so-called ugly ones. With its knotty lumps of muscle, the *Torso* has a brute power and a distinct personality despite—or because of—its rough edges. Remember this *Torso* because we'll see it again later on.

• *Enter the next, domed room.*

Round Room

This room, modeled on the Pantheon interior, gives some idea of Roman grandeur. Romans often took Greek ideas and made them bigger, like the big bronze statue of Hercules with his club, found near Pompey's Theatre (by modern-day Campo de' Fiori). The mosaic floor recreates an ancient Roman villa, and the enormous Roman hot tub/birdbath/vase, made of purple porphyry marble, is also likely from a villa. Purple was a rare, royal, expensive, and prestigious color in pre-Crayola days.

• *Enter the next room.*

Sarcophagi

These two large coffins made of porphyry marble were made for the Roman Emperor Constantine's mother and daughter. They were Christians and, therefore, criminals until Constantine made Christianity legal (A.D. 312).

• *See how we've come full circle in this building—the Egyptian Rooms are ahead on your left. Go upstairs and prepare for the Long March down the hall lined with statues toward the Sistine Chapel and Raphael Rooms.*

   Overachievers may first choose to pop into the Etruscan wing—"Museo Etrusco"—located a few steps up from the "Long March" level. (Others have permission to save their aesthetic energy for the Sistine.)

THE ETRUSCANS (800–300 B.C.)

Room I

The chariot is from 550 B.C., when crude Romans were ruled by their more civilized neighbors to the north—the Etruscans. Imagine the chariot racing around the dirt track of the Circus Maximus, through the marshy valley of the newly drained Forum, or up

Capitoline Hill to the Temple of Jupiter—all originally built by
Rome's Etruscan kings.

Room II

The golden breastplate (*Pectoral*, 650 B.C., immediately to the
right) decorated with tiny winged angels and animals shows off the
sophistication of the Etruscans. Though unwarlike and politically
decentralized, these people were able to "conquer" all of central
Italy around 650 B.C. through trade, offering tempting metalwork
goods like this.

The Etruscan vases done in the Greek style remind us of the
other great pre-Roman power—the Greek colonists who settled in
southern Italy (Magna Graecia). The Etruscans traded with the
Greeks, adopting their fashions. Rome, cradled between the two,
grew up learning from both cultures.

A Greek-style bowl (far corner of the room) depicting a man
and woman in bed together would have scandalized early Roman
farmers. He's pissing in a chamberpot, she's blowing a flute.
Etruscan art often showed husbands and wives at ease together,
giving them a reputation among the Romans as immoral, flute-
playing degenerates.

Room III

The bronze warrior whose head was sawed
off by lightning has a rare inscription that's
readable (on armor below the navel). It probably refers to the statue's former owner:
"Aha! Trutitis gave [this] as [a] gift." Archaeologists understand the Etruscans' Greek-
style alphabet and some individual words, but
they've yet to fully crack the code. As you
look around at beautiful bronze pitchers,
candlesticks, shields, and urns, ponder yet

another of Etruria's unsolved mysteries—no one is sure where
these sophisticated people came from.

Room IV

Most of our knowledge of the Etruscans is from sarcophagi and
art in Etruscan tombs. Their funeral art is solemn but hardly
morbid—check out the sarcopha-guy with the bulging belly,
enjoying a banquet for all eternity.

The Etruscans' origins are obscure, but their legacy is clear.
In 509 B.C., the Etruscan king's son raped a Roman. The king
was thrown out, the Republic was declared, Etruscan cities were
conquered by Rome's legions, and their culture was swallowed up

in Roman expansion. By Julius Caesar's time, the few remaining ethnic Etruscans were reduced to serving their masters as flute players, goldsmiths, surgeons— and street-corner soothsayers, like the one that Caesar brushed aside when he called out, "Beware the Ides of March...."

• *Return to the long hall leading to the Sistine Chapel and Raphael Rooms.*

THE LONG MARCH — SCULPTURE, TAPESTRIES, MAPS, AND VIEWS

Remember, this building was originally a series of papal palaces. They loved beautiful things, and as heirs of Imperial Rome, they felt they deserved such luxury. This quarter-mile walk gives you a sense of the scale that Renaissance popes built on. The palaces and art represent both the peak and the decline of the Catholic Church in Europe. It was extravagant spending like this that inspired Martin Luther to rebel, starting the Protestant Reformation.

Gallery of the Candelabra — Classical Sculpture

In the second "room" of the long hall, stop at the statue *Diana the Huntress* on the left. Here, the virgin goddess goes hunting. Roman hunters would pray and give offerings to statues like this to get divine help in their hunt for food.

Farmers might pray to another version of the same goddess, *Artemis*, on the opposite wall. This billion-breasted beauty stood for fertility. "Boobs or bulls' balls?" Some historians say that bulls were sacrificed and castrated, with the testicles draped over the statues as symbols of fertility.

• *Shuffle along to the* Bacchus *in the next "room" on the left with a baby on his shoulders.*

Fig Leaves

Why do the statues have fig leaves? Like *Bacchus*, many of these statues originally looked much different than they do now. First off, they were painted, usually in gaudy colors. *Bacchus* may have had brown hair, rosy cheeks, purple grapes, and a leopard-skin sidekick at his feet. Even the *Apollo Belvedere*, whose cool grey tones we now admire as "classic Greek austerity," may have had a paisley pink cloak for all we know. Also, many statues had glass eyes like *Bacchus*.

And the fig leaves? Those came from the years 1550 to

THE LONG MARCH

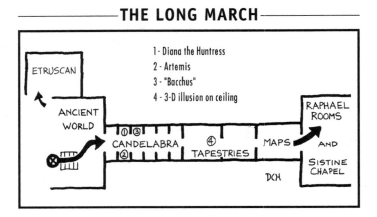

ETRUSCAN

1 - Diana the Huntress
2 - Artemis
3 - "Bacchus"
4 - 3-D illusion on ceiling

ANCIENT WORLD

CANDELABRA

TAPESTRIES

MAPS

RAPHAEL ROOMS

AND

SISTINE CHAPEL

DCH

1800, when the church decided that certain parts of the human anatomy were obscene. (Why they didn't pick the feet, which are universally ugly, I'll never know.) Perhaps church leaders associated these full-frontal statues with the outbreak of Renaissance humanism that reduced their power in Europe. Whatever; they reacted by covering classical crotches with plaster fig leaves, the same leaves Adam and Eve had used when the concept of "privates" was invented.

Note: The leaves could be removed at any time if the museum officials were so motivated. There are suggestion boxes around the museum. Whenever I see a fig leaf, I get the urge to pick-et. We could start an organ-ized campaign…

• *Cover your eyes in case they forgot a fig leaf or two and continue to the tapestries.*

Tapestries

Along the left wall are tapestries designed by Raphael and his workshop and made in Brussels. They show scenes from the life of Christ, starting with the baby Jesus in the manger.

Check out the beautiful sculpted reliefs on the ceiling, especially the lavender panel near the end of the first tapestry room showing a centurion ordering Eskimo Pies from a vendor. Admire the workmanship of this relief, then realize that it's not a relief at all—it's painted on a flat surface! Illusions like this were proof that painters had mastered the 3-D realism of ancient statues.

Map Gallery—View of Vatican City

This gallery still feels like a pope's palace. The crusted ceiling is pure papal splendor. The maps on the walls are decorations from the 16th century. You can plan the next leg of your trip with the two maps of Italy at the far end of the hall—"New Italy" and "Old Italy"—both with a smoking Mount Vesuvius next to Napoli/Neapolis/Naples. There's an interesting old map of Venice on the right as you exit.

The windows give you your best look at the tiny country of Vatican City, formed in 1929. It has its own radio station, as you see from the tower on the hill. What you see here is pretty much all there is—these gardens, the palaces you're in, and St. Peter's. If you lean out and look left you'll see the dome of St. Peter's the way Michelangelo would have liked you to see it—without the bulky Baroque facade.

• *Exit the map room and take a breather in the next small tapestry hall before turning left into the crowded Raphael Rooms.*

RENAISSANCE ART

Raphael Rooms — Papal Wallpaper

We've seen art from the ancient world; now we'll see its rebirth in the Renaissance. We're entering the living quarters of the great Renaissance popes—where they slept, worked, and worshiped. The rooms reflect the grandeur of their position. They hired the best artists—mostly from Florence—to paint the walls and ceilings, combining classical and Christian motifs.

• *Entering, you'll immediately see . . .*

The huge non-Raphael painting shows Sobieski liberating Vienna from the Muslim Turks in 1683, finally tipping the tide in favor of a Christian Europe. See the Muslim tents on the left and the spires of Christian Vienna on the right.

The second room's paintings celebrate the doctrine of the Immaculate Conception, establishing that Mary herself was conceived free from original sin. This medieval idea wasn't actually made dogma until a century ago. The largest fresco shows how the inspiration came straight from heaven (upper left) in a ray of light directly to the pope. Modern popes have had to defend this and other doctrines against the onslaught of the modern world, which questions "superstitions," the divinity of Jesus . . . and the infallibility of the pope.

RAPHAEL ROOMS

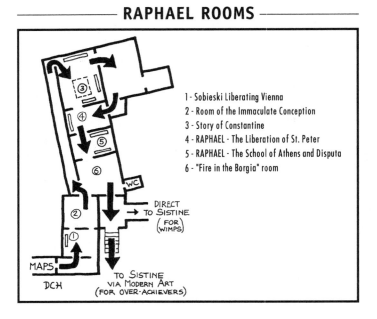

1 - Sobieski Liberating Vienna
2 - Room of the Immaculate Conception
3 - Story of Constantine
4 - RAPHAEL - The Liberation of St. Peter
5 - RAPHAEL - The School of Athens and Disputa
6 - "Fire in the Borgia" room

WC

DIRECT
→ TO SISTINE
(FOR)
(WIMPS)

MAPS

DCH

TO SISTINE
VIA MODERN ART
(FOR OVER-ACHIEVERS)

• *Next, you'll pass along an outside ramp overlooking a courtyard (is that the pope's Fiat?), finally ending up in the first of the Raphael Rooms—the Constantine Room.*

Constantine Room

The frescoes (by Raphael and assistants) celebrate the passing of the baton from one culture to the next. Remember, Rome was a pagan empire persecuting a fanatic cult from the East— Christianity.

Then, on the night of October 27, A.D. 312 (left wall), as Constantine (in gold, with crown) was preparing his troops for a coup d'état, he looked up and saw something strange. A cross appeared in the sky with the words, "You will conquer in this sign."

Next day (long wall), his troops raged victoriously into battle with the Christian cross atop their Roman eagle banners. There's Constantine in the center, slashing through the enemy, with God's warrior angels riding shotgun overhead.

Constantine was supposedly baptized a Christian (right wall), even stripping and kneeling before the pope. As emperor, he legalized Christianity and worked hand in hand with the pope (window wall). Rome soon became a Christian empire that would dominate Europe. When Rome's government fell, its glory lived on through the Dark Ages in the pomp, pageantry, and learning of the Catholic Church.

Look at the ceiling painting. A classical statue falls and crumbles before the overpowering force of the cross. Whoa! Christianity triumphs over pagan Rome. (This was painted, I believe, by Raphael's surrealist colleague, Salvadorus Dalio.)

RAPHAEL

Raphael was only 25 when Pope Julius II invited him to paint the walls of his private apartments. Julius was so impressed by Raphael's talent that he had the work of earlier masters scraped off and gave Raphael free rein to paint what he wanted.

Raphael lived a charmed life. He painted masterpieces effortlessly. He was handsome and sophisticated, and soon became Julius' favorite. In a different decade, he might have been thrown out of the Church as a great sinner, but his love affairs and devil-may-care personality seemed to epitomize the optimistic pagan spirit of the Renaissance. His works are graceful, but never lightweight or frilly—they're strong, balanced, and harmonious in the best Renaissance tradition. When he died young in 1520, the High Renaissance died with him.

• *Continue through the next room and bookshop. In the following room, block the sunlight with your hand to see...*

The Liberation of St. Peter

Peter, Jesus' right-hand man, was thrown into prison in Jerusalem for his beliefs. In the middle of the night, an angel appeared and rescued him from the sleeping guards (Acts 12). The chains miraculously fell away (and were later brought to the St. Peter-in-Chains church in Rome) and the angel led him to safety (right) while the guards took hell from their captain (left). This little "play" is neatly divided into three separate acts that make a balanced composition.

Raphael makes the miraculous event even more dramatic with the use of three kinds of light illuminating the dark cell—half-moonlight, the captain's torch, and the radiant angel. Raphael's mastery of realism, rich colors, and sense of drama made him understandably famous.

• *Enter the next room . . .*

The School of Athens

In both style and subject matter, this fresco sums up the spirit of the Renaissance, which was not only the rebirth of classical art, but a rebirth of learning, of discovery, of the optimistic spirit that man is a rational creature. Raphael pays respect to the great thinkers and scientists of ancient Greece, gathering them together at one time in a mythical school setting.

In the center are Plato and Aristotle, the two greatest. Plato points up, indicating his philosophy that mathematics and pure ideas are the source of truth, while Aristotle points down, showing his preference for hands-on study of the material world. There's their master, Socrates (midway to the left, in green), ticking off arguments on his fingers. And in the foreground at right, Euclid bends over a slate to demonstrate a geometrical formula.

Raphael shows that Renaissance thinkers were as good as the ancients. There's Leonardo da Vinci, whom Raphael worshiped, in the role of Plato. Raphael himself (next to last on the far right, with the black beret) looks out at us. And the "school" building is actually an early version of St. Peter's basilica (under construction at the time).

Raphael balances everything symmetrically—thinkers to the left, thinkers to the right, with Plato and Aristotle dead center—

showing the geometrical order found in the world. Look at the square floor tiles in the foreground. If you laid a ruler over them and extended the line upward, it would run right to center of the picture. Similarly, the tops of the columns all point down to the middle. All the lines of sight draw our attention to Plato and Aristotle, and to the small arch over their heads—a halo over these two secular saints in the divine pursuit of knowledge. While Raphael was painting this room, Michelangelo was at work down the hall in the Sistine Chapel. Raphael popped in on the sly to see the master at work. He was astonished. When he saw Michelangelo's powerful figures and dramatic scenes, he began to beef up his delicate, graceful style to a more heroic level. In *The School of Athens*, perhaps Raphael's greatest work, he tipped his brush to the master by adding Michelangelo to the scene—the brooding, melancholy figure in front leaning on a block of marble.

The Disputa

As if to underline the new attitude that pre-Christian philosophy and church thinking could co-exist, Raphael painted *The Disputa* facing the *School of Athens*. Christ and the saints in heaven are overseeing a discussion of the Eucharist (the communion wafer) by mortals below. The classical-looking woman in blue looks out as if to say, "There's the School of Athens," while pointing toward the center of the painting she's in, as if to say, "But here's the School of Heaven." Balance and symmetry reign, from the angel trios in the upper corners to the books littering the floor.

In Catholic terms, the communion wafer miraculously becomes the body of Christ when it's eaten, bringing a little bit of heaven into the material world. Raphael's painting also connects heaven and earth, with descending circles: Jesus in a halo, down to the dove of the Holy Spirit in a circle, which enters the communion wafer in its holder. The composition drives the point home. By the way, these rooms were the papal library, so themes featuring learning, knowledge, and debate were appropriate.

Moving along, the last Raphael Room (called the "Fire in the Borgia" Room) shows work done mostly by Raphael's students, who were influenced by the muscularity and dramatic, sculptural poses of Michelangelo.

• *Get ready. It's decision time. From here there are two ways to get to the Sistine Chapel. Leave the final Raphael Room and you'll soon see two arrows—one pointing left to the Sistine (Cappella Sistina) and one pointing right to the Sistine. Left goes directly to the Sistine. But going right (5 minutes and a few staircases longer) has a quiet room at the foot of the stairs with a bench where you can sit in peace to read ahead before entering the hectic Sistine Chapel. Also, you get to stroll through the impressive Modern Religious Art collection on the way (signs will direct you to the Sistine). Your call.*

THE SISTINE CHAPEL

The Sistine Chapel contains Michelangelo's ceiling and his huge *Last Judgment*. The Sistine is the personal chapel of the pope and the place where new popes are elected. When Pope Julius II asked Michelangelo to take on this important project, he said, "No, *grazie.*"

Michelangelo insisted he was a sculptor, not a painter. The Sistine ceiling was a vast undertaking and he didn't want to do a half-vast job. But the pope pleaded, bribed, and threatened until Michelangelo finally consented on the condition he be able to do it all his own way.

Julius had asked for only 12 Apostles along the sides of the ceiling, but Michelangelo had a grander vision—the entire history of the world until Jesus. He spent the next four years (1508–1512) lying on his back on scaffolding six stories up, covering the ceiling with frescoes of Bible scenes. In sheer physical terms, it's an astonishing achievement: 600 square yards, and every inch done by his own hand. (Raphael only designed most of his rooms, letting assistants do the grunt work.)

First he had to design and erect the scaffolding. Any materials had to be hauled up on pulleys. Then a section of ceiling would be plastered. With fresco—painting on wet plaster—if you don't get it right the first time, you have to scrape the whole thing off and start over. And if you've ever struggled with a ceiling light fixture or worked underneath a car for even five minutes, you know how heavy your arms get. The physical effort, the paint dripping in his eyes, the creative drain, and the mental stress from a pushy pope combined to almost kill Michelangelo.

But when it was finished and revealed to the public, it simply blew 'em away. Like the *Laocoön* statue discovered six years earlier, it was unlike anything seen before. It both caps the Renaissance and turns it in a new direction. In perfect Renaissance spirit, it mixes Old Testament prophets with classical figures. But the style is more dramatic, shocking, and emotional than the balanced Renaissance works before it. This is a very personal work—the Gospel according to Michelangelo—but its themes and subject matter are universal. Almost without exception, art critics concede that the Sistine ceiling is the single greatest work of art by any one human being.

The Sistine Ceiling — Understanding What You're Standing Under

The ceiling shows the history of the world before the birth of Jesus. We see God creating the world, creating man and woman, destroying the earth by flood, and so on. Along the sides (where the ceiling starts to curve) we see the Old Testament prophets and pagan Greek prophetesses that foretold the coming of Christ. Dividing these scenes and figures is a painted architectural framework (a 3-D illusion) decorated with nude, statue-like figures with symbolic meaning.

THE SISTINE CEILING

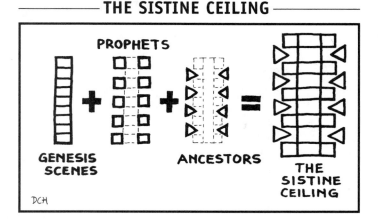

PROPHETS

GENESIS SCENES + **ANCESTORS** = **THE SISTINE CEILING**

DCH

The key is to see three simple divisions in the tangle of bodies:

(1) The central spine of nine rectangular Bible scenes

(2) The line of prophets on either side

(3) The triangles in between the prophets showing the ancestors of Christ

• *Ready? Within the Chapel, grab a seat along the side (if possible). Face the altar with the big* Last Judgment *on the wall (more on that later). Now look up to the ceiling and find the central panel of...*

The Creation of Adam

God and Man are equal in this Renaissance version of creation. Adam, newly formed in the image of God, lounges dreamily in perfect naked innocence. God, with his entourage, swoops in in a swirl of activity. Their reaching hands are the center of this work. Adam's is limp and passive; God's is strong and forceful, His finger twitching upward with energy. Here is the very moment of creation, as God passes the spark of life to man, the crowning work of His creation.

This is the spirit of the Renaissance. God is not a terrifying giant reaching down to puny and helpless man from way on high. Here they are on an equal plane, co-creators, divided only by the diagonal patch of sky. God's billowing robe and the patch of green upon which Adam is lying balance each other. They are like two pieces of a jigsaw puzzle, or two long-separated continents, or like

THE SISTINE CEILING

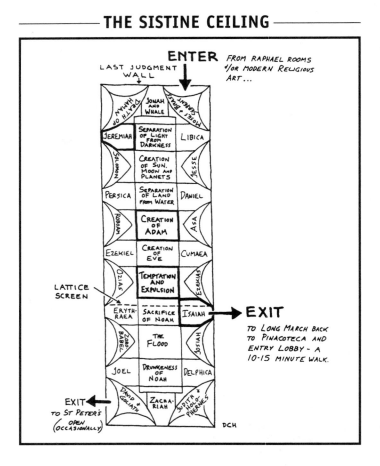

the yin and yang symbols finally coming together—uniting, complementing each other, creating wholeness. God and man work together as equals in the divine process of creation.

• *This celebration of man permeates the ceiling. Notice the Adonises-come-to-life on the pedestals that divide the central panels. And then came woman.*

The Garden of Eden: Temptation and Expulsion

In one panel we see two scenes from the Garden of Eden. On the left is the leafy garden of paradise where Adam and Eve lie around blissfully. But the devil comes along—a serpent with a woman's torso—and winds around the forbidden Tree of Knowledge. The temptation to gain new knowledge is too great for these Renaissance people. They eat the forbidden fruit.

At right, the sword-wielding angel drives them from Paradise into the barren plains. They're grieving, but they're far from helpless. Adam's body is thick and sturdy, and we know they'll survive in the cruel world. Adam firmly gestures to the angel, like he's saying, "All right, already! We're going!"

The Nine Scenes from Genesis

Take some time with these central scenes to understand the story the ceiling tells. They run in sequence, starting at the front:

(1) God, in purple, divides the light from darkness.
(2) God creates the sun (burning orange) and the moon (pale white, to the right). Oops, I guess there's another moon.
(3) God bursts towards us to separate the land and water.
(4) The Creation of Adam
(5) God creates Eve, who springs out of Adam's side.
(6) The Garden of Eden: Temptation and Expulsion
(7) Noah kills a ram and stokes the altar-fires to make a sacrifice to God.
(8) The great Flood, sent by God, destroys the wicked, who desperately head for higher ground. In the distance, the Ark carries Noah's family to safety.
(9) Noah's sons come across Noah drunk. (Perhaps Michelangelo chose to end it with this scene as a reminder that even the best of men are fallible.)

Prophets

By 1510 Michelangelo had finished the first half of the ceiling, the end farthest from the *Last Judgment* wall. When they took the scaffolding down and could finally see what he'd been working on for two years, everyone was awestruck—except Michelangelo. As powerful as his figures are, from the floor they didn't look dramatic enough for Michelangelo. For the other half he pulled out all the stops.

Compare the many small figures in the Noah scenes with, say, Adam and God at the other end. Or compare an early prophet with a later one. Isaiah ("Esaias," in purple) is shown in a pose like a Roman senator. He is a stately, sturdy, balanced, composed Renaissance Man. Now look at Jeremiah ("Hieremias") in the corner by the *Last Judgment*. This prophet, who witnessed the destruction of Israel, is a dark, brooding figure. He slumps his chin in his hand and ponders the fate of his people. The difference between the small, dignified Isaiah and the large, dramatic Jeremiah is like the difference between *Apollo Belvedere* and the *Laocoön*. This sort of emotional power was a new element in Renaissance painting.

The Cleaning Project

The ceiling and the *Last Judgment* have been cleaned, removing centuries of preservatives, dirt, and soot from candles, oil lamps, and the annual Papal Barbecue (just kidding). The bright, bright colors that emerged are a bit shocking, forcing many art experts to reevaluate Michelangelo's style.

The Last Judgment

When Michelangelo was asked to paint the altar wall 23 years later (1535), the mood of Europe—and of Michelangelo—was completely different. The Protestant Reformation had forced the Catholic Church to clamp down on free thought, and religious wars raged. Rome had recently been pillaged by roving bands of mercenaries. The Renaissance spirit of optimism was fading. Michelangelo himself had begun to question the innate goodness of mankind.

It's Judgment Day, and Christ—the powerful figure in the center, raising his arm to strike down the wicked—has come to find out who's naughty and nice. Beneath him, a band of angels blows its trumpets Dizzy Gillespie–style to wake the dead. The dead at lower left leave their graves and prepare to be judged. The righteous, on Christ's right hand (the left side of the picture), ascend to the glories of Heaven. The wicked on the other side are hurled down to Hell where demons wait to torture them. Charon, from the underworld of Greek mythology, waits below to ferry the souls of the damned to Hell.

It's a grim picture. No one, but no one, is smiling. Even many of the righteous being resurrected (lower left) are either skeletons or cadavers with ghastly skin. The angels have to play tug-of-war with subterranean monsters to drag them from their graves.

Over in Hell, the wicked are tortured by gleeful demons. One of the damned (to the right of the trumpeting angels) has an utterly lost expression, as if saying, "Why did I cheat on my wife?!" Two demons grab him around the ankles to

THE LAST JUDGMENT

1 - Christ with Mary at his side
2 - Trumpeting Angels
3 - The dead come out of their graves, the righteous ascend
4 - One of the damned
5 - Charon in his boat
6 - The demon/critic of nudity
7 - St. Bartholomew with flayed skin containing Michelangelo's self-portrait

pull him down to the bowels of Hell, condemned to an eternity of constipation.

But it's the terrifying figure of Christ who dominates this scene. As He raises His arm to smite the wicked, He sends a ripple of fear through everyone, and they recoil. Even the saints around Him—even Mary beneath His arm (whose interceding days are clearly over)—shrink back in terror. His expression is completely closed, and He turns his head, refusing to even listen to the whining alibis of the damned. Look at Christ's bicep. If this muscular figure looks familiar to you, it's because you've seen it before— the *Belvedere Torso*.

When *The Last Judgment* was unveiled to the public in 1544, it caused a sensation. The pope is said to have dropped to his knees and cried, "Lord, charge me not with my sins when thou shalt come on the Day of Judgment." And it changed the course of art. The complex composition with more than 300 figures swirling around the figure of Christ was far beyond traditional Renaissance balance. The twisted figures shown from every angle imaginable challenged other painters to try and top this master of 3-D illusion.

And the sheer terror and drama of the scene was a striking contrast to the placid optimism of, say, Raphael's *School of Athens*. Michelangelo had Baroque-en all the rules of the Renaissance, signaling a new era of art.

With the Renaissance fading, the fleshy figures in *The Last Judgment* aroused murmurs of discontent from Church authorities. Michelangelo rebelled by painting his chief critic into the scene— in Hell. He's the demon in the bottom right corner wrapped in a serpent. Look how Michelangelo covered his privates. Sweet revenge.

(After Michelangelo's death, there was no defense, and prudish church authorities painted the wisps of clothing we see today.)

Now move up close. Study the details of the lower part of the painting from right to left. Charon, with Dr. Spock ears and a Dalí

moustache, paddles the damned in a boat full of human turbulence. Look more closely at the J-Day band. Are they reading music or is it the Judgment Day tally? Before the cleaning, these details were lost in murk.

The Last Judgment marks the end of Renaissance optimism epitomized in *The Creation of Adam*, with its innocence and exaltation of man. There he was the equal of a fatherly God. Here, man cowers in fear and unworthiness before a terrifying, wrathful deity.

Michelangelo himself must have wondered how he would be judged— had he used his God-given talents wisely? Look at St. Bartholomew, the bald bearded guy at Christ's left foot (our right). In the flayed skin he's holding is a barely recognizable face—the twisted self-portrait of a self-questioning Michelangelo.

• *Exiting the Sistine you'll soon find yourself facing the Long March back to the museum's entrance. You're one floor down from the long corridor you walked to get here.*

(Or consider the Sistine–St. Peter's shortcut: From the back of the Sistine Chapel there's a tour group exit that shortcuts you directly to St. Peter's Basilica. If you're going there next and a group is leaving, you can slip out with them and save a 30-minute walk—it's worth waiting. Occasionally a guard can be sweet-talked into opening the door for an individual. Note that if you take the shortcut, you'll miss the Pinacoteca.)

THE LONG MARCH BACK

Along this corridor you'll see some of the wealth amassed by the popes, mostly gifts from royalty. Find your hometown on the map of the world from 1529—look in the land called "Terra Incognita." The elaborately decorated library that branches off to the right contains rare manuscripts.

• *The corridor eventually spills out back outside. Follow signs to the . . .*

PINACOTECA (PAINTING GALLERY)

How would you like to be Lou Gehrig—always batting behind Babe Ruth? That's the Pinacoteca's lot in life, following Sistine & Co. But after the Vatican's artistic feast, this little collection of paintings is a delicious 15-minute after-dinner mint.

See this gallery of paintings as you'd view a time-lapse blossoming of a flower, walking through the evolution of painting from medieval to Baroque with just four stops.

• *Enter and stroll up to Room IV.*

Melozzo Da Forli — Musician Angels

Salvaged from a condemned church, this playful series of frescoes shows the delicate grace and nobility of Italy during the time known fondly as the *quattrocentro* (1400s). Notice the detail and the classical purity given these religious figures.

• *Walk on to the end room (Room VIII) where they've turned on the dark to let Raphael's* Transfiguration *shine. Take a seat.*

Raphael — *The Transfiguration*

Raphael's *Transfiguration* shows Christ on a mountaintop visited in a vision by the prophets Moses and Elijah. Peter, James, and John cower in awe under Jesus, "transfigured before them, his face shining as the sun, his rainment white as light." (As described by the evangelist Matthew—taking notes in the painting's lower left.)

The nine remaining Apostles try in vain to heal a boy possessed by demons. Jesus is gone, but "Lady Faith" in the center exhorts them to carry on.

Raphael died in 1520, leaving this final work to be finished by his pupils. The last thing Raphael painted was the beatific face of Jesus, perhaps the most beautiful Christ in existence.

• *Heading back down the parallel corridor, stop in Room IX at the brown unfinished work by Leonardo.*

Leonardo da Vinci — *St. Jerome* (c. 1482)

This unfinished work gives us a glimpse behind the scenes at Leonardo's technique. Even in the brown undercoating we see

the psychological power of Leonardo's genius. The intense penitence and painful ecstasy of the saint comes through loud and clear in the anguished body on the rocks and in Jerome's joyful eyes, which see divine forgiveness. Leonardo wrote that a good painter must paint two things: "man and the movements of his spirit." (The patchwork effect is due to Jerome's head having been cut out and used as the seat of a stool in a shoemaker's shop.)

• *Roll on through the sappy sweetness of the Mannerist rooms into the shocking ultra-realistic world of Caravaggio, Room XII.*

Caravaggio — *Deposition*

Caravaggio was the first painter to intentionally shock his viewers. By exaggerating the contrast between light and dark, shining a brutal third-degree-interrogator-type light on his subjects, and using everyday models in sacred scenes, he takes a huge leap away from the Raphael-pretty past and into the "expressive realism" of the modern world.

A tangle of grief looms out of the darkness as Christ's heavy, dead body nearly pulls the whole group with him from the cross into the tomb.

• *Walk through the rest of the gallery's canvas history of art, enjoy one last view of the Vatican grounds and Michelangelo's dome, then follow the grand spiral staircase down. Go in peace.*

ST. PETER'S BASILICA TOUR

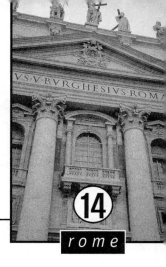

St. Peter's is the greatest church in Christendom. It represents the power and splendor of Rome's 2,000-year domination of the Western world. Built on the memory and grave of the first pope, St. Peter, this is where the grandeur of ancient Rome became the grandeur of Christianity.

Orientation

Cost: Free (L8,000 to climb dome)

Hours: Daily May–Sept 7:00–19:00, Oct–Apr 7:00–18:00. Mass is held daily at 9:00, 10:00, 11:00, 12:00, and 17:00. The lift to the dome opens at 8:30 and closes one hour before the church closes. The best time to visit is early or late. Strictly enforced dress code: no shorts or bare shoulders (men or women), no miniskirts.

Getting there: Subway to "Ottaviano," then a 15-minute walk south on Via Ottaviano. Several city buses go right to St. Peter's Square (#64 is convenient for pickpockets). Taxis are reasonable.

Information: There's a guide booth just inside the front door. The tourist office on the left (south) side of square is excellent (Mon–Sat 8:30–18:30, closed Sun, free Vatican and church map, tel. 06-6988-4466). This TI conducts special insider tours for L18,000 of the Vatican Gardens, offering the only way to see the gardens (other than the shuttle bus service between St. Peter's and the Vatican Museum which may resume in 2000)—book tours at least one day ahead in person or by fax at 06-6988-5100 (not by phone). Free, 90-minute English "Pilgrim Service" church tours usually leave at 10:00 and 12:30 (confirm schedule at TI). WCs are to the right and left (near TI) of the church and on the roof. Drinking fountains are at the obelisk and near WCs. The post office is next to the TI (Vatican post is more reliable than Italian).

Vatican City

This tiny independent country of just over 100 acres, contained entirely within Rome, has its own postal system, armed guard, helipad, mini–train station, and radio station (KPOP). Politically powerful, the Vatican is the religious capital of 800 million Roman Catholics. If you're not one already, become a Catholic for your visit.

Tourist Information: A helpful TI is just to the left of St. Peter's Basilica (Mon–Sat 8:30–18:30, closed Sun, tel. 06-6988-4466, Vatican switchboard tel. 06-6982, www.vatican.va). Telephone the Vatican TI if you're interested in their sporadic but good tours of the Vatican grounds or the church interior, or the pope's schedule. If you don't care to see the pope, minimize crowd problems by avoiding these times.

Seeing the Pope: The pope will be in Rome throughout this Holy Year except for a short trip to the Holy Land. Each evening (God willing) he'll lead a prayer and bless the pilgrims on St. Peter's Square. In normal summers, the pope (when in town) reads a prayer and blesses the gathered masses from his library window overlooking St. Peter's Square Sundays at noon and Wednesday mornings. In the winter this happens in the 7,000-seat Aula Paola VI Auditorium (free, Wed at 11:00, call 06-6988-3273 for details and reservations). Smaller ceremonies celebrated by the pope require reservations. The weekly entertainment guide *Romanc'e* always has a "Seeing the Pope" section.

Holy Year at the Vatican: At midnight on December 24, 1999, the pope hit the Holy Door with a silver hammer, symbolically opening it and kicking off the Holy Year. The door stays open throughout the year 2000, which starts and ends with all the world's Catholic churches ringing their bells. Among the many Church festivities planned, the biggies are June 29 (St. Peter and Paul Day, when 250,000 will pack Piazza San Pietro) and August 19 (the start of a weeklong Youth Jubilee, when 2 million young pilgrims gather to pray).

Getting to Vatican City: The neighborhood's Ottaviano Metro stop is closer to St. Peter's while the new Metro stop, Cipro-Musei Vaticani, is closer to the Vatican Museum. Between St. Peter's and the Vatican Museum it's a 15-minute walk around the wall (or a two-minute bus ride through the pleasant Vatican grounds—that is, if the shuttle bus starts running again; the stop is outside St. Peter's TI, to the left as you face the church).

Tour length: One hour, plus another hour if you climb the dome (300 feet).
Cloakroom: Free, usually mandatory bag check is outside at right of entrance.
Starring: Michelangelo, Bernini, Bramante, St. Peter, a heavenly host, and, occasionally, the pope.

OLD ST. PETER'S

• *Find a shady spot where you like the view under the columns around St. Peter's oval-shaped "square." If the pigeons left a clean spot, sit on it.*

Nearly 2,000 years ago this area was the site of Nero's Circus—a huge Roman chariot racecourse. The obelisk you see in the middle of the square stands where the chariots made their hairpin turns. The Romans had no marching bands, so for halftime entertainment they killed Christians. This persecuted minority was forced to fight wild animals and gladiators, or they were simply crucified. Some were tarred up, tied to posts, and burned—human torches to light up the evening races.

One of those killed here, around 65 A.D., was Peter, Jesus' right-hand man who had come to Rome to spread the message of love. Peter was crucified on an upside-down cross at his own request because he felt unworthy to die as his master had. His remains were buried in a nearby cemetery where, for 250 years, they were quietly and secretly revered.

When Christianity was finally legalized in 312, the Christian emperor Constantine built a church on the site of the martyrdom of this first "pope," or bishop of Rome, from whom all later popes claimed their authority as head of the Church. "Old St. Peter's" lasted 1,200 years (A.D. 324–1500).

By the time of the Renaissance, Old St. Peter's was falling apart and was considered unfit to be the center of the Western Church. The new, larger church we see today was begun in 1506, and actually built around the old one. As it was completed 120 years later, after many changes of plans, Old St. Peter's was dismantled and carried out the doors of the new one.

• *Ideally you should head out to the obelisk to view the square and read this. But let me guess—it's 95 degrees, right? Okay, read on in the shade of these stone sequoias.*

ST. PETER'S SQUARE

St. Peter's Square, with its ring of columns, symbolizes the arms of the church "maternally embracing Catholics, heretics, and the faithless." It was designed by the Baroque architect Bernini, who also did much of the work we'll see inside. Numbers first: 284 columns, 50 feet high, in stern Doric style. Topping them are

ST. PETER'S SQUARE

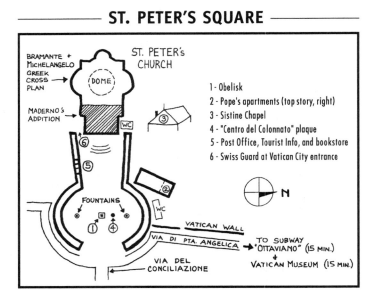

ST. PETER'S CHURCH

BRAMANTE + MICHELANGELO GREEK CROSS PLAN → (DOME)

MADERNO'S ADDITION

WC

1 - Obelisk
2 - Pope's apartments (top story, right)
3 - Sistine Chapel
4 - "Centro del Colonnato" plaque
5 - Post Office, Tourist Info, and bookstore
6 - Swiss Guard at Vatican City entrance

FOUNTAINS

WC

N

VATICAN WALL

VIA DI PTA. ANGELICA → TO SUBWAY "OTTAVIANO" (15 MIN.)
↓
VATICAN MUSEUM (15 MIN.)

VIA DEL CONCILIAZIONE

Bernini's 90 favorite saints, each 10 feet tall. The "square" itself is elliptical, 200 by 150 yards.

The obelisk in the center is 80 feet of solid granite weighing over 300 tons. Think for a second of how much history this monument has seen. Erected originally in Egypt over 2,000 years ago, it witnessed the fall of the pharoahs to the Greeks and then to the Romans. It was then moved to Imperial Rome, where it stood impassively watching the slaughter of Christians at the racecourse and the torture of Protestants by the Inquisition (in the yellow and rust building just outside the square, to the left of the church). Today it watches over the church, a reminder that each civilization builds on the previous ones. The puny cross on top reminds us that

our Christian culture is but a thin veneer over our pagan origins.
• *Now venture out across the burning desert to the obelisk which provides a narrow sliver of shade.*

Face the church, then turn about-face and say "*Grazie, Benito.*" I don't make a habit of thanking Fascist dictators, but in the

1930s Benito Mussolini did open up this broad boulevard, finally letting people see the dome of St. Peter's, which had been hidden for centuries by the facade. From here at the obelisk, Michelangelo's magnificent dome can only peek its top over the bulky Baroque front entrance.

The grey building at two o'clock to the right (as you face the church), rising up behind Bernini's colonnade, is where the pope lives. The last window on the right of the top floor is his bedroom. The window to the left of that is his study, where he appears occasionally to greet the masses. If you come to the square at night as a Poping Tom, you might see the light on—the pope burns much midnight oil.

On more formal occasions (which you may have seen on TV) the pope appears from the church itself, on the small balcony above the central door.

The Sistine Chapel is just to the right of the facade—the small grey-brown building with the triangular roof topped by an antenna. The tiny chimney (the pimple along the roofline midway up the left side) is where the famous smoke signals announce the election of each new pope. If the smoke is black, a 75 percent majority hasn't been reached. White smoke means a new pope has been selected.

Walk to the right, five pavement plaques from the obelisk, to one marked "Centro del Colonnato." From here all of Bernini's columns on the right side line up. The curved Baroque square still pays its respects to Renaissance mathematical symmetry.

• *Climb the gradually sloping stairs past crowd barriers and the huge statues of St. Mark with his two-edged sword and St. Peter with his bushy hair and keys.*

You'll pass two of the entrances to Vatican City—one to the left of the facade, one to the right in the crook of Bernini's "arm." Guarding this small but powerful country's border crossing are the mercenary guards from Switzerland. You have to wonder if they really know how to use those pikes. Their colorful uniforms are said to have been designed by Michelangelo, though he was not known for his sense of humor.

• *Enter the atrium (entrance hall) of the church. You'll pass by the dress-code enforcers and a gaggle of ticked-off guys in shorts.*

THE BASILICA

The Atrium

The atrium is itself bigger than most churches. Facing us are the five famous bronze doors, leading into the main church. The central door, made from the melted-down bronze of the original door of Old St. Peter's, is only opened on special occasions.

The far right entrance is the Holy Door, opened only during Holy Years. At midnight on Christmas Eve every 25 years the pope knocks three times with a silver hammer and the door is opened, welcoming pilgrims to pass through. (This ceremony occurred on Christmas 1999 for 2000.) At the end of the year, he bricks it up again from the inside with a ceremonial trowel to await another 24 years. On the door, note Jesus' shiny knees, polished by pious pilgrims who touch them for a blessing.

The other doors are modern, reminding us that amid all this tradition the Catholic Church has changed enormously even within our lifetimes. Door #2 (second from left) commemorates the kneeling pope, John (Giovanni) XXIII, who opened the landmark Vatican II Council in the early 1960s. This meeting of church leaders brought the medieval church into the modern age—they dropped outdated rituals—like the use of Latin in the Mass—and made old doctrines "relevant" to modern times.

• *Now for one of Europe's great wow experiences. Enter the church. Gape for a while. But don't gape at Michelangelo's famous* Pietà *(on the right). That's this tour's finale. I'll wait for you at the round maroon pavement stone between the entrance and exit doors.*

The Church

While ancient Rome fell, its grandeur survived. Roman basilicas became churches, senators became bishops, and the Pontifex Maximus (Emperor)...remained the Pontifex Maximus (Pope). This church is appropriately huge.

Size before beauty: The golden window at the far end is two football fields away. The dove in the window above the altar has the wingspan of a 747 (okay, maybe not quite, but it is big). The church covers six acres— if planted with wheat it could feed a small city. The babies at the base of the pillars along the main hall (the nave) are adult-size. The lettering in the gold band along the top

ST. PETER'S BASILICA

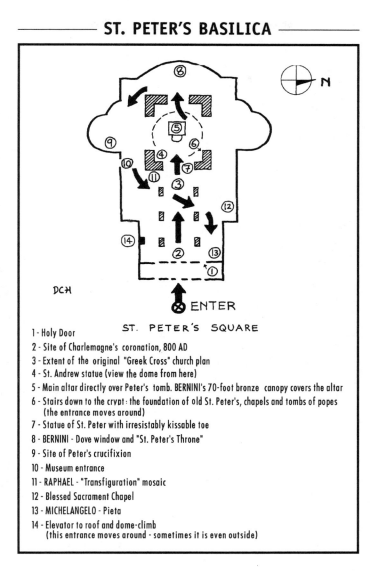

ST. PETER'S SQUARE

DCH

1 - Holy Door
2 - Site of Charlemagne's coronation, 800 AD
3 - Extent of the original "Greek Cross" church plan
4 - St. Andrew statue (view the dome from here)
5 - Main altar directly over Peter's tomb. BERNINI's 70-foot bronze canopy covers the altar
6 - Stairs down to the crypt: the foundation of old St. Peter's, chapels and tombs of popes
   (the entrance moves around)
7 - Statue of St. Peter with irresistably kissable toe
8 - BERNINI - Dove window and "St. Peter's Throne"
9 - Site of Peter's crucifixion
10 - Museum entrance
11 - RAPHAEL - "Transfiguration" mosaic
12 - Blessed Sacrament Chapel
13 - MICHELANGELO - Pieta
14 - Elevator to roof and dome-climb
   (this entrance moves around - sometimes it is even outside)

of the pillars is six feet high. Really. The church has a capacity of 95,000 worshipers standing (that's over 2,000 tour groups).

The church is huge and it feels huge, but everything is actually designed to make it seem smaller and more intimate than it really is. For example, the statue of St. Theresa near the bottom of the first pillar on the right is 15 feet tall. The statue above her near the top looks the same size but is actually six feet taller, giving the impression that it's not as far away as it really is. Similarly, the fancy bronze canopy over the altar at the far end is as tall as a seven-story building. That makes the great height of the dome seem smaller.

Looking down the nave we get a sense of the grandeur of ancient Rome that was carried on by the Catholic Church. The floor plan is based on the ancient Roman basilica, or law-court building, with a central aisle (nave) flanked by two side aisles.

The goal of this unprecedented building project was to "put the dome of the Pantheon atop the Forum's Basilica Maxentius." If you've seen these two Roman structures you have an idea of this

megavision. In fact, many of the stones used to build St. Peter's were scavenged from the ruined law courts of ancient Rome.

On the floor near the central doorway is a round slab of porphyry stone in the maroon color of ancient Roman officials. This is the spot where, on Christmas night in A.D. 800, the French King Charlemagne was crowned "Holy Roman Emperor." Even in the Dark Ages, when Rome was virtually abandoned and visitors reported that the city "had more thieves and wolves than decent people," its imperial legacy made it a fitting place to symbolically establish a briefly united Europe.

You're surrounded by marble, gold, stucco, mosaics, columns of stone, and pillars of light. This is Baroque, the decorative style popular at the height of the wars between Protestants and Catholics. It was intended to overwhelm and impress the masses with the authority of the church. St. Peter's was very expensive to build and decorate. The popes financed it by selling "indulgences," allowing the rich to literally buy forgiveness from the church. This kind of corruption inspired an obscure German monk named Martin Luther to rebel and start the Protestant Reformation. The Baroque interior by Bernini was part of the church's "Counter"-Reformation, a time when the church aggressively defended itself and art became a powerful propaganda tool. Here we see a glorious golden vision of heaven available to anyone—who remained a good Catholic.

• *Now, walk straight up the center of the nave toward the altar.*

"Michelangelo's Church" — The Greek Cross

The plaques on the floor show where other, smaller churches of the world would end if they were placed inside St. Peter's: St. Paul's Cathedral in London (Londinense), the Florence Cathedral, and so on.

You'll also walk over circular golden grates. Stop at the second one (at the third pillar from the entrance). Look back at the entrance and realize that if Michelangelo had had his way, this whole long section of the church wouldn't exist. The nave was extended after his death.

Michelangelo was 72 years old when the pope persuaded him to take over the church project and cap it with a dome. He agreed, intending to put the dome over Bramante's original "Greek Cross" floor plan (+), with four equal arms. In optimistic Renaissance times this symmetrical arrangement symbolized perfection—the orderliness of the created world and the goodness of man (who was created in God's image). But Michelangelo was a Renaissance Man in Counter-Reformation times. The church, struggling against Protestants and its own corruption, opted for a plan designed to impress the world with its grandeur—the Latin cross of the Crucifixion with its extended nave to accommodate the grand religious spectacles of the Baroque period.

• *Continue toward the altar, entering Michelangelo's Church. Park yourself in front of the statue of St. Andrew to the left of the altar, the guy holding an X-shaped cross. Like Andrew, gaze up into the dome. Gasp if you must—never stifle a gasp.*

The Dome

The dome soars higher than a football field on end, 390 feet to the top of the lantern. It glows with light from its windows, the blue and gold mosaics creating a cool, solemn atmosphere. In this majestic vision of heaven we see (above the windows) Jesus, Mary, and a ring of saints, more rings of angels above them, and way up in the ozone, God the Father (a blur of blue and red, without binoculars).

Listen to the hum of visitors echoing through St. Peter's. Churches are an early form of biofeedback where we can become aware of ourselves, our own human sounds, and can reflect on our place in the cosmos. Half animal, half angel, stretched between heaven and earth, born to live only a short while, a bubble of foam on a great cresting wave of humanity.

• *But I digress.*

Peter

The base of the dome is ringed with a gold banner telling us in blue letters six feet tall why this church is so important. According to

Catholics, Peter was selected by Jesus to head the church. The banner in Latin quotes from the Bible where Jesus says to him, "You are Peter *(Tu es Petrus)* and upon this rock I will build my church" (Matthew 16:18). Peter was the first bishop of Rome, and his authority has supposedly passed in an unbroken chain to each succeeding bishop of Rome—that is, the 250-odd popes that followed.

Under the dome, under the bronze canopy, under the altar, some 20 feet under the marble floor rest the bones of St. Peter, the "rock" upon which this particular church was built. Go to the railing

and look down into the small lighted niche eight feet below the altar with a box containing bishops' shawls—a symbol of how Peter's authority spread to the other churches. Peter's tomb is several feet below this box.

Are they really the bones of Jesus' apostle? According to a papal pronouncement: definitely maybe. The traditional site of his tomb was sealed up when Old St. Peter's was built on it in A.D. 326, and it remained sealed until 1940 when it was opened for archaeological study. Bones were found, dated from the first century, of a robust man who died in old age. His body was wrapped in expensive cloth. Various inscriptions and graffiti in the tomb indicate that second- and third-century visitors thought this was Peter's tomb. Does that mean it's really Peter? Who am I to disagree with the pope? Definitely maybe.

If you line up the cross on the altar with the dove in the window you'll notice that the niche below the cross is a foot-and-a-half off-center left with the rest of the church. Why? Because Michelangelo built the church around the traditional location of the tomb, not the actual location discovered by modern archaeology.

Back in the nave sits a bronze statue of Peter under a canopy. This is one of a handful of pieces of art that was in the earlier church. In one hand he holds the keys, the symbol of the authority given him by Christ, while with the other he blesses us. He's wearing the toga of a Roman senator. It may be that the original statue was of a senator and the bushy head and keys were added later to make it Peter. His big right toe has been worn smooth by the lips of pilgrims. Stand in line and kiss it, or, to avoid hoof and mouth disease, touch your

hand to your lips, then rub the toe. This is simply an act of reverence with no legend attached, though you can make one up if you like.

The Main Altar

The main altar beneath the dome and canopy (the white marble slab with cross and candlesticks) is used only when the pope himself says Mass. He often conducts the Sunday morning service when he's in town, a sight worth seeing. I must admit, though, it's a little strange being frisked at the door for weapons at the holiest place in Christendom.

The tiny altar would be lost in this enormous church if it weren't for Bernini's seven-story bronze canopy which "extends" the altar upward and reduces the perceived distance between floor and ceiling.

Gian Lorenzo Bernini (1598–1680) is the man most responsible for the interior decoration of the church. The altar area was his masterpiece, a "theater" for holy spectacles. Bernini did: (1) the bronze canopy, (2) the dove window in the apse surrounded by bronzework and statues, (3) the statue of lance-bearing St. Longinus (which became the model for the other three statues), (4) the balconies above the four statues, incorporating the actual corkscrew columns looted from Solomon's Temple in Jerusalem, and (5) much of the marble floor decoration. Bernini, the father of Baroque, gave an impressive unity to an amazing variety of pillars, windows, statues, chapels, and aisles.

The bronze canopy is his crowning touch. The Baroque-looking corkscrew columns are enlarged copies of the ancient columns from Solomon's Temple. The bronze used was stolen and melted down from the ancient Pantheon. On the marble base of the columns you see three bees on a shield, the symbol of the Bar-

berini family who commissioned the work and ordered the raid on the Pantheon. As the saying went, "What the barbarians didn't do, the Barberini did."

Starting from the column to the left of the altar, walk clockwise around the canopy. Notice the female faces on the marble bases, about eye-level above the bees. Someone in the Barberini family was pregnant during the making of the canopy, so Bernini put the various stages of childbirth on the bases. Continue clockwise to the last base to see how it came out.

• *Walk into the apse (it's the front area with the golden dove window) and take a seat.*

The Apse

Bernini's dove window shines above the smaller front altar used for everyday services. The Holy Spirit in the form of a six-foot dove pours sunlight onto the faithful through the alabaster windows, turning into artificial rays of gold and reflecting off swirling gold clouds, angels, and winged babies. This is the epitome of Baroque—a highly decorative, glorious, mixed-media work designed to overwhelm the viewer.

Beneath the dove is the centerpiece of this structure, the so-called "Throne of Peter," an oak chair built in medieval times for a king. Subsequently it was encrusted with tradition and encased in bronze by Bernini as a symbol of papal authority. Statues of four early church fathers support the chair, a symbol of how bishops should support the pope in troubled times—times like the Counter-Reformation. Bernini's Baroque was great propaganda for the power of the Catholic Church.

This is a good place to remember that this is a church, not a museum. In the apse, Mass is said daily (Mon–Sat at 17:00, Sun at 17:45) for pilgrims and Roman citizens alike. Wooden confessional booths are available for Catholics to tell their sins to a listening ear and receive forgiveness and peace of mind. The faithful renew their faith and the faithless gain inspiration. Sit here, look at the light streaming through the windows, turn and gaze up into the dome, and quietly contemplate your god.

Or...

Contemplate this: the mystery of empty space. The bench you're sitting on and the marble at your feet, solid as they may seem, consist overwhelmingly of open space—99.9999 percent open space. The atoms that form these "solid" benches are themselves mostly open space. If the nucleus of your average atom were as large as the period at the end of this sentence, its electrons would be specks of dust orbiting around it—at the top of

Michelangelo's dome. Empty space. Perhaps matter is only an aberration in an empty universe.

• *Like wow.*

Now head to the left of the main altar into the south transept. At the far end, look left at the dark painting of St. Peter crucified upside down.

Left Transept

The painting is at the exact spot (according to tradition) where Peter was killed 1,900 years ago.

The Romans were actually quite tolerant of other religions. All they required of their conquered peoples was allegiance to the empire by worshiping the emperor as a god. For most religions this was no problem, but monotheistic Christians were children of a jealous God who would not allow worship of any others. They refused to worship the emperor and valiantly stuck by their faith even when burned alive, crucified, or thrown to the lions. Their bravery, optimism in suffering, and message of love struck a chord among slaves and members of the lower classes. The religion started by a poor carpenter grew despite occasional "pogroms" by fanatical emperors. In three short centuries, Christianity went from a small Jewish sect in Jerusalem to the official religion of the world's greatest empire.

Admire this painting, and realize it's the only true "painting" in the church. All the others you see are actually mosaic copies made from thousands of colored chips the size of your little fingernail. Smoke and humidity would damage real paintings. Around the corner on the right (heading back towards the central nave), pause at the copy of Raphael's huge "painting" (mosaic) of *The Transfiguration*, especially if you won't be seeing the original in the Vatican Museum.

• *Back near the entrance to the church, in the far corner, behind bullet-proof glass is . . .*

The Pietà

Michelangelo was 24 years old when he completed this *Pietà* (pee-ay-TAH), of Mary with the dead body of Christ taken from the cross.

Michelangelo, with his total mastery of the real world, captures the sadness of the moment. Mary cradles her crucified son in her lap. Christ's lifeless right arm drooping down lets us know how heavy this corpse is. His smooth skin is accented by the rough folds of Mary's robe. Mary tilts her head downward, looking at her dead son with sad tenderness. Her left hand is upturned as if asking, "How could they do this to you?"

Michelangelo didn't think of sculpting as creating a figure, but as simply freeing the God-made figure from the prison of marble around it. He'd attack a project like this with an inspired passion, chipping away to reveal what God put inside.

Realistic as this work is, its true power lies in the subtle "unreal" features. Look how small and childlike Christ is compared with the massive Mary. Unnoticed at first, this accentuates the subconscious impression of Mary enfolding Jesus in her maternal love. Notice how young Mary is. She's the mother of a 33-year-old man, but here she's portrayed as a teenage girl. Michelangelo did it to show how Mary was the eternally youthful "handmaiden" of the Lord, always serving Him even at this moment of supreme sacrifice. She accepts God's will, even if it means giving up her own son.

The statue is a solid pyramid of maternal tenderness. Yet within this, Christ's body tilts diagonally down to the right and Mary's hem flows with it. Subconsciously we feel the weight of this dead God sliding from her lap to the ground.

On Christmas morning, 1972, a madman with a hammer entered St. Peter's and began hacking away at the *Pietà*. The damage was repaired, but that's why there's a shield of bulletproof glass today.

This is Michelangelo's only signed work. The story goes that he overheard some pilgrims praising his finished *Pietà*, but attributing it to a second-rate sculptor from a lesser city. He was so enraged he grabbed his chisel and chipped "Michelangelo Buonarotti of Florence did this" in the ribbon running down Mary's chest.

On your right is the inside of the Holy Door. It's open all Jubilee Year, then bricked up until it will next be opened: on Christmas Eve, 2024. If there's a prayer inside you, maybe ask that when it's opened for the next Holy Year, St. Peter's will no longer need security checks or bulletproof glass.

Up to the Dome (Cupola)

A good way to finish a visit to St. Peter's is to go up to the dome for the best view of Rome anywhere.

There are two levels, the rooftop of the church and the very top of the dome. An elevator (L8,000) takes you to the first level, on the church roof just above the facade. Even from there you have a commanding view of St. Peter's Square, the statues on the colonnade, Rome across the Tiber in front of you, and the dome itself—almost terrifying in its nearness—looming behind you.

From here you can also go inside to the gallery ringing the interior of the dome, where you can look down inside the church. Notice the dusty top of Bernini's seven-story-tall canopy far below, study the mosaics up close—and those six-foot letters! It's worth the elevator ride for this view alone.

From this level, if you're energetic, continue all the way up to the top of the dome itself. The staircase (free at this point) actually winds between the outer shell and the inner one. It's a long, sweaty, stuffy, claustrophobic 15-minute climb, but worth it. The view from the summit is great, the fresh air even better. Find the big white Victor Emmanuel Monument with the two statues on top and the Pantheon with its large light shallow dome. The large rectangular building to the left of the obelisk is the Vatican Museum, stuffed with art. Survey the Vatican grounds with its mini-train system and lush gardens. Look down into the square on the tiny pilgrims buzzing like electrons around the nucleus of Catholicism.

(The dome opens daily at 8:30 and closes at 18:00 Apr–Sept and at 17:00 Oct–Mar. Allow one hour for the full trip up and down, a half hour to go only to the roof and gallery. The entrance to the elevator varies. Sometimes it's inside the church, opposite the *Pietà*. Other times it's just outside the church. Look for signs to the *cupola*.)

THE REST OF THE CHURCH

The Crypt: You can go down to the foundations of Old St. Peter's, containing tombs of popes and memorial chapels. But you won't see St. Peter's tomb...it's off-limits. The staircase entrance moves around, but it's usually inside the church near St. Andrew or one of his three fellow statues. Seeing the crypt is free, but the visit takes you back outside the church, a 15-minute detour. (Do it when you're ready to leave.)

The Museum (Museo-Tesoro): If you like old jewels and papal robes, you'll find the treasures and splendors of Roman Christianity, a marked contrast to the poverty of early Christians. It's located near (but not in) the left transept, through a grey portal.

Blessed Sacrament Church: You're welcome to step through the metal-work gates into this oasis of peace reserved for prayer and meditation. It's located on the right-hand side of the church, about midway to the altar.

BERNINI BLITZ

Nowhere is there such a conglomeration of works by the flamboyant genius who remade the church—and the city—in the Baroque style. Here's your scavenger-hunt list. You have 20 minutes. Go.

1. St. Peter's Square: design and statues
2. Constantine equestrian relief (right end of atrium)
3. Decoration (stucco, gold-leaf, marble, etc.) of side aisles (flanking the nave)
4. Tabernacle (the temple-like altarpiece) inside Blessed Sacrament Chapel
5. Much of the marble floor throughout church
6. Bronze canopy over the altar
7. St. Longinus statue (holding a lance) near altar
8. Balconies (above each of the four statues) with corkscrew, Solomonic columns
9. Dove window, bronze sunburst, angels, "Throne," and Church Fathers (in the apse)
10. Tomb of Pope Urban VIII (far end of the apse, right side)
11. Tomb of Pope Alexander VII (near the left transept, over a doorway, with the gold skeleton smothered in jasper poured like maple syrup). Bizarre . . . Baroque . . . Bernini.

PILGRIM'S
ROME

Pilgrims to Rome try to visit four great basilicas: St. Peter's (of course), Santa Maria Maggiore, San Giovanni in Laterano, and San Paolo Fuori Le Mura. For your sightseeing pleasure, we've replaced inconvenient San Paolo with the fascinating and more handy San Clemente.

The pilgrim industry helped shape Rome. Ancient Rome's population peaked at about 1.2 million. When Rome fell in 476, barbarians cut off the water supply by breaking the aqueducts, Romans fled the city, and the Tiber silted up. During the Dark Ages, mosquitos ruled over a pathetic village of 50,000... bad news for pilgrims, bad news for the Vatican. Back then the Catholic Church was the Christian church. Because popes needed a place fit for pilgrimages, the Church revitalized the city. Hotel and restaurant owners cheered.

In 1587 Pope Sixtus V reconnected aqueducts and established boulevards connecting the great churches and pilgrimage sites. To make his Renaissance capital easy to navigate, he built long straight streets for pilgrims. Obelisks served as markers. As you explore the city, think like a pilgrim. Look down long roads and you'll see either a grand church or an obelisk from where you'll see a grand church. For example, Via XX Settembre is a montage of pilgrimage churches connecting the Catacombs of St. Agnese (to the east) with the pope's home on the Quirinal (to the west).

SAN GIOVANNI IN LATERANO

Imagine the jubilation when this church—the first Christian church in the city of Rome—was opened in A.D. 313. Persecuted Christians could finally "come out" and worship openly without fear of reprisal. After that glorious beginning, the church has

PILGRIM'S ROME

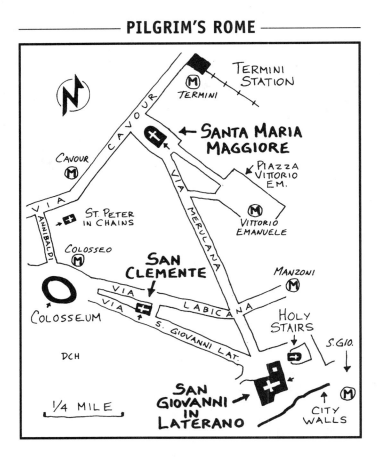

served as the center of Catholicism and the home of the popes up until the Renaissance renovation of St. Peter's. Until 1870, all popes were "crowned" here. Even today, it's the home church of the Bishop of Rome—the pope. (Free, Mon–Sat 6:15-12:00, 15:00–18:15, Sun 6:15–12:00, 15:30–18:45, on Piazza San Giovanni in Laterano, Metro: San Giovanni.)

Exterior

The massive facade is 18th century, with Christ triumphant on the top. The blocky adjacent building on the right is the Lateran Palace, residence of popes until about 1300. Across the street to your right is the pope's private chapel and the popular-with-pilgrims Holy Stairs (Scala Santa). Behind you, through the gate

SAN GIOVANNI IN LATERANO

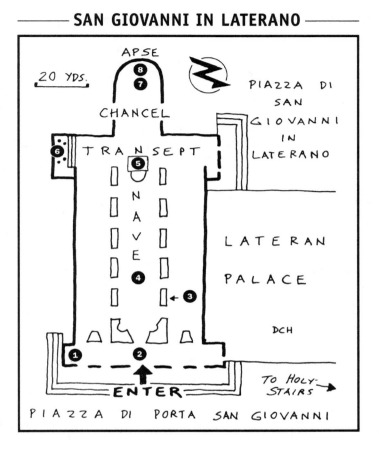

in a well-preserved chunk of the ancient Roman wall, is the San Giovanni Metro stop.

1. Statue of Constantine
(inside the portico, far left end)

It's October 28, A.D. 312, and Constantine—sword tucked under his arm and leaning confidently on a (missing) spear—has conquered Maxentius and liberated Rome. Constantine marched to this spot where his enemy's personal bodyguards lived, trashed their pagan idols, and dedicated the place to the god who gave him his victory—Christ. The holes in Constantine's head once held a golden halo-like crown for the emperor who legalized Christianity.

2. Central Doorway (in the portico)

These bronze doors, with their floral designs and acorn studs, are the original doors from ancient Rome's Senate House (Curia) in the Forum. The Church appropriated these to show that they were now Europe's lawmakers. The star borders were added later to make these big doors bigger.

3. Giotto Fresco
(inside church, second pillar in right aisle)

Pope Boniface VIII proclaims the first (modern) Jubilee Year in 1300 in this fading fresco attributed to the first "modern" painter, Giotto. A servant holds the pope's cue cards.

4. Basilica Floor Plan

San Giovanni was the first public church in Rome and the model for all later churches, including St. Peter's. The floor plan—a large central hall (nave) flanked by two side aisles—was based on the ancient Roman basilica (law courts) floor plan. These buildings were big enough to accommodate the large Christian congregations.

5. Baldacchino (canopy over altar)

In the upper cage are two silver statues of saints Peter (with keys) and Paul (sword), containing their... heads.

6. Golden Columns from Temple of Jupiter
(left transept)

Tradition says that these gilded bronze columns once stood in pagan Rome's holiest spot—the Temple of Jupiter, the King of all Gods, on the summit of Capitol Hill (c. 50 B.C.). Now they support a pediment topped by a bearded, Jupiter-like God the Father.

7. Bishop's Chair (in apse)

The chair (or "cathedra") reminds visitors that this is the cathedral of Rome... and the pope himself is the bishop that sits here.

8. Mosaic (in semicircular dome of apse)

The original design dates from about 450. (The mosaic was remodeled with saints added in the 13th century.) You see a cross, animals, plants, and the River Jordan running along the base. Mosaic, of course, was an ancient Roman specialty adapted by medieval Christians. The figure of Christ (above the cross) must have been a glorious sight to early worshipers— one of the first legal images of Christ ever seen in formerly pagan Rome.

Holy Stairs (Scala Santa)

The stairs are outside the church and across the street.

In 326 Emperor Constantine's mother (St. Helena) brought home the 28 marble steps of Pilate's residence. Jesus climbed these steps on the day he was sentenced to death. Each day hundreds of "penitent faithful" climb these steps on their knees (reciting a litany of prayers, available at the desk to the right of the entry). The steps—covered with walnut wood with small glass-covered holes showing stains from Jesus' blood—

lead to the "Holy of Holies" (Sancta Sanctorum) which was the private chapel of the popes in the Middle Ages. With its world-class relics, this chapel was considered the holiest place on earth. While the relics are now in the Vatican and the chapel is locked up, you can look through the grated windows in the doors atop the staircase.

On September 20, 1870, as nationalist forces unifying Italy took Rome and ended the pope's temporal power, Pope Pius IX left his Quirinal Palace home for the last time. He stopped here to climb the steps, pray in his chapel, and bless his supporters from the top of the steps. Then he fled to the Vatican where he spent the rest of his days.

SANTA MARIA MAGGIORE

The basilica of Santa Maria celebrates Holy Mary, the mother of Jesus. One of Rome's oldest and best-preserved churches, its fifth-century mosaics give it the feel of the early Christian community. (It's on Piazza Santa Maria Maggiore, Metro: Vittorio.)

Exterior

Mary's column originally stood in the Forum's Basilica Maxentius. The fifth-century church built in her honor proclaims she was indeed the Mother of God—a fact disputed by hair-splitting theologians of the day. When you step inside the church, you'll be exiting Italy and entering the Vatican—the "Maggiore" indicates this land is a Vatican possession.

Interior

Despite the Renaissance ceiling and Baroque crusting, you still feel like you're walking into an early Christian church. The stately rows of columns, the simple layout, the cheery colors, the spacious nave—it's easy to imagine worshipers finding an oasis of peace here as the Roman Empire crashed around them.

SANTA MARIA MAGGIORE

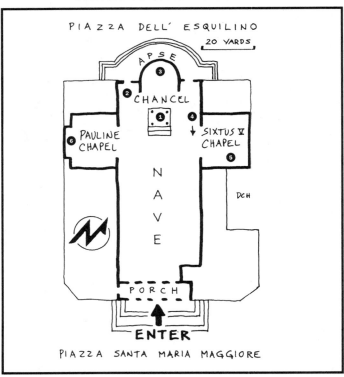

PIAZZA DELL' ESQUILINO

20 YARDS

APSE

❸

CHANCEL

❷

❶

❹

↓ SIXTUS V
CHAPEL

❻ PAULINE
CHAPEL

❺

N
A
V
E

DCH

PORCH

ENTER

PIAZZA SANTA MARIA MAGGIORE

1. Manger Fragments
(under altar in lighted niche)
A kneeling pope prays before a glass case with an urn that contains several pieces of wood, bound by iron and said to be from Jesus' crib. The church was built around these relics of Mary's motherhood. Are they the real thing? Look into the eyes of pilgrims who visit.

2. Mosaics in Chancel Arch
(the ceiling arch that "frames" the altar's purple canopy)
Colorful panels tell Mary's story in fifth-century Roman terms. Mary (upper left panel) sits on a throne in royal purple like an empress, surrounded by haloed senator-saints in white togas. The angel Gabriel swoops down to announce to Mary she'll conceive Jesus, and the Dove of the Holy Spirit follows. Below (bottom left

panel) are sheep, representing the Apostles, entering the city of Jerusalem ("Hiervsalem").

3. Apse Mosaic
(in semicircular dome of apse)
The 13th-century mosaic shows Mary being crowned by Jesus. By the Middle Ages, her cult status was secure.

4. Nave Mosaics
(right side of nave, starting near altar)
The church contains some of the world's oldest and best-preserved mosaics from Christian Rome. Those with good eyesight or binoculars will enjoy watching the story of Moses unfold in a series of surprisingly colorful and realistic scenes—more sophisticated than anything that would be seen for a thousand years.

The mosaic panels are above the columns, on the right-hand side of the nave. Start at the altar and work back toward the entry.

1. It's a later painting, skip it.
2. Pharaoh's daughter (upper left) and her maids take baby Moses from the Nile.
3. Moses (lower half of panel) sees a burning bush that reconnects him with his Hebrew origins.
4. The Israelites (left side) flee Egypt through a path in the Red Sea, while Pharaoh's troops drown.
5. Moses leads them across the Sinai desert (upper half), and God provides for them with a flock of quail (lower half).
6. Moses (upper half) sticks his magic rod in a river to desalinate it.
7. The Israelites battle their enemies while Moses commands from a hillside.
8. Moses (upper left) brings the Ten Commandments, then goes with Joshua (upper right) to die.
9. Joshua crosses the (rather puny) Jordan River . . .
10. . . . attacks Jericho . . .
11. . . . and the walls come a-tumblin' down.

5. Tomb of Sixtus V
(right transept, the praying pope on right-hand wall)
The Rome we see today is largely due to Pope Sixtus V (or was it Fiftus VI)? This energetic pope (1585–1590) leveled shoddy medieval Rome and erected grand churches connected by long broad boulevards spiked with obelisks as focal points. (The city of Rome has 13 Egyptian obelisks—all of Egypt has only five.) The relief panels (upper right) show some of the obelisks and buildings he commissioned.

6. Madonna Painting and Miracle Relief
(left transept, over altar)

The altar, a geologist's delight, is adorned with jasper, agate, amethyst, lapis lazuli, and gold angels. Amid it all is a simple, iconic version of the lady this church is dedicated to: Mary.

Above the painting is a bronze relief panel showing a pope and amazed bystanders shoveling snow. In 352 Mary appeared to Pope Liberius in a dream, telling him: "Build me a church where the snow falls." The next morning, they discovered a small patch of snow here on the Esquiline Hill—on August 5—and this church, dedicated to Santa Maria, was begun.

SAN CLEMENTE
Here, like nowhere else, you'll enjoy the layers of Rome—a 12th-century basilica sits atop a fourth-century Christian basilica which sits atop a second-century Mithraic Temple and some even earlier Roman buildings. (L5,000, Mon–Sat 9:00–12:30, 15:00–18:00, Sun opens at 10:00, on Via di San Giovanni in Laterano, Metro: Colosseo.)

Upper Church — 12th Century
The church (at today's ground level) is dedicated to the fourth pope, Clement, who was martyred by drowning around A.D. 100—tied to an anchor by angry Romans and tossed overboard. You'll

see his symbol, the anchor around the church. While today's entry is on the side, the original entry was through the courtyard in back—a kind of defensive atrium common in medieval times.

The carved marble choir enclosure in the middle of the church (Schola Cantorum) was where dignitaries sat. About 1,500 years ago, it stood in the old church beneath us. The (hard-to-find) carvings on its small pillars were early-Christian code to fool Roman persecutors—the dove meant peace, the vine was the bread-and-wine ritual, and the fish (Greek word "Ichthus") was an acronym for "Jesus Christ, Son of God, Savior."

In the apse, study the fine 12th-century mosaics. The delicate Crucifixion—with Christ sharing the cross with a dozen Apostles as doves—is engulfed by a richly inhabited Tree of Life. Above it all, a triumphant Christ, one hand on the Bible, blesses the congregation.

Lower Church — Fourth Century

Buy a ticket in the bookshop and descend 800 years to the time when Christians were razzed on their way to church by pagan neighbors. The first room you enter was the original atrium (entry-hall)—the nave extends to the right.

Pagan Inscription (in atrium)

This two-sided marble burial slab—one side for a Christian, the other for a pagan (you can turn it)—shows the two Romes that lived side by side in the fourth-century.

Fresco of St. Clement and Sisinnius
(in nave near altar, on left wall)

Clement (center) holds a secret mass for early Christians back when it was a capital crime. Theodora, a prominent Roman (in yellow, to the right), is one of the undercover faithful. Her pagan husband Sisinnius has come to retrieve and punish her when—zap!—he's struck blind and has to be led away (right side).

But Sisinnius is still unconvinced. When Clement cures his blindness, Sisinnius (lower panel, far right) orders two servants to drag Clement off to the authorities. But the package they carry is not really Clement, who lives to die another day—notice the anchor carved into the church's altar nearby.

Presumed Burial Place of St. Cyril
(in far left corner of church)

Cyril, who died in A.D. 869 (see the icon-like mosaic of him), was an inveterate traveler who spread Christianity to the Slavic lands and Russia—today's Russian Orthodox faithful. Along the way he introduced the Cyrillic alphabet used by Russians and Slavs.

Temple of Mithras (Mithreum) — Second Century

Now descend farther to the Mithraic Temple (Mithreum). Nowhere in Rome is there a better place to experience this weird cult.

Worship Hall (the barred room to the left)

Worshipers of Mithras—men only—sat on the benches on either side of the room. At the far end is a small statue of the god Mithras. In the center sits an altar carved with a relief showing Mithras fighting with a bull that contains all life. A scorpion, a dog, and a snake try to stop Mithras, but he wins, running his sword through the bull. The blood spills out, bringing life to the world.

Mithras' fans gathered here in this tiny microcosm of the universe (the ceiling was decorated with stars) to celebrate the victory with a ritual meal of bread (the bull's flesh) and wine (blood). Every spring, Mithras brings new life again, and so they ritually kept track of the seasons—the four square shafts in the ceiling represent the seasons, the seven round ones were the great constellations. Initiates went through hazing rituals representing the darkness of this world, then emerged into the light-filled world brought by Mithras.

The religion, stressing loyalty and based on the tenuousness of life, was popular among soldiers. It dates back to the time of Alexander the Great, who brought it from Persia. By Imperial times it was one of several mystery cults from the East (like Christianity) that filtered into Rome. When Christians gained power, they found the beliefs abhorrently similar to their own—a saviour bringing life, a life-giving sacrifice, a ritual meal—and banished it.

Facing the barred room are two Corinthian pilasters supporting three arches of the temple's entryway, decorated with a fine stucco, coffered ceiling. At the far end of the hallway another barred door marks the equivalent of a Mithraic Sunday School room. Exit signs direct you down several steps into a vast Roman public area. Look down at the stream—part of the aqueduct system which brought fresh drinking water to first-century Rome. Now climb 2,000 years back to today's street level.

DAY TRIPS
FROM ROME

While the eternal city can keep you busy for ages, here are a few excuses to leave Rome for a day. Tivoli (with a villa of Roman ruins and a villa of Baroque fountains) is famous but a pain to get to. Its tired fountains have a certain nostalgic charm and the ruins are impressive. But for ruins, those at Ostia Antica—Rome's ancient port—are better, and it's easier to visit. While Ostia rivals Pompeii for a look at the ruins of a Roman town, Pompeii is the ultimate. A trip south to Naples and Pompeii is the most demanding of the day trips listed (six hours of train travel) but also the most rewarding, with a chance to wander Rome's most evocative ruins and go on an urban safari in perhaps Europe's most intense city.

TIVOLI

At the edge of the Sabine Hills, 30 kilometers east of Rome, sits the medieval hilltown of Tivoli, a popular retreat since ancient times. Today it's famous for two very different attractions: Hadrian's Villa—an emperor's hot and dusty retirement villa, and Villa D'Este—the lush and watery villa of a cardinal in exile.

The town of Tivoli, with Villa d'Este in its center, is about four kilometers from Hadrian's Villa (Villa Adriana). The TI is on Largo Garibaldi near the garden entry (closed Mon, tel. 0774-21249).

You can get from Rome to Tivoli either by a Metro/bus combination or a shuttle bus. **By Metro and bus:** Ride Metro line B to Ponte Mammolo, then take the local Cotral bus (3/hrly, get off at Via Tiburtina for Hadrian's Villa—Villa Adriana—500 meters away); the same bus continues to Tivoli and Villa d'Este (end of the line). **By shuttle bus:** Rome's Stop-'n'-Go City Tours offers a shuttle bus daily except Monday (L20,000 round-trip, departs Rome at 9:30 from Piazza dei Cinquecento in front of train station; stops at both Villa d'Este and Hadrian's Villa but

you only have time to see one, picks up about 2 hrs later, back in Rome by 13:30, tel. 06-321-7054, e-mail: csr@progleonard.it).
Villa d'Este—Ippolito d' Este's grandfather was the pope . . . probably the only reason Ippolito became a cardinal. Ippolito's claim to fame: his pleasure palace at Tivoli. In the 1550s Ippolito destroyed a Benedictine monastery to build this fanciful late-Renaissance palace. Like Hadrian's Villa, it's a large residential villa. But this one features hundreds of fountains, all gravity-powered. The Aniene river, frazzled into countless threads, weaves its way entertainingly through the villa. At the bottom of the garden, the exhausted little streams once again team up to make a sizable river.

The cardinal had a political falling out with Rome and was exiled. With this watery wonderland on a cool hill with fine views, he made sure Romans would come to visit. It's symbolic of the luxury and secular interests of the cardinal. Today it's tired. Construction barricades make it ugly and many of the best fountains no longer function. Senior travelers—the least able to handle its many stairs—like it best (L8,000, Tue–Sun 9:00–19:30, last ticket at 18:30, closed Mon, shorter hours off-season, tel. 077-431-2070).
▲**Hadrian's Villa**—Built at the peak of the Empire by Hadrian (ruled A.D. 125–134), this was the emperor's retreat from the political complexity of court life in Rome. The Spanish-born Hadrian—an architect, lover of Greek culture (nicknamed "the Little Greek"), and great traveler—created a microcosm of cosmopolitan Rome. In the spirit of Legoland, Disneyworld, and Las Vegas, he re-created famous structures from around the world, making the largest and richest Roman villa anywhere as a retreat and retirement home. Today, the ruins of Hadrian's Villa sprawl over 300 evocative acres. Start your visit at the plastic model. Find the Egyptian Canopus (Sanctuary of the god Serapis, a canal lined with statues), the Greek Pecile (from Athens), and the Teatro Marittimo (a circular palace, favorite retreat on an island where Hadrian did his serious thinking). This "Versailles of ancient Rome" was plundered by barbarians. The marble was burned to make lime for cement. The art was scavenged, ending up in museums throughout Europe (L8,000, daily 9:00–19:00, audioguide L7,000). Getting there is complicated and time-consuming, and the site is hot and comes with lots of unavoidable walking.

OSTIA ANTICA
Rome's ancient seaport, less than an hour from downtown Rome, is the next best thing to Pompeii. Ostia had 80,000 people at the time of Christ, later became a ghost town, and is now excavated. Start at the 2,000-year-old theater, buy a map, explore the town,

and finish with its fine little museum (note that museum closes at 14:00). To get there take the Metro's B Line to the Piramide stop (consider popping out to see pyramid, page 44), then catch the Lido train to Ostia Antica (2/hrly), walk over the overpass, go straight to the end of that road, and follow the signs to (or ask for) "*scavi* Ostia Antica" (L8,000, Tue–Sun 9:00 until an hour before sunset, closed Mon, museum closes at 14:00, tel. 06-5635-8099). Just beyond is Rome's filthy beach (*lido*).

NAPLES AND POMPEII

If you like Italy as far south as Rome, go farther south. It gets better. If Italy is getting on your nerves, don't go farther. Italy intensifies as you plunge deeper. Naples is Italy in the extreme—its best (birthplace of pizza and Sophia Loren) and its worst (home of the Camorra, Naples' "family" of organized crime).

Italy's third-largest city (with more than 2 million people) has almost no open spaces or parks, which makes its position as Europe's most densely populated city plenty evident. Watching the police try to enforce traffic sanity is almost comical in Italy's grittiest, most polluted, and most crime-ridden city. But Naples surprises the observant traveler with its impressive knack for living, eating, and raising children in the streets with good humor and decency. Overcome your fear of being run down or ripped off long enough to talk with people—enjoy a few smiles and jokes with the man running the neighborhood tripe shop or the woman taking her day-care class on a walk through the traffic.

Twenty-five hundred years ago, Neapolis ("new city") was a thriving Greek commercial center. It remains southern Italy's leading city, offering a fascinating collection of museums, churches, eclectic architecture, and volunteers needing blood for dying babies. The pulse of Italy throbs in Naples. Like Cairo or Bombay, it's appalling and captivating at the same time, the closest thing to "reality travel" you'll find in Western Europe. But this tangled mess still somehow manages to breathe, laugh, and sing—with a captivating Italian accent.

For those with a week in Rome and interested in maximum travel thrills, I'd spend a day visiting Naples and Pompeii.

Planning Your Time

Breakfast on the early Rome–Naples express (7:10–9:00), catch the Circumvesuviana (commuter train from the central train station basement) to Pompeii, tour the excavation (11:00–13:00), ride the same train back to Naples, visit the National Museum, do the Naples urban jungle walk, have pizza in its birthplace, and ride the late evening train (2 hrs) back to Rome. In the afternoon, Naples'

NAPLES

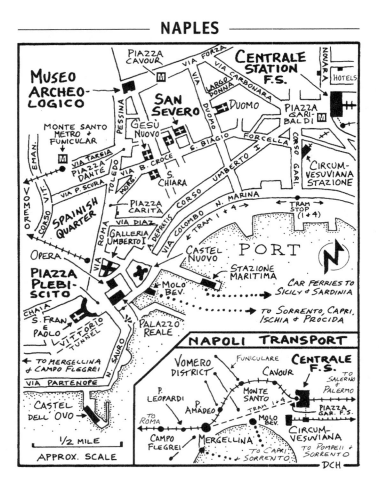

street life slows and many sights close as the temperature soars. The city comes back to life in the early evening.

Arrival in Naples

There are several Naples stations. You want Naples Centrale (facing Piazza Garibaldi), which has a Circumvesuviana stop for commuter trains to Pompeii, baggage check, and a TI.

Continuing to Pompeii on the Circumvesuviana: Naples and Pompeii are on the handy commuter train, the Ferrovia Circumvesuviana. Catch it in the basement of Naples' Central Station; it's clearly signposted (get tickets near the train turnstiles). Two

trains per hour marked "Sorrento" get you to Pompeii in 40 minutes (L3,500, no passes; check schedule carefully or confirm with a
local before boarding to make sure the train is going to Pompeii).
When returning to Naples Central Station on the Circumvesuviana,
get off at the second-to-the-last station, the Collegamento FS or
Garibaldi stop (Central Station and Metro stop are right there).

Getting around Naples

Naples' simple one-line subway, the Servizio Metropolitano, runs
from the Centrale station through the center of town (direction:
Pozzouli), stopping at Piazza Cavour (Archaeology Museum). The
L1,500 tickets are good for 90 minutes. If you can afford a taxi,
don't mess with the buses. A short taxi ride costs L6,000 to
L10,000 (insist on the meter).

Sights—Naples

▲▲▲**Museo Archeologico**—For lovers of antiquity, this
museum alone makes Naples a worthwhile stop; it offers the only
possible peek into the artistic jewelry boxes of Pompeii and Her-
culaneum. The actual sights are impressive but barren; the best art
ended up here.

Paintings and artifacts: Climb the grand stairs to the top
floor and, from the grand ballroom, go left into a Pompeiian art
gallery lined with paintings, bronze statues, artifacts, and an interesting model of the town of Pompeii (room LXXXIII), all of
which make the relative darkness of medieval Europe obvious and
clearly show how classical art inspired the Renaissance greats.

Mosaics: From the same staircase, one floor (several flights)
down on the opposite side, you'll find a smaller but exquisite collection of Pompeiian mosaics (note the fourth-century B.C. Battle
of Alexander showing the Macedonians defeating the Persians).

Farnese Collection: The ground floor (on the distant left as
you leave the stairs) has enough Greek, Roman, and Etruscan art
to put any museum on the map, but its highlight is the Farnese
Collection—a giant hall of huge, bright, and wonderfully restored
statues excavated from Rome's Baths of Caracalla. You can almost
hear the Toro Farnese snorting. This largest intact statue from
antiquity (a third-century copy of a Hellenistic original) was
carved out of one piece of marble and restored by Michelangelo.
Read the worthwhile descriptions on the walls.

Cost and Hours: L12,000, Wed–Mon 9:00–22:00, closed
Tue and at 14:00 in winter, tel. 081-440-166, call to confirm times
if visiting in the afternoon. To get to the museum from the
Centrale train station, follow signs to Metropolitano and ride
the subway one stop.

— NAPLES WALK —

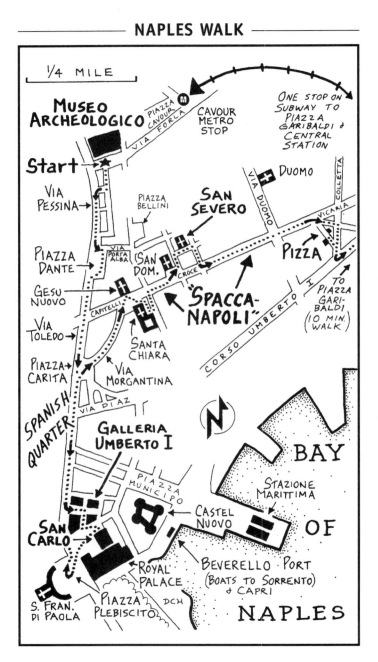

1/4 MILE

MUSEO ARCHEOLOGICO

PIAZZA CAVOUR

Ⓜ

VIA FORIA

CAVOUR METRO STOP

ONE STOP ON SUBWAY TO PIAZZA GARIBALDI & CENTRAL STATION

Start

VIA PESSINA →

PIAZZA BELLINI

SAN SEVERO

DUOMO

VIA DUOMO

COLLETTA

VICARIA

PIAZZA DANTE →

VIA PORTA ALBA

SAN DOM.

CROCE

"SPACCA-NAPOLI"

PIZZA

GESU NUOVO

CAPITELLI

TO PIAZZA GARI-BALDI (10 MIN. WALK)

VIA TOLEDO →

SANTA CHIARA

CORSO UMBERTO I

PIAZZA→ CARITA

VIA MORGANTINA

VIA DIAZ

SPANISH QUARTER

N

BAY

GALLERIA UMBERTO I

PIAZZA MUNICIPO

STAZIONE MARITTIMA

OF

SAN CARLO →

CASTEL NUOVO

ROYAL PALACE

BEVERELLO PORT (BOATS TO SORRENTO) & CAPRI

S. FRAN. DI PAOLA

PIAZZA PLEBISCITO

DCH

NAPLES

▲▲▲**The Slice-of-Neapolitan-Life Walk**—Walk from the museum through the heart of town and back to the station (allow at least two hours plus pizza and sightseeing stops). Sights are listed in the order you'll see them on this walk.

Naples, a living medieval city, is its own best sight. Couples artfully make love on Vespas here surrounded by more fights and smiles per cobble than anywhere else in Italy. Rather than seeing Naples as a list of sights, see the one great museum, then capture its essence by taking this walk through the core of the city. Should you become overwhelmed or lost, step into a store and ask for help (*"Dov'è il stazione centrale?"*, DOH-vay eel staht-zee-OH-nay chen-TRAH-lay) or point in this book to the next sight.

Via Toledo and the Spanish Quarter (city walk, first half): Leaving the Archaeological Museum at the top of Piazza Cavour (Metro: Piazza Cavour), cross the street and dip into the ornate galleria on your way to Via Pessina. The first part of this walk is a straight one-mile ramble down the boulevard to Galleria Umberto I near the Royal Palace. Coffee will be waiting.

Busy Via Pessina leads downhill to Piazza Dante. After two blocks, a tiny pedestrian street (Via Micco Spadaro) to your left dead-ends at the **Academy of Fine Arts** (Belle Arti). Sneak a peek inside. Isn't that Michelangelo's *David*?! (The bar/pizzeria in front serves a decent quick lunch with pleasant outdoor seating.)

At Piazza Dante, notice poor old Dante in the center, looking out over the chaos with a hopeless gesture. Past the square, Via Pessina becomes Via Toledo, Naples' principal shopping street. About five blocks below Piazza Dante, at Via Maddaloni, you cross the long straight street called Spaccanapoli (literally, "split Naples"). Look left and right. Since ancient times, this thin street (which changes names several times) has bisected the city. (We'll be coming back to this point later. To abbreviate this walk, turn left here and skip down to the Spaccanapoli section.)

Via Toledo runs through **Piazza Carita** with its Fascist architecture (from 1938) overlooking the square. Wander down Via Toledo a few blocks past the Fascist architecture of two banks (both on the left). Try robbing the second one (Banco di Napoli, Via Toledo 178).

Up the hill to your right is the **Spanish Quarter**—Naples at its rawest, poorest, and most historic. Thrill seekers (or someone in need of a $20 prostitute) will take a stroll up one of these streets and loop back to Via Toledo.

The only thing predictable about this Neapolitan tidepool is the ancient planned grid of its streets, the friendliness of its shop-keepers, and the boldness of its mopeds. Concerned locals will tug on their lower eyelid, warning you to be wary. Pop into a grocery shop and ask the man to make you his best ham and mozzarella sandwich. Trust him for the price—it should be around L5,000.

Continue down Via Toledo to the Piazza Plebiscito. From here you'll see the church of **San Francesco di Paola** with its Pantheon-inspired dome and broad, arcing colonnades. Opposite is the **Royal Palace**, which has housed Spanish, French, and even Italian royalty. The lavish interior is open for tours (L8,000, 9:00–14:00, closed Mon or Tue). Next door, peek inside the neoclassical **Teatro San Carlo**, Italy's second-most-respected opera house (after Milan's La Scala). The huge castle on the harborfront just beyond the palace houses government bureaucrats and is closed to tourists.

Under the Victorian iron and glass of the 100-year-old Galleria Umberto I, enjoy a coffee break or sample a unique Neapolitan pastry called *sfogliatella* (crispy, scallop shell–shaped pastry filled with sweet ricotta cheese). Go through the tall yellow arch at the end of Via Toledo or across from the opera house. Gawk up.

Spaccanapoli back to the station (city walk, second half): To continue your walk, double back up Via Toledo past Piazza Carita to Via Maddaloni. (Consider going via the back streets.) Look east and west to survey the straight-as-a-Roman-arrow Spaccanapoli. Formerly the main thoroughfare of the Greek city of Neapolis, it starts up the hill near the Montesanto funicular (a colorful and safer Spanish Quarter neighborhood from where you can see how strictly Spaccanapoli splits Naples' historic center).

Turn right off Via Toledo and walk down Via Maddaloni to two bulky old churches (and a TI) on Piazza Gesu Nuovo. Check out the austere, fortresslike church of **Gesu Nuovo**, with its peaceful but brilliant Baroque interior. Across the street, the simpler Gothic church of **Santa Chiara** offers a stark contrast (free, Mon–Sat 8:30–12:30, 15:30–18:30, Sun 8:30–12:30). Its bright-tiled cloisters are a peaceful refuge (to reach cloisters, exit church and go right, walk alongside church to separate entrance, donation requested).

The rest of this walk is basically a straight line (all of which locals call Spaccanapoli). Continue down traffic-free Via B. Croce to the next square, Piazza S. Domenico Maggiore. Detour behind the castlelike **San Domenico Maggiore** church (to the right as you face the church, take the first right after that), following yellow signs to the **Capella Sansevero** (L8,000, Jul–Oct Mon, Wed–Sat 10:00–18:00, Sun 10:00–13:30, closed Tue; Nov–Jun closes weekdays at 16:40, Via de Sanctis 19). This small chapel is a Baroque explosion mourning the body of Christ, who lies on a soft pillow under an incredibly realistic veil. It's all carved out of marble and is like no statue I've seen (by Giuseppe "howdeedoodat"

Pizza in Naples

Drop by one of the two most traditional pizzerias. Naples, where just the right combination of fresh dough, mozzarella, and tomatoes is baked in traditional wood-burning ovens, is the birthplace of pizza. A few blocks from the train station, **Antica Pizzeria da Michele** is for purists (Mon–Sat 8:00– 23:00, closed Sun, cheap, filled with locals, 50 yards off Corso Umberto on Via Cesare Sersale, look for the vertical red "Antica Pizzeria" sign, tel. 081-553-9204). It serves two kinds: *margherita* (tomato sauce and mozzarella) or *marinara* (tomato sauce, oregano, and garlic, with no cheese). A pizza with beer costs L8,000. Some locals prefer **Pizzeria Trianon** (daily 10:00–15:30, 18:30–23:00, across the street at Via Pietro Colletta 42, tel. 081-553-9426). Da Michele's arch-rival offers more choices, higher prices, air conditioning, and a cozier atmosphere. For legendary pizza near the museum, try **Pizzeria Port Alba** (a block from the Cavour Metro stop on Via Port Alba).

Sammartino, 1750). Lovely statues, carved from a single piece of marble, adorn the altar. Despair struggles with a marble rope net (on the right, opposite Chastity). No photos are allowed in the chapel (postcards are available in the gift shop).

For the ghoul in all of us, walk down the stairway to the right for a creepy look at two 200-year-old studies in varicose veins. Was one decapitated? Was one pregnant?

Back on Via B. Croce, turn left and continue the Spaccanapoli cultural scavenger hunt. As Via B. Croce becomes Via S. Biagio dei Librai, notice the gold and silver shops and the Ospedale delle Bambole (doll hospital) at #81.

Cross busy Via Duomo. The street and side-street scenes along Via Vicaria intensify. Paint a picture with these thoughts: Naples has the most intact street plan of any ancient Roman city. Imagine life here as in a Roman city (retain these images as you visit Pompeii) with streetside shop fronts that close up after dark to become private homes. Today is just one more page in a 2,000-year-old story of city activity: all kinds of meetings, beatings, and cheatings, kisses and near misses, and little-boy pisses.

You name it, it occurs right on the streets today, as it has since Roman times. People ooze from crusty corners. Black-and-white death announcements add to the clutter on the walls. Widows sell cigarettes from buckets. For a peek behind the scenes in the shade of wet laundry, venture down a few side streets (two blocks before the Y in the road). Buy two carrots as a gift for the woman on the fifth floor if she'll lower her bucket to pick them up. The neighborhood action seems best around 18:00.

At the tiny fenced-in triangular park, veer right onto Via Forcella. Turning right on busy Via Pietro Colletta, walk 50 meters and step into the North Pole. Reward yourself for surviving this safari with a stop at the Polo Nord Gelateria (at Via Pietro Colletta 41, sample their Kiss flavor before ordering). Via Pietro Colletta leads past Napoli's two most competitive pizzerias (see "Pizza in Naples" sidebar, page 175) to Corso Umberto.

To finish the walk, turn left on the grand-boulevardian Corso Umberto, and walk through all kinds of riffraff to the vast and ugly Piazza Garibaldi. On the far side is the Central Station. Run for it! (If you're tired or late, any bus coming down the meridian is Central Station–bound.)

Pompeii

Stopped in its tracks by the eruption of Mount Vesuvius in A.D. 79, Pompeii offers the best look anywhere at what life in Rome must have been like 2,000 years ago. An entire city of well-preserved ruins is yours to explore. Once a thriving commercial port of 20,000, Pompeii grew from Greek and Etruscan roots to become an important Roman city. Then, Pompeii was buried under 30 feet of hot mud and volcanic ash. For archaeologists this was a shake-'n'-bake windfall, teaching them almost all they know about daily Roman life. It was rediscovered in the 1600s, and the first excavations began in 1748 (L12,000, daily 9:00 until an hour before sunset, 20:30 in summer, ticket office closes an hour before closing time).

Get off the Circumvesuviana train at the Villa dei Misteri, Pompei Scavi stop. (The modern town is Pompei, the ancient site is Pompeii.) Allow at least two hours to tour Pompeii and consider the following route, starting at the Porta Marina (town gate) after the ticket booth.

Tour of Pompeii: Remember this was a booming trading city. Most streets would have been lined with stalls and jammed with customers from sunup to sundown. Chariots vied for street space with shoppers and many streets were off-limits to chariots during shopping hours. (You'll still see street signs with pictures of men carrying vases—this meant pedestrians only.)

Fountains overflowed into the streets, flushing the gutters into the sea (thereby cleaning the streets). The stones you see at intersections allowed pedestrians to cross the constantly gushing streets. A single stone designated a one-way street (just enough room for one

POMPEII

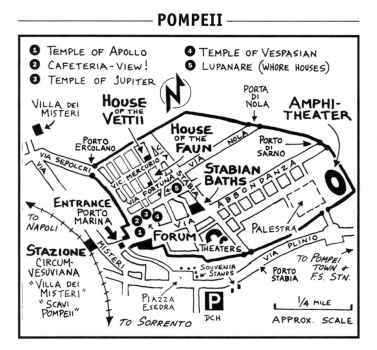

❶ TEMPLE OF APOLLO
❷ CAFETERIA - VIEW!
❸ TEMPLE OF JUPITER
❹ TEMPLE OF VESPASIAN
❺ LUPANARE (WHORE HOUSES)

VILLA DEI MISTERI
HOUSE OF THE VETTII
PORTA DI NOLA
AMPHI-THEATER
HOUSE OF THE FAUN
PORTO ERCOLANO
NOLA
PORTO DI SARNO
VIA SEPOLCRI
VIA
VIC. MERCURIO
STABIAN BATHS
VIA STABIA
ABBONDANZA
ENTRANCE PORTO MARINA
VIA FORTUNA
❷❸❹
❶
FORUM
VIA
PALESTRA
TO NAPOLI
MISTERI
THEATERS
VIA PLINIO
STAZIONE CIRCUM-VESUVIANA
SOUVENIR STANDS
PORTO STABIA
TO POMPEI TOWN + F.S. STN.
"VILLA DEI MISTERI"
"SCAVI POMPEII"
PIAZZA ESEDRA
P
DCH
¼ MILE
APPROX. SCALE
TO SORRENTO

chariot) and two stones meant a two-way chariot street. There were no posh neighborhoods. Rich and poor mixed it up as elegant homes existed side by side with simple homes throughout Pompeii. With most buildings covered by a brilliant white ground-marble stucco, Pompeii in A.D. 79 was a fine town. Remember, Pompeii's best art is in the Naples museum, described above.

After buying your ticket, stop before the archway into Pompeii. This was the Porta Marina—the sea came right to Pompeii's door here before Vesuvius blew. There would have been large public baths below. Approaching the Porta Marina, notice two openings—big for chariots, small for pedestrians.

From the Porta Marina, Via Marina leads to the **Temple of Apollo** (Tempio di Apollo), surrounded by 48 columns. Enter on your left just before the Forum and face the altar. The Forum is just to your right (beyond the wall). Exit, turn left, and the Forum is in front of you again.

The Forum (Foro), Pompeii's commercial, religious, and political center, is the most ruined part of Pompeii. It's grand nonetheless with several temples, the "basilica" (Pompeii's largest building, used for legal and commercial business), and some eerie casts of volcano victims displayed with piles of pottery (behind the roofed area with the iron fences on the left as you walk through the Forum).

At the far end of the Forum, take the gate to your right (as you walk toward the volcano)—past the convenient 20th-century cafeteria (decent value, gelati, overpriced cards and books, WCs with great rooftop views) down Via del Foro—and enter into the impressive baths, Terme del Foro (on left, past cafeteria). Here, three rooms offered clients a hot bath *(caldarium)*, a warm bath *(tepidarium)*, and a cold-plunge bath *(frigidarium)*.

Exit the baths through the back door; you'll be on Via della Fortuna. Straight in front of you is an ancient fast-food stand (notice the holes in the counters for pots); to your left a few doors down is the **Casa de Poeta Tragico** with its famous "Beware of Dog" mozaic in the entryway; and to your right—down the street—is the **House of Faun** (Casa del Fauno, Danzante). The faun is still dancing just inside the door.

One of Pompeii's largest homes, the House of Faun provided Naples' Archaeological Museum with many of its top treasures, including the famous mosaic of the Battle of Alexander. Wander through the many courtyards. Exit to the rear, turning right on to Vicolo di Mercurio, then left on Vicolo dei Vetti (notice the exposed 2,000-year-old lead pipes in the wire cage on the right as you turn left) and enter Pompeii's best-preserved home, the House of Vetti (Casa dei Vetti).

The House of Vetti, which has retained its mosaics and frescoes, was the home of two wealthy merchant brothers who were into erotic wallpaper (cover your eyes as you enter). An immediate right upon entering (open your eyes now) takes you into the slave's sleeping quarters and through to the kitchen and the little hanky-pantry off the kitchen with erotic art. Enjoy the beautifully preserved rooms as you walk counterclockwise around the central courtyard.

Leaving the **House of Vetti**, go left past the pipes again. Then turn right onto the Vicolo dei Vetti and peek into the **Casa degli Scienziati** (#43, view mosaic chapel in back). Next turn left onto the Via della Fortuna. From there a quick right on Vicolo Storto leads down a curving street to the bakery and mill *(forno e mulini)*. The ovens look like modern-day pizza ovens. Take the first left after the bakery onto Via degli Augustali, checking out the mosaics on the left at the **Taberna Hedones** (must be the tavern of hedonism), then turn right and follow the signs to the brothel *(lupanare)* at #18. Wander into the brothel, a simple place with stone beds, stone pillows, and art to get you in the mood.

If you're tired after the brothel, you've seen the essentials and can head on out. Otherwise, Pompeii's last great sight is a worthwhile 10-minute stroll away. Exiting the brothel, turn right onto the same street you entered from, then turn left on the Via della Abbondanza, which leads to the well-preserved **Stabian baths** (Terme Stabiane—about 25 yards down on the left and worth the detour). At the end of Via della Abbondanza, turn right at the *"uscita/per l'anfiteatro"* sign and walk down the pine tree–lined lane to the huge, rebuilt amphitheater *(anfiteatro)*. This is the oldest (80 B.C.) and best-preserved Roman amphitheater in Italy. From the top, look into the giant rectangular Palestra, where athletes used to train. Retrace your steps all the way down the Via della Abbondanza to the entrance of Pompeii.

SLEEPING
IN ROME

The absolute cheapest doubles in Rome are L70,000, without shower or breakfast. You'll pay L30,000 in a backpacker-filled dorm or hostel. A nicer hotel (L240,000 with a bathroom and air conditioning) provides an oasis and refuge, making it easier to enjoy this intense and grinding city. If you're going door to door, prices are soft—so bargain. Built into a hotel's official price list is a kickback for a room-finding service or agency; if you're coming direct, they pay no kickback and may lower the price for you. Many hotels have high-season (mid-Mar–Jun, Sept–Oct) and low-season prices. Easter and September are most crowded and expensive. Room rates are lowest in sweltering August.

Most of my recommended hotels are small, with huge, murky entrances that make you feel like a Q-Tip in a gas station. English works in all but the cheapest places. Traffic in Rome roars, so my challenge has been to find friendly places on quiet streets. With the recent arrival of double-paned windows and air conditioning, night noise is not the problem it was. Even so, light sleepers should always ask for a *tranquillo* room. Many prices here are promised only to people who show this book, pay in lire (no credit cards), and come direct without using a room-finding service. On Easter, April 25, and May 1, the entire city gets booked up.

Scala Reale, the company that runs tours (see "Tours of Rome," page 30), can help you find short-term accommodations in private apartments (U.S. tel. 888/467-1986, Italy tel. 06-445-1477, fax 06-4470-0898, www.scalareale.org).

Your hotel can point you to the nearest Laundromat (usually open daily 8:00–22:00, about L12,000 to wash and dry a 15-pound load). The Bolle Blu chain now comes with Internet access (L8,000/hr, near train station at Via Palestro 59, Via Milazzo 20, and Via Principe Amedeo 116, tel. 06-4470-3098).

Sleep Code

S = Single, **D** = Double/Twin, **T** = Triple, **Q** = Quad,
b = bathroom, **t** = toilet only, **s** = shower only, **CC** = Credit
Card (Visa, MasterCard, Amex), **SE** = Speaks English,
NSE = No English. Breakfast is normally included in the
expensive places.
Exchange rate: L1,900 = about $1

Sleeping on Via Firenze (zip code: 00184)

I generally stay on Via Firenze because it's tranquil, safe, handy, and
central. It's a 10-minute walk from the central train station and airport shuttle, and two blocks beyond the Piazza della Repubblica and
TI. The defense ministry is nearby, and you've got heavily armed
guards all night. Virtually all the orange buses that rumble down
Via Nazionale (#64, #70, #115, #640) take you to Piazza Venezia
(Forum) and Largo Argentina (Pantheon). From Largo Argentina,
#8 goes to Trastevere (first stop after crossing the river) and #64
(jammed with people and thieves) continues to St. Peter's.

Hotel Oceania is a peaceful slice of air-conditioned
heaven. This nine-room manor house–type hotel is spacious
and quiet, with newly renovated and spotless rooms, run by a
pleasant father-and-son team (Sb-L190,000, Db-L240,000,
Tb-L300,000, Qb-L355,000, these prices through 2000 with this
book only, additional 20 percent off in Aug and winter, breakfast
included, phones, English newspaper, CC:VMA, Via Firenze 38,
tel. 06-482-4696, fax 06-488-5586, www.hoteloceania.it, e-mail:
hoceania@tin.it, son Stefano SE, dad Armando serves world-
famous coffee).

Hotel Aberdeen is classier and more professional for about
the same price. It has mini-bars, phones, and showers in its 36
modern, air-conditioned, and smoke-free rooms; includes a fine
breakfast buffet; and is warmly run by Annamaria, with support
from her cousins Sabrina and Cinzia, and trusty Reda riding shotgun after dark (Sb-L180,000, Db-L240,000, Tb-L280,000, prices
through 2000 with this book only, L50,000 less per room in Aug
and winter, CC:VMA, garage-L40,000, Via Firenze 48, tel. 06-
482-3920, fax 06-482-1092, e-mail: hotel.aberdeen@travel.it, SE).

Residence Adler, with its wide halls, garden patio, and eight
quiet, elegant, and air-conditioned rooms in a great locale, is
another good deal. It's run the old-fashioned way by a charming
family (Db-L200,000, Tb-L280,000, Qb-L340,000, includes
breakfast, prices through 2000 with this book only, CC:VMA,

HOTELS NEAR TRAIN STATION

TAXI STAND — Ⓣ
METRO STN — Ⓜ

1/4 MILE

1. HOTEL OCEANIA & NARDIZZI
2. HOTEL ABERDEEN
3. RESIDENCE ADLER
4. HOTEL REX
5. HOTEL BRITTANIA
6. HOTEL SONYA
7. HOTEL PENSIONE ITALIA
8. HOTEL CORTINA
9. YMCA CASA STUDENTESSE
10. SUORE SANTA ELISABETTA
11. HOTEL MONTREAL
12. HOTEL FENICIA & MAGIC
13. ALBERGO SILEO & FAWLTY TOWERS
14. HOTEL DUCA D'ALBA
15. HOTEL GRIFO
16. SUORE DI SANT ANNA
17. SNACK BAR GASTRONOMIA
18. PASTICCERIA DAGNINO
19. HOSTARIA ROMANA
20. RISTORANTE GIOVANNI
21. GRILL TARGET PIZZA
22. EST EST EST PIZZERIA
23. RIST. CINESE INT'L.
24. BEEHIVE HOSTEL
25. CASA OLMATA HOSTEL

additional 5 percent off if you pay cash, elevator, Via Modena 5, tel. 06-484-466, fax 06-488-0940, NSE).

Here are three basic and sleepable hotels each wonderfully located on Via Firenze: **Hotel Nardizzi Americana** has a back-packer-friendly roof terrace and decent rooms. But it won't win any cleanliness awards and traffic noise can be a problem in the front rooms (Sb-L150,000, Db-L200,000, Tb-L240,000, Qb-L260,000, prices through 2000 with this book only, includes breakfast, discounts for off-season and long stays, CC:VMA, additional 10 percent off with cash, air con, elevator, drinks available evenings, Via Firenze 38, tel. 06-488-0368, fax 06-488-0035, SE). **Hotel Seiler** is a quiet, serviceable place with 30 basic rooms (Sb-L190,000, Db-L250,000, Tb-L300,000, CC:VMA, fans, elevator, Via Firenze 48, tel. 06-485550, fax 06-4880688, e-mail: acropoli@rdn.it, Silvio SE). **Hotel Texas Seven Hills**, a stark institutional throwback to the 1960s, rents 18 quiet but depressing rooms (D-L160,000, Db-L200,000, CC:VMA, often soft prices, Via Firenze 47, elevator, tel. 06-481-4082, fax 06-481-4079, e-mail: what's that?, NSE).

Sleeping between Via Nazionale and Basilica Santa Maria Maggiore

Hotel Rex is a business-class Art Deco fortress—a quiet, plain, and stately four-star place with all the comforts but too many sconces (48 rooms, Sb-L300,000, Db-L400,000, Tb-L500,000, prices through 2000 with this book only, CC:VMA, elevator, air conditioning, some smoke-free rooms, just off Via Nazionale at Via Torino 149, tel. 06-482-4828, fax 06-488-2743, e-mail: hotel.rex@alfanet.it, SE).

Hotel Britannia stands like a marble fruitcake offering all the comforts in tight quarters on a quiet and safe-feeling street. Lushly renovated with over-the-top classical motifs, its 32 air-conditioned rooms are small but comfortable with bright, modern bathrooms (Db-L410,000 in May–Jun and Sept–Oct, Db-L360,000 the rest of the year, even less in Aug, CC:VMA, extra bed-L90,000, children up to 10 stow away for free, babysitting service, free parking, Via Napoli 64, tel. 06-488-3153, fax 06-488-2343, e-mail: britannia@venere.it).

Hotel Sonya is a small, family-run but impersonal place with a dozen comfortable, well-equipped rooms, a great location, and low prices; reserve well in advance (Db-L200,000, Tb-L240,000, Qb-L290,000, CC:VMA, air conditioning, elevator, facing the Opera at Via Viminale 58, tel. 06-481-9911, fax 06-488-5678, Francesca SE).

Hotel Pensione Italia, in a busy, interesting, handy locale and placed safely on a quiet street next to the Ministry of the Interior, is comfortable, airy, bright, clean, and thoughtfully run by English-speaking Andrea and Abdul (31 rooms, Sb-L130,000, Db-L180,000, Tb-L240,000, Qb-L280,000, includes breakfast, prices through 2000 with this book and cash only, all rooms 20 percent off in Aug and winter, elevator, air conditioning for L15,000 extra, Via Venezia 18, just off Via Nazionale, tel. 06-482-8355, fax 06-474-5550, e-mail: hitalia@pronet.it). Their singles are all on the quiet courtyard and the nine annex rooms across the street are a cut above the rest.

Hotel Cortina rents 14 simple, comfortable, air-conditioned rooms for a decent price (Db-L240,000, includes breakfast, CC:VMA, 10 percent discount with this book and cash, Via Nazionale 18, 00184 Roma, tel. 06-481-9794, fax 06-481-9220, e-mail: hotelcortina@pronet.it, John Carlo and Angelo SE).

YWCA Casa Per Studentesse accepts men and women. It's an institutional place, filled with white-uniformed maids, more-colorful Third World travelers, and 75 single beds. It's closed from midnight to 7:00 in the morning; the locked doors with no way out trouble some travelers (L40,000 per person in 3- and 4-bed rooms, S-L60,000, Sb-L80,000, D-L100,000, Db-L120,000, includes breakfast except on Sun, Via C. Balbo 4, 00184 Roma, tel. 06-488-0460, fax 06-487-1028). The YWCA faces a great little street market.

Suore di Santa Elisabetta is a heavenly Polish-run convent booked long in advance, but it's an incredible value (Sb-L63,000, Db-L115,000, Tb-L148,000, Qb-L180,000, includes breakfast, CC:VM, elevator, fine view roof terrace, a block south of Basilica Santa Maria Maggiore at Via dell' Omata 9, tel. 06-488-8271, fax 06-488-4066).

Hotel Montreal is a bright, solid business-class place on a big street a block in front of Santa Maria Maggiore (Db-L220,000, CC:VMA, 18 of its 22 rooms have air con, a block from Metro: Vittorio at Via Carlo Alberto 4, 00185 Roma, tel. 06-445-7797, fax 06-446-5522, www.venere.it, e-mail: info@hotelmontrealroma.com).

Sleeping Cheap, Northeast of the Train Station

The cheapest hotels in town are northeast of the station. Some travelers feel this area is weird and spooky after dark. With your back to the train tracks, turn right and walk two blocks out of the station.

Hotel Fenicia rents 11 comfortable well-equipped rooms at a fine price. Some are on fourth floor—quiet but there's no elevator (Sb-L80,000, Db-L130,000, Tb-L180,000, prices through 2000 with this book only, air con-L20,000/day, breakfast-L10,000,

CC:VMA, 2 blocks from station at Via Milazzo 20, tel. & fax 06-490-342, Anna and Georgio).

Hotel Magic, a tiny place run by a mother-daughter team, is clean and high enough off the road to escape the traffic noise (10 rooms, Sb-L90,000, Db-L130,000, Tb-L170,000, prices through 2000 with this book only, less in Aug, CC:VM, no breakfast, thin walls, midnight curfew, Via Milazzo 20, 3rd floor, 00185 Roma, tel. & fax 06-495-9880, little English spoken, reportedly unreliable for reservations).

Albergo Sileo is a shiny-chandeliered, 10-room place with an elegant touch that has a contract to house train conductors who work the night shift. With maids doing double-time, they offer rooms from 19:00 to 9:00 only. If you can handle this it's a great value. During the day they store your luggage, and though you won't have access to a room, you're welcome to hang out in their lobby or bar (D-L75,000, Db-L90,000, Tb-L115,000, breakfast extra, elevator, Via Magenta 39, tel. & fax 06-445-0246, Allesandro and Maria Savioli NSE).

Fawlty Towers is a backpacker-type place well run by the Aussies from Enjoy Rome. It's young, hip, and English-speaking, with a rooftop terrace, lots of information, and no curfew (shared co-ed 4-bed dorms for L30,000 per bed, S-L60,000, Sb-L75,000, D-L90,000, Ds-L100,000, Db-L120,000, Ts-L130,000, Tb-L145,000, reservations by credit card but pay in cash, dorm beds reserved only to those calling at 21:00 the night before, elevator, Internet access, Via Magenta 39, tel. & fax 06-445-0374, e-mail: info@enjoyrome.com).

Sleeping near the Colosseum (zip code: 00184)

One stop on the subway from the train station (to Metro: Cavour), these places are buried in a very Roman world of exhaust-stained medieval ambience. The handy electrico bus line #117 connects you with the sights.

Hotel Duca d'Alba is a tight and modern pastel-marble-hardwood place just half a block from the Metro station (Sb-L260,000, Db-L350,000, extra bed-L40,000, breakfast buffet, CC:VMA, air con, Via Leonina 14, tel. 06-484-471, fax 06-488-4840, e-mail: duca.dalba@venere.it, SE).

Hotel Grifo has a homey but tangled floor plan with 20 simple, modern rooms and a roof terrace. The double-paned windows don't quite keep out the Vespa noise (Db-L230,000, L210,000 in Jul–Aug, CC:VMA, elevator, air con planned for 2000, 2 blocks off Via Cavour at Via del Boschetto 144, tel. 06-487 1395, fax 06-474 2323, e-mail: zuccale@freemail.it, son Alessandro SE).

Suore di Sant Anna was built for Ukrainian pilgrims. The sisters are sweet. It's clumsy and difficult (23:00 curfew), but once you're in, you've got a comfortable home in a classic Roman-village locale (Sb-L60,000, Db-L120,000, Tb-L180,000, includes breakfast, consider a monkish dinner for L26,000, off the corner of Via dei Serpenti and Via Baccina at Piazza Madonna dei Monti 3, Metro: Cavour, tel. 06-485-778, fax 06-487-1064).

Sleeping near Campo de' Fiori and Piazza Navona (zip code: 00186)

Hotel Campo de' Fiori is ideal for wealthy bohemians who value centrality over peace and comfort. It's just off Campo de' Fiori and has an unreal rooftop terrace and rickety windows and furniture (D-L160,000, Db-L220,000, includes breakfast, CC:VM, lots of stairs and no elevator, Via del Biscione 6, tel. 06-6874886, fax 06-687-6003, SE). They also have apartments nearby that can house five or six people (L250,000 for 2 people, extra person-L50,000).

Albergo del Sole is impersonal and filled with German groups but well located (D-L150,000, small Db-L180,000, Db-L220,000, no breakfast, Via del Biscione 76, tel. 06-6880-6873, fax 06-689-3787, e-mail: sole@italyhotel.com).

Casa di Santa Brigida, also near the characteristic Campo de' Fiori, overlooks the elegant Piazza Farnese. With soft-spoken sisters gliding down polished hallways, and pearly gates instead of doors, this lavish convent makes the exhaust-stained Roman tourist feel like he's died and gone to heaven. If you're unsure of your destiny (and don't need a double bed), this is worth the splurge (Sb-L125,000, Db-L250,000, 4 percent extra with CC, great-value dinners, roof garden, plush library, air con, walk-in address: Monserrato 54, mailing address: Piazza Farnese 96, reserve long in advance, tel. 06-6889-2596, fax 06-6889-1573, www.brigidine.org, e-mail: brigida@mclink.it, many of the sisters are from India and speak English).

Piazza Navona: Hotel Navona, a ramshackle 25-room hotel occupying an ancient building in a perfect locale a block off Piazza Navona, is a fine value (S-L90,000, D-L130,000, Db-L160,000, Db with air con-L200,000, breakfast, family rooms, lots of student groups, Via dei Sediari 8, tel. 06-686-4203, fax 06-6880-3802, run by an Australian named Corry).

Hotel Nazionale, a four-star landmark, is a 16th-century palace sharing a well-policed square with the national parliament. Its 87 rooms are served by lush public spaces, fancy bars, and a uniformed staff. I think it's the only place with a revolving front door I've ever recommended, but if you want security, comfort and the heart of old Rome at your doorstep (the Pantheon is

——SLEEPING IN THE HEART OF ROME——

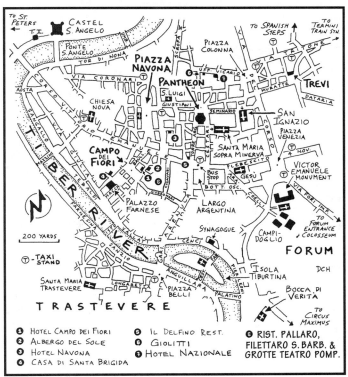

- ❶ Hotel Campo dei Fiori
- ❷ Albergo del Sole
- ❸ Hotel Navona
- ❹ Casa di Santa Brigida
- ❺ Il Delfino Rest.
- ❻ Giolitti
- ❼ Hotel Nazionale
- ❽ Rist. Pallaro, Filettaro S. Barb. & Grotte Teatro Pomp.

3 blocks away, Rome's top gelateria is just around the corner), this is a worthy splurge. Its room furnishings are a bit tired, keeping the price out of orbit (Sb-L340,000, Db-L400,000-500,000, extra person-L100,000, fancier rooms and suites available for much more, CC:VMA, air con, elevator, Piazza Montecitorio 131, tel. 06-695-001, fax 06-678-6677, www.nazionaleamontecitorio.it, e-mail: nazionale@micanet.it).

Sleeping "Three Stars" near the Vatican Museum (zip code: 00192)

To locate hotels, see map on page 41.

Hotel Alimandi is a good value, run by the friendly and entrepreneurial Alimandi brothers: Paolo, Enrico, Luigi, and Germano (35 rooms, Sb-L160,000, Db-L220,000, Tb-L260,000, 5 percent discount with this book and cash, CC:VMA, grand breakfast-L15,000 extra, elevator, great roof garden, self-service washing machines, internet access, pool table, parking-L30,000/day, down the stairs directly in front of Vatican Museum, Via Tunisi 8, near Metro: Cipro–Musei Vaticani, reserve by phone, no reply to fax means they are full, tel. 06-3972-6300, toll-free in Italy tel. 800-12212, fax 06-3972-3943, www.lcnet.it/initaly/alimandi/hoteling.htm, e-mail: alimandi@tin.it, SE). They offer their guests free airport pick-up and drop-off (saving you L80,000 if you were planning on taking a taxi), though you must reserve when you book your room and conform to their schedule (which can mean waiting). Maria Alimandi rents out three rooms in her apartment a 20-minute bus ride from the Vatican (Db-L140,000, see Web site above).

Hotel Spring House, offering fine rooms with balconies and refrigerators, has an impersonal staff. Confirm prices and mention this book ("superior" Db-L250,000, includes breakfast, 5 percent discount for cash payment, 15 percent discount Jul–Aug, simple doubles a bit cheaper, CC:VMA, air con, elevator, parking-L25,000/day, Metro: Cipro–Musei Vaticani, Via Mocenigo 7, a block from Alimandi, tel. 06-3972-0948, fax 06-3972-1047, www.hotelspringhouse.com).

Hotel Gerber is sleek, modern, air conditioned, business-like, and set in a quiet residential area (27 rooms, S-L120,000, Sb-L180,000, Db-L235,000, Tb-L285,000, Qb-L330,000, 10 percent discount with this book, includes breakfast buffet, CC:VMA, 1 block from Lepanto subway stop, Via degli Scipioni 241, tel. 06-321-6485, fax 06-321-7048, Peter SE).

Sleeping in Hostels and Dorms

Rome's one real youth hostel is big, institutional, and not central or worth the trouble. For cheap dorm beds, consider **Fawlty Towers** (above) or these places: **Casa Olmata** is a laid-back backpackers' place midway between the Termini train station and Colosseum (beds in shared quads-30,000, S-L60,000, D-L60,000, lots of stairs, laundry service, Internet access, games, communal dinners and kitchen, English dominant language, a block south of Basilica Santa Maria Maggiore at Via dell 'Omata 36, tel. 06-483-019, fax 06-474-2854, www.casaolmata.com, e-mail: casaolmata@inbox.ilink.it).
The Beehive is the best of these dorms for older travelers. This tidy little place, with three six-bed dorms and a guests' kitchen on one floor, is thoughtfully run by a friendly young American couple, Steve and Linda (L30,000 beds, CC:VMA, closed 13:00-16:00, 2 blocks south of Basilica Santa Maria Maggiore at Via Giovanni Lanza 99, tel. 06-474-719, www.the-beehive.com). **Pensione Ottaviano** offers a fun, easygoing clubhouse feel and a good

location near the Vatican (25 beds in 2- to 7-bed rooms, L30,000 per bed with sheets, D-L90,000, 6 blocks from Ottaviano Metro stop, Via Ottaviano 6, reservations only after 21:00 the night before, tel. 06-3973-7253). The same slum visionaries run the dumpier **Pensione Sandy** (L30,000 beds, south of station, up a million depressing stairs, Via Cavour 136, tel. 06-488-4585).

EATING
IN ROME

Romans spend their evenings eating rather than drinking and the preferred activity is to simply enjoy a fine, slow meal buried deep in the old city. Rome's a fun and cheap place to eat, with countless little eateries serving fine $20 meals. Tourists wander the streets just before midnight wondering, "Why did I eat so much?"

Although I've listed a number of restaurants, I recommend that you just head for a scenic area and explore. Piazza Navona, the Pantheon area, Campo de' Fiori, and Trastevere are neighborhoods full of places ranging from expensive sit-down to cheap take-out.

Eating in Trastevere

Guidebooks list Trastevere's famous places, but I'd wander the fascinating maze of streets near Piazza Santa Maria in Trastevere and find a mom-and-pop place with barely a menu. Check out the tiny streets north of the church. You might consider these places before making a choice:

For outdoor seating on romantic Piazza della Scala, check out **Taverna della Scala**, the local choice for pizza (closed Tue, tel. 06-581-4100) and **La Scala Restaurant**, chic and popular with Generation X Romans. Don't miss the fine little *gelatería* with oh-wow pistachio (north end of Piazza della Scala).

At **Taverna del Moro**, Tony scrambles—with a great antipasta table—to keep his happy eaters well fed and returning (but too much mayo on bruschetta, off Via del Moro at Vicolo del Cinque 36, tel. 06-580-9165). For a basic meal with lots of tourists, you can eat cheap at **Mario's** (Mon–Sat 19:00–24:00, closed Sun, 3 courses with wine and service for L18,000, Via del Moro 53, tel. 06-580-3809).

Ristorante Alle Fratte di Trastevere is lively and inexpensive (closed Tue, Via dell Fratte di Trastevere, tel. 06-583-5775). **La Cisterna**—bragging it's the oldest restaurant in Rome and has served the rich and famous—is more expensive but serves tasty food in a lively pleasant setting (Via Della Cisterna 13, tel. 06-581-2543).

Eating on and near Campo de' Fiori

For the ultimate romantic square setting, eat at whichever place looks best on Campo de' Fiori. Circle the square, considering each place. **La Carbonara** claims to be the birthplace of pasta carbonara (closed Tue). Meals on small nearby streets are a better value but lack that Campo de' Fiori magic. Bars and pizzerias seem to be overwhelming the popular square. The **Taverna** or **Vineria** at numbers 16 and 15 offer good perches from which to people watch and nurse a glass of wine.

Nearby, on the more elegant and peaceful Piazza Farnese, **Ostaria Da Giovanni Ar Galletto** has a dressier local crowd, great outdoor seating, moderate prices, and fine food (closed Sun, tucked in corner of Piazza Farnese at #102, tel. 06-686-1714).

Dar Filettaro a Santa Barbara is a tradition for many Romans. Basically a fish bar with paper tablecloths and cheap prices, its grease-stained, hurried waiters serve old-time favorites—fried cod fillets, a strange bitter *puntarelle* salad, and delightful anchovies with butter—to nostalgic locals (Mon–Sat 17:30–23:10, closed Sun, a block east of Campo de' Fiori tumbling onto a tiny and atmospheric square, Largo dei Librari 88, tel. 06-686-4018).

Ristorante del Pallaro has no menu but plenty of return eaters. Paola Fazi, with a towel wrapped around her head turban-style, and her family serve up a five-course festival of typically Roman food for L33,000, including wine, coffee, and a wonderful mandarin liquor. Their slogan: "Here, you'll eat what we want to feed you." Look like Oliver asking for more soup and get seconds on the mandarin liqueur (Tue–Sun 12:00–15:30, 19:30–24:00, closed Mon, indoor/outdoor seating on quiet square, a block south of Corso Vittorio Emanuele down Largo del Chiavari to Largo del Pallaro 15, tel. 06-6880-1488).

Ristorante Grotte del Teatro di Pompeo, sitting atop an ancient theater, serves good food at fair prices with a smile (closed Mon, Via del Biscione 73, tel. 06-6880-3686).

For interesting bar munchies, try **Cul de Sac** on Piazza Pasquino (a block southwest of Piazza Navona). **L'Insalata Ricca**, a popular chain that specializes in hearty and healthy salads, is next door (Piazza Pasquino 72, tel. 06-6830-7881). Another branch is nearby with more spacious outdoor seating (just off Corso Vitorio Emanuele on Largo del Chiavari).

Near the Pantheon, facing Largo Argentina, **Il Delfino** is a handy self-service cafeteria (daily 7:00–21:00, not cheap but fast). Across the side street, **Frullati Bar** sells refreshing fruity frappés. The *alimentari* (grocery store) on the Pantheon square will make you a sandwich for a temple-porch picnic.

Eating near Via Firenze and Via Nazionale Hotels

Snack Bar Gastronomia is a great local hole-in-the-wall for lunch or dinner (open until 20:00, closed Sun, really cheap hot meals dished up from under glass counter, tap water with a smile, Via Firenze 34). There's an *alimentari* across the street.

Pasticceria Dagnino, popular for its top-quality Sicilian specialties—especially pastries and ice cream—is where those who work at my recommended hotels eat (daily 7:00–22:00, in Galleria Esedra off Via Torino, a block from hotels, tel. 06-481-8660). Their *arancino*—a rice, cheese, and ham ball—is a greasy Sicilian favorite. Direct the construction of your meal at the bar, pay for your trayful at the cashier, and climb upstairs, where you'll find the dancing Sicilian girls (free).

➤ **Hostaria Romana** is a great place for traditional Roman cuisine. For an air-conditioned, classy local favorite run by a jolly group of men who enjoy their work, eat here (closed Sun, midway between Trevi fountain and Piazza Barberini, Via del Boccaccio 1, at intersection with Via Rasella, no reservations needed before 20:00, tel. 06-474-5284). Go ahead and visit the antipasto bar in person to assemble your plate. They're happy to serve an antipasti *misto della casa* and pasta dinner. Take a hard look at their Specialita Romane list.

Ristorante da Giovanni is a serviceable, hardworking place feeding locals and travelers now for 50 years (L23,000 menu, Mon–Sat 12:00–15:00, 19:00–22:30, closed Sun, just off Via XX Septembre at Via Antonio Salandra 1, tel. 06-485-950).

Restaurant Grill Target Pizza is a modern, efficient place with a good antipasti buffet (L7,000 per plate) and a mix-and-match pasta and sauce menu, offering a fast alternative to the burger joints (daily 12:00–15:00, 18:00–23:00, air con, Via Torino 33, tel. 06-474-0066).

Est Est Est Antica Pizzeria, with a traditional old Roman ambience and quiet streetside tables outside, serves good pizza and *crostini* as well as heavier meals (Tue–Sun 19:00–24:00, closed Mon, 32 Via Genova, a block off Via Nazionale, tel. 06-4881107).

Ristorante Cinese Internazionale is your best neighborhood bet for Chinese (daily 18:00–23:00, inexpensive, no pasta, just off Via Nazionale behind Hotel Luxor at Via Agostino de Pretis 98, tel. 06-474-4064).

The **McDonald** restaurants on Piazza della Repubblica

(free piazza seating outside), Piazza Barberini, and Via Firenze offer air-conditioned interiors and salad bars.

Flann O'Brien Irish Pub is a great place for a quick light meal (pasta or something *other* than pasta), fine Irish beer, and the most Italian crowd of all (daily 7:00–24:00, Via Nazionale 18, at intersection with Via Napoli, tel. 06-488-0418).

Eating near the Vatican Museum

Antonio's Hostaria dei Bastioni is tasty and friendly. It's conveniently located midway between your walk from St. Peters' to the Vatican Museum, with noisy streetside seating and a quiet interior (hot when hot—no air con, Mon–Sat 12:00–15:00, 19:00–23:30, closed Sun, L10,000–12,000 pastas, L15,000 *secondi*, no cover charge, at corner of Vatican wall, Via Leone IV 29, tel. 06-3972-3034).

La Rustichella has a great and fresh antipasti buffet (L15,000, enough for a meal) and fine pasta dishes. Arrive when they open at 19:30 to avoid a line and have the pristine buffet to yourself (Tue–Sun 12:30–15:00, 19:30–23:00, closed Mon, near new Metro: Cipro–Musei Vaticani stop, opposite church at end of Via Candia, Via Angelo Emo 1, tel. 06-3972-0649). Consider the fun and fruity **Gelatería Millennium** next door.

Avoid the restaurant pushers handing out fliers near the Vatican: bad food, expensive menu tricks. Viale Giulio Cesare is lined with cheap **Pizza Rustica** shops and fun eateries, such as **Cipriani Self-Service Rosticcería** (closed Mon, pleasant outdoor seating, near Ottaviano subway stop, Viale Guilio Cesare 195).

Turn your nose loose in the wonderful **Via Andrea Doria** open-air market three blocks north of the Vatican Museum (Mon–Sat roughly 7:00–13:30, later on Tue and Fri, between Via Tunisi and Via Andrea Doria). If the market is closed, try the nearby **Meta supermarket** (Mon–Wed and Fri–Sat 8:30–13:15, 16:15–19:30, Thu 8:30–13:15, closed Sun, a half block straight out from Via Tunisi entrance of open-air market, Via Francesco 18).

Sorry, but Rome is not a great place for little kids. Parks are rare. Kid-friendly parks are more rare. The low-tech museums lack hands-on fun.

The good news for kids? Pizza and gelato. Any person under a meter (39 inches) tall travels free on the public transit. And Italians are openly fond of kids, and you'll probably get lots of friendly attention from locals.

Here are some tips:
- Take advantage of local information. *Romanc'e*, the periodical entertainment guide, has a children's section in English. Ask at Rome's TIs about kid-friendly activities.
- Rome's hotels often give price breaks for kids. (Air conditioning can be worth the splurge.)
- Eat dinner early (around 19:00) and you'll miss the romantic crowd. Skip the famous places. Look instead for self-serve cafeterias, bars (kids are welcome), or even fast-food restaurants where kids can move around without bothering others. Picnic lunches and dinners work well. For ready-made picnics, try the *rosticceríe* (delis) and Pizza Rustica shops (cheap take-out pizza; *diavola* is the closest thing on the menu to kid-friendly pepperoni).
- Public WCs are hard to find: Try museums, bars, gelato shops, and fast-food restaurants.
- Follow this book's crowd-beating tips to a tee. Kids don't like standing in a long line for a museum (which they might not even want to see).

Sights to Consider

Rome's many squares are traffic-free with plenty of space to run and pigeons to feed while Mom and Dad enjoy a coffee at an outdoor table.

When visiting the ancient sites, have some fun with *Ancient Rome—Then and Now*, a fun book for kids, with plastic overlays showing how the ruins used to look. It's available at stalls near the entrance of ancient sites.

The Vatican Museum comes with mummies and fun statues of animals. There's an entire hall of statues with their penises broken off that my kids found entertaining.

Villa Borghese is Rome's sprawling central park. The best kids' zone is near Porta Pinciana where you'll find bikes for rent, pony rides, and other amusements.

The ghoulish Cappucin Crypt (decorated with skeletons) and the Catacombs tunnels are goblin-pleasers. (✪ For Crypt, see page 40, for Catacombs, page 46.)

The Church of St. Ignazio with its false dome can fascinate kids and adults. ✪ See page 89.

Rome feels safe at night, and you can easily take your kids on the walks suggested in this book (✪ see Night Walk Across Rome on page 50 and Dolce Vita Stroll on page 198).

The Luna Park at E.U.R. is a tired old amusement park (Metro to Magliana, then bus to Via delle Tre Fontana, tel. 06-592-5933). And Rome has three big water parks: Piscina delle Rose, Hydromania, and Acquapiper (your hotel will have details).

SHOPPING
IN ROME

Shops are open from 9:00 to 13:00 and from 16:00 to 19:00. They're often closed on summer Saturday afternoons and winter Monday mornings.

If all you need are souvenirs, a surgical strike at any souvenir shop will do. Otherwise, try...

Department Stores

Large department stores offer relatively painless one-stop shopping. A good upscale department store is **La Rinascente.** Its main branch is on Piazza Fiume, and there's a smaller store on Piazza Colonna. **COIN,** near Piazza Fiume, is also fashionable (like an Italian Bon Marche). **UPIM** is the Roman Kmart (many branches, including Via Nazionale 111, Piazza Santa Maria Maggiore, and Via del Tritone 172).

Boutiques

For top fashion, stroll the streets around the Spanish Steps, including **Via Condotti, Via Borgognona** (for the big-name shops), and **Via del Babuino** (trendy design shops and galleries). For antiques, stroll **Via de Coronari** (between Piazza Navona and the bend in the river), **Via Giulia** (between Campo de' Fiori and the river), or **Via Margutta** (classier, with art galleries too, from Spanish Steps to Piazza del Popolo).

Open-Air Produce Markets

Rome's outdoor markets provide a fun and colorful dimension of the city even the most avid museum-goer should not miss. Wander through the easygoing neighborhood produce markets that clog certain streets and squares every morning except Sunday. Consider the huge **Mercato Andrea Doria** (3 blocks in front of the Vatican Museum at Via Andrea Doria). Smaller but equally charming slices of everyday Roman life are at markets on these streets and squares: **Piazza delle Coppelle** (near the Pantheon), **Via Balbo** (near recommended hotels off Via Nazionale near the Termini station), and **Via della Pace** (near Piazza Navona). The covered **Mercato di Testaccio** is mostly produce and a hit with photographers and people watchers (Piazza Testaccio, near Metro: Piramide). And **Campo de' Fiori,** while newly renovated to fit Euro-standards, is still a fun scene. These produce markets are generally open from 7:00 to 13:00 and closed Sunday.

Flea Market
For antiques and fleas, the granddaddy of markets is the **Porta Portese** *mercato delle pulci* (flea market, Via Portuense and Via Ippolito Nievo, tram #8 from Largo Argentina, 6:30–13:00 Sun only).

Airport Souvenirs
Leonardo da Vinci Airport ("Fiumicino") sells Italian specialty foods vacuum-packed to clear U.S. customs. Most shops are near the departure gates (after you check your bags and pass through security). Try Parmigiano-Reggiano cheese, dried porcini mushrooms or peppers, and better olive oil than you can buy at home.

NIGHTLIFE
IN ROME

Romans get dressed up and eat out in casual surroundings for their evening entertainment. For most visitors, the best after-dark entertainment is to simply stroll the medieval lanes that connect the romantic, floodlit squares and fountains. Head for Piazza Navona, the Pantheon, Campo de' Fiori, Trevi Fountain, Spanish Steps, Via del Corso, Trastevere, or Monte Testaccio. (✪ See Night Walk across Rome, page 50, and Dolce Vita Stroll, below.)

For concerts and opera, see local newspaper and the periodical entertainment guides (such as *Romanc'e*, sold at newsstands, or *L'Evento*, free at TI, www.comune.roma.it/comunicazione /evento/). The famous open-air opera at the Baths of Caracalla has been discontinued to protect the ruins.

An interesting place for club-hopping is **Monte Testaccio**. After 21:00, ride the Metro to Piramide and follow the noise. Monte Testaccio was once an ancient trash heap and now a small hill whose cool caves are funky restaurants and trendy clubs.

At **Pasquino,** Rome's English movie theater, you'll find movies in English daily (in Trastevere at Vicolo del Piede 19, tel. 06-580-3622). Some theaters around town run movies in their original language (look for "V.O."—*versione originale*).

The Dolce Vita Stroll down Via del Corso
This is the city's chic and hip "cruise" from **Piazza del Popolo** (Metro: Flaminio) down a wonderfully traffic-free section of **Via del Corso** and up **Via Condotti** to the **Spanish Steps** each evening around 18:00 (Sat and Sun are best). Strollers, shoppers, and flirts on the prowl fill this neighborhood of Rome's most fashionable stores (open after siesta 16:30–19:30).

Throughout Italy, early evening is time to stroll. While

elsewhere in Italy this is called the *passeggiata*, in Rome it's a cruder big-city version called the *struscio*. (Struscio means "to rub.") Unemployment among Italy's youth is very high; many stay with their parents even into their thirties. They spend a lot of time being trendy and hanging out. Hardcore cruisers from the suburbs, which lack pleasant public spaces, congregate on Via del Corso to make the scene. The hot *vroom vroom* motorscooter is their symbol; haircuts and fashion are follow-the-leader. They are the *coatto*. In a more genteel small town, the *passeggiata* comes with sweet whispers of *"bella"* and *"bello"* ("pretty" and "handsome"). In Rome, the admiration is stronger, oriented toward consumption— they say *"buona"* and *"buono"*—meaning "good" (terms used to describe food).

Historians: Note that Piazza del Popolo was just inside medieval Rome's main entry. The delightfully car-free square is marked by an obelisk that was brought to Rome by Augustus after he conquered Egypt. (It once stood in the Circus Maximus.) The Baroque Church of Santa Maria del Popolo (with Raphael's Chigi Chapel and two Caravaggio paintings) is next to the gate in the old wall, on the far side of Piazza del Popolo. Augustus' Ara Pacis is a 5-minute detour west of Via del Corso.

Non-shoppers should hike a mile down Via del Corso— straight since Roman times—to the Victor Emmanuel Monument. Climb Michelangelo's stairway to his glorious (especially when floodlit) square atop Capitol Hill and catch the lovely views of the Forum (from either side of the mayor's palace) as the horizon reddens and cats prowl the unclaimed rubble of ancient Rome.

TRANSPORTATION
CONNECTIONS
㉒
`r o m e`

ROME'S TRAIN STATION

Rome's main train station, Termini, is a minefield of tourist services: a late-hours bank, public showers, luggage lockers, 24-hour thievery, the city bus station, a subway stop, and Chef Express (a handy and cheery self-service restaurant, daily 11:00–22:30). Multilingual charts make locations fairly clear. The station is crawling with sleazy sharks with official-looking cards. In general, avoid anybody selling anything at the station if you can.

Most of my hotel listings are easily accessible by foot (those near the train station) or by Metro (those in the Colosseum and Vatican neighborhoods). The train station has its own Metro stop (Termini).

Types of Trains

You'll encounter several types of trains in Italy. Along with the various milk-run trains, there are the slow IR (Interregional) and *directo* trains, the medium *expresso*, the fast IC (Intercity), and the bullet-train Eurostar Italia (supplement costs L30,000 even with train pass). Fast trains, even with supplements, are affordable (e.g., a second-class Rome-to-Venice ticket costs about $50 with an express supplement). Buying supplements on the train comes with a nasty penalty. Buying them at the station can be a time-waster. Try to buy them at travel agencies (CIT or AmExCo) in towns. The cost is the same, the lines and language barrier are smaller, and you'll save time.

Schedules

Newsstands sell up-to-date regional and all-Italy timetables (L7,000, ask for the *orario ferroviaro*). There is now a single all-Italy telephone number for train information—1478-88088 (daily 7:00–21:00, English generally spoken). On the Web, check www.fs-on-line.com, www.itwg.com/trains, or http://bahn.hafas .de/english.html. Strikes are common. Strikes generally last a day, and train employees will simply say *"Sciopero"* (strike). But actually, sporadic trains—following no particular schedule—lumber down the tracks during most strikes.

By train from Rome to: Venice (6/day, 5–8 hrs, overnight possible), **Florence** (12/day, 2 hrs), **Pisa** (8/day, 3–4 hrs), **Genova** (7/day, 6 hrs, overnight possible), **Milan** (12/day, 5 hrs, overnight possible), **Naples** (6/day, 2 hrs, L33,000 2nd class), **Brindisi** (2/day, 9 hrs), **Amsterdam** (2/day, 20 hrs), **Bern** (5/day, 10 hrs), **Frankfurt** (4/day, 14 hrs), **Munich** (5/day, 12 hrs), **Nice** (2/day, 10 hrs), **Paris** (5/day, 16 hrs), **Vienna** (3/day, 13–15 hrs).

ROME'S AIRPORT

A slick, direct train link connects Rome's Fiumicino (a.k.a. Leonardo da Vinci) airport and the central Termini train station. Trains run once hourly and take 30 minutes. From the airport, trains depart at :07 past the hour (from airport's arrival gate, follow signs to "Stazione/Railway Station"; buy ticket from a machine or the Biglieteria office; L16,000 or free with first-class railpass). From Termini, trains depart at :20 past the hour from Track 22 (but ticket from machine at Alitalia desk for L16,000; trains run 7:20–21:20). Your hotel can arrange a taxi to the airport at any hour for about L80,000. To get from the airport into town cheaply by taxi, try teaming up with any tourist also just arriving (most are heading for hotels near yours in the center). Splitting a taxi and hopping out once downtown at a taxi stand to take another to your hotel will save you L30,000. You could also save money taking the train to the station, then catching a taxi to your hotel, but you probably won't save time since the airport train runs only once hourly. Avoid unmarked, unmetered taxis.

Airport information (tel. 06-65951) can connect you directly to your airline. (British Air tel. 06-6595-4195, Alitalia tel. 06-65643, Delta tel. 06-6595-4104, KLM tel. 06-652-9286, SAS tel. 06-6501-0771, TWA tel. 06-6595-4901, United tel. 0266-7481, Lufthansa tel. 06-6595-4156, Swiss Air tel. 06-6595-4099.)

DRIVING IN ROME

Greater Rome is circled by the Grande Raccordo Anulare. This ring road has spokes that lead you into the center. Entering from the north, leave the *autostrada* at the Settebagni exit. Following the ancient Via Salaria (and the black-and-white "Centro" signs), work your way doggedly into the Roman thick of things. This will take you along the Villa Borghese park and dump you right on Via

Veneto (where there's an Avis office). Avoid rush hour, and drive defensively: Roman cars stay in their lanes like rocks in an avalanche. Parking in Rome is dangerous. Park near a police station or get advice at your hotel. The Villa Borghese underground garage is handy (L35,000/day, Metro: Spagna).

Consider this: Your car is a worthless headache in Rome. Avoid a pile of stress and save money by parking at the huge, easy, and relatively safe lot behind the Orvieto station (follow "P" signs from autostrada), and catch the train to Rome (every 2 hrs, 75 min).

APPENDIX
ROME

ROMAN HISTORY—THREE MILLENNIA IN FOUR PAGES

History in a Hurry

Ancient Rome lasted a thousand years (500 B.C.–500 A.D.), half as an expanding republic, half as a dominating empire. When Rome fell to invaders, all Europe suffered a thousand years of poverty and ignorance (500–1500 A.D.), though Rome's influence could still be felt in the Catholic Church. Popes rebuilt Rome for pilgrims, in Renaissance then Baroque and neoclassical styles (1500–1800). As capital of a newly united Italy, Rome followed Fascist Mussolini into World War II (and lost), but rebounded in Italy's post-War economic boom.

Want more?

Legendary Birth (1200–500 B.C.)

Aeneas flees burning Troy (1200 B.C.), wanders like Odysseus, and finally finds a home along the Tiber. His descendants, Romulus and Remus—orphaned at birth, suckled by a she-wolf, raised by shepherds—grow up to steal wives and build a wall, traditionally founding Rome (753 B.C.).

Closer to fact, the local agrarian tribes were dominated by more sophisticated neighbors to the north (Etruscans) and south (Greek colonists). Their convenient location on the Tiber was perfect for a future power.

Sights:
- Romulus' "hut" and wall (Palatine Hill)
- She-wolf statue (Capitol Museum)
- Frescoes of Aeneas and Romulus (National Museum of Rome)
- Bernini's Aeneas statue (Borghese Gallery)

- Etruscan wing (Vatican Museum)
- Etruscan Museum (in Villa Borghese gardens)
- Etruscan legacy (the original Circus Maximus, the drained Forum)

The Republic (509–27 B.C.)

The city expands throughout the Italian peninsula (500–300 B.C.), then defeats Hannibal's North African Carthaginians (the Punic Wars, 264–146 B.C.) and Greece (168 B.C.). Rome is master of the Mediterranean, and booty and captured slaves pour in. Romans bicker among themselves over their slice of the pie, pitting wealthy landowners (the ruling Senate) against the working class (plebes) and rebellious slaves (Spartacus' revolt, 73 B.C.). In the chaos, charismatic generals like Julius Caesar, who can provide wealth and security, become dictators. Change is necessary . . . and coming.

Sights:
- Forum's Curia, Temple of Saturn, Temple of Castor and Pollux, Rostrum, Basilica Aemilia, Temple of Julius Caesar, and Basilica Julia (all rebuilt later)
- Appian Way built, lined with tombs
- Aqueducts, which carry water to a growing city
- Portrait busts of citizens (National Museum of Rome)
- The Republic's "S.P.Q.R." belief and motto, seen today on statues, buildings, and even manhole covers: the **S**enatus and **P**ublicus **Q** (which constitute) **R**omanus

The Empire — The "Roman Peace," or Pax Romana (A.D. 1–200)

After Julius Caesar was killed by disgruntled Republicans, his adopted son Augustus took undisputed control, ended the civil wars, declared himself emperor, and established his family to succeed him, setting the pattern of rule for the next 500 years.

Rome ruled an empire of 54 million people, stretching from Scotland to Africa, from Spain to Turkey. The city, with over a million inhabitants, was decorated with Greek-style statues and monumental structures faced with marble . . . it was the marvel of the known world. The empire prospered on a (false) economy of booty, slaves, and trade, surviving the often turbulent and naughty behavior of emperors like Caligula and Nero.

Sights:
- Colosseum
- Forum
- Palatine Hill palaces
- Poems by Virgil, Catullus, Horace, and Ovid (from time of Augustus)

- Augustus' house (Casa di Livia) on Palatine Hill
- Pantheon
- Trajan's Column and Forum
- Greek and Greek-style statues (National Museum of Rome, Vatican Museum)
- Piazza Navona (former stadium)
- Hadrian's Villa (Tivoli) and tomb (now Castel Sant' Angelo, in Rome)

Rome Falls (200–476)
Corruption, disease, and the constant pressure of barbarians pecking away at the borders slowly drained the unwieldy empire. Despite Diocletian's division of the empire and Constantine legalizing Christianity (312), the city was sacked (410) and the last emperor checked out (476). Rome fell like a huge column, kicking up dust that would plunge Europe into a thousand years of darkness.
Sights:
- Arch of Constantine
- The Forum's Basilica Maxentius
- Baths of Diocletian
- Old Roman Wall (gates at Via Veneto or Piramide)

Medieval Rome (500–1500)
The once-great city of a million people dwindled to a rough village of 10,000 with a corrupt pope, forgotten ruins, and malaria-carrying mosquitoes. Cows grazed in the ruined Forum and wolves prowled the Vatican at night. During the 1300s even the popes left Rome to live in France. What little glory Rome retained was in the pomp, knowledge, and wealth of the Catholic Church.
Sights:
- The damage done to ancient Roman monuments caused by disuse, barbarian looting, and pillaging for pre-cut stones
- Early Christian churches built before Rome fell (Santa Maria Maggiore, San Giovanni in Laterano, San Clemente)
- Churches of Santa Maria sopra Minerva and Santa Maria in Trastevere
- Castel Sant' Angelo

Renaissance and Baroque Rome (1500–1800)
As Europe's economy recovered, energetic popes rebuilt Rome to attract pilgrims. The best artists decorated palaces and churches, carved statues, and built fountains. The city was not a great political force, but as the center of Catholicism during the struggle against Protestants (c. 1520–1648), it was an influential religious and cultural capital.

Renaissance Sights:
- Michelangelo's Sistine Chapel (Vatican Museum), dome of St. Peter's, *Pietà* (St. Peter's), Moses (St. Peter-in-Chains church), Christ statue (Santa Maria sopra Minerva), Campidoglio Square on Capitol Hill, Santa Maria degli Angeli church (in former Baths of Diocletian)
- Raphael's *School of Athens* and *Transfiguration* (Vatican Museum)
- Paintings by Raphael, Titian, others (Borghese Gallery)

Baroque Sights:
- St. Peter's Square and interior (largely by Bernini)
- Bernini statues (at Borghese Gallery, and *St. Teresa in Ecstasy* at Santa Maria della Vittoria church) and fountains (Piazza Navona, Piazza Barberini)
- Ancient obelisks erected in squares (Piazza del Popolo, Piazza Navona)
- Trevi fountain
- Gesu and St. Ignazio churches
- Caravaggio's *Calling of St. Matthew* (San Luigi dei Francesi church) and other paintings (Borghese Gallery and Vatican Museums)
- Baroque paintings (Borghese Gallery)
- Borromini's facade of Santa Agnese church (Piazza Navona)

Modern Rome (1800–2000)

Rome becomes the capital of a newly-reunited Italy (1870), is modernized by Fascist Mussolini, and survives the destruction of World War II. Italy's post-War "economic miracle" makes Rome a world-class city of cinema, banking, and tourism.

Sights:
- Victor Emmanuel II Monument, which honors modern Italy's first (democratic) king
- Mussolini: The balcony he spoke from (Palazzo Venezia), his planned city (E.U.R.), grand boulevards (Via dei Fori Imperiali, Via Conciliazione), Olympic Stadium
- Cinecitta film studios and Via Veneto nightlife, which have faint echoes of Fellini's "La Dolce Vita" Rome
- Subway system, broad boulevards, smog.

Rome Today

After surviving the government-a-year turbulence and Mafia-tainted corruption of the post-war years, Rome is stabilizing. Today, the average Roman makes more money than the average Englishman. The city is less polluted and more organized. For the millennium, this eternal city has given its monuments a facelift—it's ready for pilgrims, tourists, and you to come and make more history.

Let's Talk Telephones

International Access Codes

When dialing direct, first dial the international access code of the country you're calling from. From the U.S. and Canada, it's 011. Virtually all European countries (including Italy) use "00" as their international access code; the only exceptions are Finland (990), Estonia (800), and Lithuania (810).

Country Codes

After you've dialed the international access code, then dial the code of the country you're calling.

Austria—43	Finland—358	Norway—47
Belgium—32	France—33	Portugal—351
Britain—44	Germany—49	Spain—34
Canada—1	Greece—30	Sweden—46
Czech Rep.—420	Ireland—353	Switzerland—41
Denmark—45	Italy—39	U.S.A.—1
Estonia—372	Netherlands—31	

Useful Italian Phone Numbers

Emergency (English-speaking police help): 113
Emergency (military police): 112
Road Service: 116
Directory Assistance (for L1,000, an Italian-speaking robot gives the number twice, very clearly): 12
Telephone help (in English; free directory assistance): 170

Rome's Climate

1st line, avg. daily low; 2nd line, avg. daily high; 3rd line, days of no rain.

J	F	M	A	M	J	J	A	S	O	N	D
39°	**39°**	42°	**46°**	55°	**60°**	64°	**64°**	61°	**53°**	46°	**41°**
54°	**56°**	62°	**68°**	74°	**82°**	88°	**88°**	83°	**73°**	63°	**56°**
23	**17**	26	**24**	25	**28**	29	**28**	24	**22**	22	**22**

Numbers and Stumblers

- Europeans write a few of their numbers differently than we do. 1 = 1 , 4 = 4 , 7 = 7 . Learn the difference or miss your train.
- In Europe, dates appear as day/month/year, so Christmas is 25-12-00.
- Commas are decimal points and decimals commas. A dollar and a half is 1,50 and there are 5.280 feet in a mile.
- When pointing, use your whole hand, palm downward.

- When counting with fingers, start with your thumb. If you hold up your first finger to request one item, you'll probably get two.
- What we Americans call the second floor of a building is the first floor in Europe.
- Europeans keep the left "lane" open for passing on escalators and moving sidewalks. Keep to the right.

Metric Conversions (approximate)

1 inch = 25 millimeters

1 foot = 0.3 meter

1 yard = 0.9 meter

1 mile = 1.6 kilometers

1 centimeter = 0.4 inch

1 meter = 39.4 inches

1 kilometer = .62 mile

32 degrees F = 0 degrees C

82 degrees F = about 28 degrees C

1 ounce = 28 grams

1 kilogram = 2.2 pounds

1 quart = 0.95 liter

1 square yard = 0.8 square meter

1 acre = 0.4 hectare

Public Holidays and Festivals

Italy has more than its share of holidays. Each town has a local festival honoring its patron saint. Italy (including most major sights) closes down on these national holidays: January 1, January 6 (Epiphany), Easter Sunday and Monday, April 25 (Liberation Day), May 1 (Labor Day), May 20 (Ascension Day), August 15 (Assumption of Mary), November 1 (All Saints Day), December 8 (Immaculate Conception of Mary), and December 25 and 26.

BASIC ITALIAN SURVIVAL PHRASES

Hello (good day).	**Buon giorno.**	bwohn **jor**-noh
Do you speak English?	**Parla inglese?**	par-lah een-**glay**-zay
Yes. / No.	**Si. / No.**	see / noh
I'm sorry.	**Mi dispiace.**	mee dee-**speeah**-chay
Please.	**Per favore.**	pehr fah-**voh**-ray
Thank you.	**Grazie.**	**graht**-seeay
Goodbye!	**Arrivederci!**	ah-ree-vay-**dehr**-chee
Where is...?	**Dov'è...?**	doh-**veh**
...a hotel	**...un hotel**	oon oh-**tehl**
...a youth hostel	**...un ostello della gioventù**	oon oh-**stehl**-loh **day**-lah joh-vehn-**too**
...a restaurant	**...un ristorante**	oon ree-stoh-**rahn**-tay
...a supermarket	**...un supermercado**	oon soo-pehr-mehr-**kah**-doh
...the train station	**...la stazione**	lah staht-seeoh-nay
...tourist information	**...informazioni per turisti**	een-for-maht-seeoh-nee pehr too-**ree**-stee
...the toilet	**...la toilette**	lah twah-**leht**-tay
men	**uomini, signori**	**woh**-mee-nee, seen-**yoh**-ree
women	**donne, signore**	**don**-nay, seen-**yoh**-ray
How much is it?	**Quanto costa?**	**kwahn**-toh **kos**-tah
Cheap(er).	**(Più) economico.**	(pew) ay-koh-**noh**-mee-koh
Is it included?	**È incluso?**	eh een-**kloo**-zoh
I would like...	**Vorrei....**	vor-**rehee**
...a ticket.	**...un biglietto.**	oon beel-**yay**-toh
...a room.	**...una camera.**	**oo**-nah **kah**-may-rah
...the bill.	**...il conto.**	eel **kohn**-toh
one	**uno**	**oo**-noh
two	**due**	**doo**-ay
three	**tre**	tray
four	**quattro**	**kwah**-troh
five	**cinque**	**cheeng**-kway
six	**sei**	**seh**ee
seven	**sette**	**seht**-tay
eight	**otto**	**ot**-toh
nine	**nove**	**nov**-ay
ten	**dieci**	dee**eay**-chee
hundred	**cento**	**chehn**-toh
thousand	**mille**	**mee**-lay
At what time?	**A che ora?**	ah kay **oh**-rah
now / soon / later	**adesso / presto / tardi**	ah-**dehs**-soh / **prehs**-toh / **tar**-dee
today / tomorrow	**oggi / domani**	**oh**-jee / doh-**mah**-nee

For more user-friendly Italian phrases, check out *Rick Steves' Italian Phrase Book and Dictionary* or *Rick Steves' French, Italian & German Phrase Book and Dictionary*.

Road Scholar Feedback For Rome 2000

*We're all in the same travelers' school of hard knocks. Your feedback
helps us improve this guidebook for future travelers. Please fill this out
(or use the online version at www.ricksteves.com/feedback), include more
info or any tips/favorite discoveries if you like, and send it to us. As
thanks for your help, we'll send you our quarterly travel newsletter free
for one year. Thanks!* **Rick**

**Of the recommended accommodations/restaurants used,
which was:**

Best _____

       Why? _____

Worst _____

       Why? _____

**Of the sights/experiences/destinations recommended by
this book, which was:**

Most overrated _____

       Why? _____

Most underrated _____

       Why? _____

Best ways to improve this book:

_____

I'd like a free newsletter subscription:

_____ Yes   _____ No   _____ Already on list

_____
Name

_____
Address

_____
City, State, Zip

_____
E-mail Address

Please send to: ETBD, Box 2009, Edmonds, WA 98020

Jubilee 2000—Let's Celebrate the Millennium by Forgiving Third World Debt

Let's ring in the millennium by convincing our government to forgive the debt owed to us by the world's poorest countries. Imagine spending over half your income on interest payments alone. You and I are creditors, and poor countries owe us more than they can pay.

Jubilee 2000 is a worldwide movement of concerned people and groups—religious and secular—working to cancel the international debts of the poorest countries by the year 2000.

Debt ruins people: In the poorest countries, money needed for health care, education, and other vital services is diverted to interest payments.

Mozambique, with a per capita income of $90 and life expectancy of 40, spends over half its national income on interest. This poverty brings social unrest, civil war, and often costly humanitarian intervention by the U.S.A. To chase export dollars, desperate countries ruin their environment. As deserts grow and rain forests shrink, the world suffers. Of course, the real suffering is among local people born long after some dictator borrowed (and squandered) that money. As interest is paid, entire populations go hungry.

Who owes what and why? Mozambique is one of 41 countries defined by the World Bank as "Heavily Indebted Poor Countries." In total, they owe $200 billion. Because these debts are unlikely to be paid, their market value is only a tenth of the face value (about $20 billion). The U.S.A.'s share is under $2 billion.

How can debt be canceled? This debt is owed mostly to the U.S.A., Japan, Germany, Britain, and France either directly or through the World Bank. We can forgive the debt owed directly to us and pay the market value (usually 10 percent) of the debts owed to the World Bank. We have the resources. (Norway, another wealthy creditor nation, just unilaterally forgave its Third World debt.) All America needs is the political will . . . people power.

While many of these poor nations are now democratic, corruption is still a concern. A key to Jubilee 2000 is making certain that debt relief reduces poverty in a way that benefits ordinary people: women, farmers, children, and so on.

Let's celebrate the new millennium by giving poor countries a break. For the sake of peace, fragile young democracies, the environment, and countless real people, forgiving this debt is the right thing for us in the rich world to do.

Tell Washington, D.C.: If our government knows this is what we want, it can happen. Learn more, write letters, lobby legislators, or even start a local Jubilee 2000 campaign. For details, contact Jubilee 2000 (tel. 202/783-3566, www.j2000usa.org). For information on lobbying Congress on J2000, contact Bread for the World (tel. 800/82-BREAD, www.bread.org).

Faxing Your Hotel Reservation

Faxing is more accurate and cheaper than telephoning. Use this handy form for your fax (or find it online at www.ricksteves.com /reservation). Photocopy and fax away.

One-Page Fax

To: _____ @ _____
        hotel   *fax*

From: _____ @ _____
        name   *fax*

Today's date: ____ /_____ /____
                    day *month* *year*

Dear Hotel _____,

Please make this reservation for me:

Name: _____

Total # of people: _____   # of rooms: _____   # of nights: _____

Arriving: ____ /_____ /____   My time of arrival (24-hr clock): _____
            day *month* *year*   (I will telephone if I will be late)

Departing: ____ /_____ /____
              day *month* *year*

Room(s):   Single___   Double___   Twin___   Triple___   Quad___

With: Toilet___   Shower___   Bath___   Sink only___

Special needs: View___   Quiet___   Cheapest Room___

Credit card: Visa___   MasterCard___   American Express___

Card #: _____

Expiration date:_____

Name on card: _____

You may charge me for the first night as a deposit. Please fax or mail me confirmation of my reservation, along with the type of room reserved, the price, and whether the price includes breakfast. Thank you.

_____
Signature

_____
Name

_____
Address

_____
City   *State*   *Zip Code*   *Country*

_____
E-mail Address

INDEX

Rick Steves' Phrase Books

Unlike other phrase books and dictionaries on the market, my well-tested phrases and key words cover every situation a traveler is likely to encounter. With these books you'll laugh with your cabby, disarm street thieves with insults, and charm new European friends.

Each book in the series is 4" x 6", with maps.

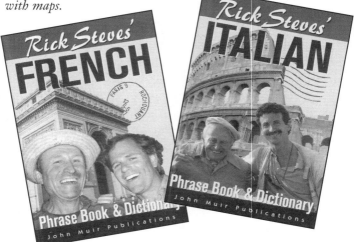

RICK STEVES' ITALIAN PHRASE BOOK & DICTIONARY
U.S. $6.95/Canada $10.75

RICK STEVES' FRENCH PHRASE BOOK & DICTIONARY
U.S. $6.95/Canada $10.75

RICK STEVES' GERMAN PHRASE BOOK & DICTIONARY
U.S. $6.95/Canada $10.75

RICK STEVES' SPANISH & PORTUGUESE PHRASE BOOK & DICTIONARY
U.S. $8.95/Canada $13.95

RICK STEVES' FRENCH, ITALIAN & GERMAN PHRASE BOOK & DICTIONARY
U.S. $8.95/Canada $13.95

FREE-SPIRITED TOURS FROM

Rick Steves'

Great Guides
Big Buses
Small Groups
No Grumps

Best of Europe I & II ■ **Turkey** ■ **Italy** ■ **Britain** ■ **Spain/Portugal**
Ireland ■ **E. France** ■ **W. France** ■ **Village France** ■ **Scandinavia**
Germany/Austria/Switz. ■ **London** ■ **Paris** ■ **Rome**

Looking for a one, two, or three-week tour in Rick Steves' lively "back door" style? *Rick Steves' Europe* has a wide selection of tours to tickle your travel bug.

We've been taking groups to Europe "through the back door" since 1978. Of the more than 3000 travelers who joined us last year, 96% who filled out post-tour surveys reported that we exceeded their expectations, our advertising was accurate, and that they'd recommend our tours to a friend. So consider yourself invited!

The "sticker price" of a Rick Steves tour includes much more than mainstream tours—which routinely dip into your pockets for hundreds of dollars in non-included sightseeing expenses and tips, and squeeze you into a bus with twice as many tourists. Here's what you'll get with a fully guided Best of Europe or regional tour...

✓ You'll travel with a small, non-smoking group—never more than 26 travelers.

✓ You'll have two guides traveling and dining with you on your tour.

✓ You'll travel in a full-size 48-to-52-seat bus, with plenty of empty seats for you to spread out and read, snooze, get away from your spouse, or whatever.

✓ You'll nearly always stay for two nights at each stop, sleeping in small, characteristic, locally-run hotels in the center of each city—within easy walking distance of the great sights of Europe you traveled so far to see.

✓ Your tour price will include all group sightseeing, with no hidden extra charges.

✓ Single travelers pay no extra supplement—they room with other singles.

✓ Tour cancellation/interruption protection coverage is included at no extra cost.

✓ All guide and driver tips are included. Because your guides are paid salaries by Rick, they'll focus 100% on giving you the best European travel experience possible—not on earning extra tips, kickbacks and commissions on the side.

Interested? Call (425) 771-8303 or visit www.ricksteves.com for a free copy of Rick Steves' **2000 Tours** booklet!